Keep being
Awesome!

"Mr Awesome"

13 STEPS TO
RICHES

Featuring Erik Swanson & Glenn Lundy

IMAGINATION
VOLUME 5

HABITUDE
WARRIOR

Foreword by Scott McKain

BEYOND

Library of Congress Control Number: 2022903512

Paperback ISBN: 978-1-63792-277-4

Hardcover ISBN: 978-1-63792-281-1

TESTIMONIALS
THE 13 STEPS TO RICHES

"What an honor to collaborate with so many personal development leaders from around the world as we Co-Author together honoring the amazing principles by Napoleon Hill in this new book series, *The 13 Steps to Riches*, by Habitude Warrior and Erik "Mr. Awesome" Swanson. Well done "Mr. Awesome" for putting together such an amazing series. If you want to up-level your life, read every book in this series and learn to apply each of these time tested steps and principles."

Denis Waitley ~ Author of *Psychology of Winning & The NEW Psychology of Winning - Top Qualities of a 21st Century Winner*

"Just as *Think and Grow Rich* reveals the 13 steps to success discovered by Napoleon Hill after interviewing the richest people around the world (and many who considered themselves failures) in the early 1900's, *The 13 Steps to Riches*, produced by Habitude Warrior and Erik Swanson takes a modern look at those same 13 steps. It brings together many of today's personal development leaders to share their stories of how *the 13 Steps to Riches* have created and propelled their own successes. I am honored to participate and share the power of Faith in my life. If you truly want to accelerate reaching the success you deserve, read every volume of *The 13 Steps to Riches*."

Sharon Lechter ~ 5 Time N.Y. Times Best-Selling Author. Author of *Think and Grow Rich for Women*, Co-Author of *Exit Rich, Rich Dad Poor Dad, Three Feet from Gold, Outwitting the Devil* and *Success and Something Greater* ~ **SharonLechter.com**

"The most successful book on personal achievement ever written is now being elaborated upon by many of the world's top thought leaders. I'm honored to Co-Author this series on the amazing principles from Napoleon Hill, in *The 13 Steps to Riches*, by Habitude Warrior, Erik "Mr. Awesome" Swanson."

> **Jim Cathcart** ~ Best-Selling Author of *Relationship Selling* and *The Acorn Principle,* among many others. Certified Speaking Professional (CSP) and Former President of the National Speakers Association (NSA)

"Some books are written to be read and placed on the shelf. Others are written to transform the reader, as they travel down a path of true transcendence and enlightenment. "*The 13 steps to Riches*" by Habitude Warrior and Erik Swanson is the latter. Profoundly insightful, it revitalizes the techniques and strategies written by Napoleon Hill by applying a modern perspective, and a fearsome collaboration of some of the greatest minds and thought leaders from around the globe. A must read for all of those who seek to break free of their current levels of success, and truly extract the greatness that lies within. It is an honor and a privilege to have been selected to participate, in what is destined to be the next historic chapter in the meteoric rise of many men and women around the world."

> **Glenn Lundy** ~ Husband to one, Father to 8, Automotive Industry Expert, Author of "The Morning 5", Creator of the popular morning show "#riseandgrind", and the Founder of "Breakfast With Champions"

"How exciting to team up with the amazing Habitude Warrior community of leaders such as Erik Swanson, Sharon Lechter, John Assaraf, Denis Waitley and so many more transformational and self-help icons to bring you these timeless and proven concepts in the fields of success and wealth. *The 13 Steps to Riches* book series will help you reach your dreams and accomplish your goals faster than you have ever experienced before!"

> **Marie Diamond** ~ Featured in *The Secret*, Modern Day Spiritual Teacher, Inspirational Speaker, Feng Shui Master

"If you are looking to crystalize your mightiest dream, rekindle your passion, breakthrough limiting beliefs and learn from those who have done exactly what you want to do - read this book! In this transformational masterpiece, *The 13 Steps to Riches*, self-development guru Erik Swanson has collected the sage wisdom and time tested truths from subject matter experts and amalgamated it into a one-stop-shop resource library that will change your life forever!"

Dan Clark ~ Speaker Hall of Fame & N.Y. Times Best-Selling Author of *The Art of Significance*

"Life has always been about who you surround yourself with. I am in excellent company with this collaboration from my fellow authors and friends, paying tribute to the life changing principles by Napoleon Hill in this amazing new book series, *The 13 Steps to Riches*, organized by Habitude Warrior's founder and my dear friend, Erik Swanson. Hill said, 'Your big opportunity may be right where you are now.' This book series is a must-read for anyone who wants to change their life and prosper, starting now."

Alec Stern ~ America's Startup Success Expert, Co-Founder of Constant Contact

"Finally a book series that encompasses the lessons the world needs to learn and apply, but in our modern day era. As I always teach my students to "Say **YES**, and then figure out how", I strongly urge you to do the same. Say YES to adding all of these 13 books in *The 13 Steps to Riches* book series into your success library and watch both your business as well as your personal life grow as a result."

Loral Langemeier ~ 5 Time N.Y. Times Best-Selling Author, Featured in *The Secret*, Author of *The Millionaire Maker* and *YES! Energy - The Equation to Do Less, Make More*

"Napoleon Hill had a tremendous impact on my consciousness when I was very young – there were very few books nor the type of trainings that we see today to lead us to success. Whenever you have the opportunity to read and harness *The 13 Steps to Riches* as they are presented in this series, be happy (and thankful) that there were many of us out there applying the principles, testing the teachings, making the mistakes, and now being offered to you in a way that they are clear, simple and concise – with samples and distinctions that will make it easier for you to design a successful life which includes adding value to others, solving world problems, and making the world work for 100% of humanity… Read on… those dreams are about to come true!"

> *Doria Cordova* ~ CEO of Money & You, Excellerated Business School, Global Business Developer, Ambassador of New Education

"Success leaves clues and the Co-Authors in this awesome book series, *The 13 Steps to Riches*, will continue the Napoleon Hill legacy with tools, tips and modern-day principals that greatly expand on the original masterpiece… *Think and Grow Rich*. If you are serious about living your life to the max, get this book series now!"

> *John Assaraf* ~ Chairman & CEO NeuroGym, MrNeuroGym.com, New York Times best-selling author of *Having It All, Innercise*, and *The Answer*. Also featured in *The Secret*

"Over the years, I have been blessed with many rare and amazing opportunities to invest my time and energy. These opportunities require a keen eye and immediate action. This is one of those amazing opportunities for you as a reader! I highly recommend you pick up every book in this series of *The 13 Steps to Riches* by Habitude Warrior and Erik Swanson! Learn from modern day leaders who have embraced the lessons from the great Napoleon Hill in his classic book from 1937, *Think and Grow Rich*."

> *Kevin Harrington* ~ Original "Shark" on *Shark Tank*, Creator of the Infomercial, Pioneer of the *As Seen on TV* brand, Co-Author of *Mentor to Millions*

"When you begin your journey, you will quickly learn of the importance of the first step of *The 13 Steps To Riches*. A burning desire is the start of all worthwhile achievements. Erik 'Mr. Awesome' Swanson's newest book series contains a wealth of assistance to make your journey both successful and enjoyable. Start today... because tomorrow is not guaranteed on your calendar."

Don Green ~ 45 Years of Banking, Finance & Entrepreneurship, Best-Selling Author of *Everything I know About Success I Learned From Napoleon Hill & Napoleon Hill My Mentor: Timeless Principles to Take Your Success to the Next Level & Your Millionaire Mindset*

Our minds become magnetized with the dominating thoughts we hold in our minds and these magnets attract to us the forces, the people, the circumstances of life which harmonize with the nature of our dominating thoughts.

(Napoleon Hill)

Global Speakers Mastermind & Habitude Warrior Masterminds

Join us and become a member of our tribe! Our Global Speakers Mastermind is a virtual group of amazing thinkers and leaders who meet twice a month. Sessions are designed to be 'to the point' and focused, while sharing fantastic techniques to grown your mindset as well as your pocket books. We also include famous guest speaker spots for our private Masterclasses. We also designate certain sessions for our members to mastermind with each other & counsel on the topics discussed in our previous Masterclasses. It's time for you to join a tribe who truly cares about **YOU** and your future and start surrounding yourself with the famous leaders and mentors of our time. It is time for you to up-level your life, businesses, and relationships.

For more information to check out our Masterminds:
Team@HabitudeWarrior.com
www.DecideTobeAwesome.com

FREE GIFT!
GRAB YOUR SPECIAL
& AWESOME FREE GIFT!

We have a very special gift for those who want to surround themselves with a tribe of people creating magic in supporting each other and their growth in their personal and professional lives! It's time for you to be up-leveled in such a fantastic way! You deserve to reward yourself and join us. "NDSO!" No Drama - Serve Others!

Visit the QR code link above to get your FREE GIFT!
www.RideAlongGuestPass.com

NAPOLEON HILL

I would like to personally acknowledge and thank the one and only Napoleon Hill for his work, dedication, and most importantly believing in himself. His unwavering belief in himself, whether he realized this or not, had been passed down from generation to generation to millions and millions of individuals across this planet including me!

I'm sure, at first, as many of us experience throughout our lives as well, he most likely had his doubts. Think about it. Being offered to work for Andrew Carnegie for a full 20 years with zero pay and no guarantee of success had to be a daunting decision. But, I thank you for making that decision years and years ago. It paved the path for countless many who have trusted in themselves and found success in their own rights. You gave us all hope and desire to bank on the most important entity in our world today - ourselves!

For this, I thank you Sir, from the bottom of my heart and the top of all of our bank accounts. Let us all follow the 13 Steps to Riches and prosper in so many areas of our lives.

~ Erik "Mr Awesome" Swanson

13 Time #1 Best-Selling Author & Student of Napoleon Hill Philosophies

CPL. DAEGAN W. PAGE, 23

It is our distinct honor to dedicate each one of our *13 Steps to Riches* book volumes to each of the 13 United States Service Members who courageously lost their lives in Kabul in August 2021. Your honor, dignity, and strength will always be cherished and remembered. ~ Habitude Warrior Team

Cpl. Daegan W. Page, 23, of Omaha, Nebraska, a rifleman.

His awards and decorations include the Korean Defense Service Medal, National Defense Service Medal, Sea Service Deployment Ribbon and Global War on Terrorism Service Medal. Additional awards pending approval may include Purple Heart, Combat Action Ribbon and Sea Service Deployment Ribbon. We honor you and thank you for your ultimate sacrifice!

THE 13 STEPS TO RICHES FEATURING:

DENIS WAITLEY ~ Author of *Psychology of Winning & The NEW Psychology of Winning - Top Qualities of a 21st Century Winner,* NASA's Performance Coach, Featured in *The Secret* ~ www.DenisWaitley.com

SHARON LECHTER ~ 5 Time N.Y. Times Best-Selling Author. Author of *Think and Grow Rich for Women,* Co-Author of *Exit Rich, Rich Dad Poor Dad, Three Feet from Gold, Outwitting the Devil* and *Success and Something Greater* ~ www.SharonLechter.com

JIM CATHCART~ Best-Selling Author of *Relationship Selling* and *The Acorn Principle,* among many others. Certified Speaking Professional (CSP) and Former President of the National Speakers Association (NSA) ~ www.Cathcart.com

MICHAEL E. GERBER ~ New York Times Bestseller of the mega best selling theory for over two consecutive decades… E-Myth books.

GLENN LUNDY ~ Husband to one, Father to 8, Automotive Industry Expert, Author of "The Morning 5", Creator of the popular morning show "#riseandgrind", and the Founder of "Breakfast With Champions" ~ www.GlennLundy.com

MARIE DIAMOND ~ Featured in *The Secret*, Modern Day Spiritual Teacher, Inspirational Speaker, Feng Shui Master ~ www.MarieDiamond.com

DAN CLARK ~ Award Winning Speaker, Speaker Hall of Fame, N.Y. Times Best-Selling Author of *The Art of Significance* ~ www.DanClark.com

ALEC STERN ~ America's Startup Success Expert, Co-Founder of Constant Contact, Speaker, Mentor, Investor ~ www.AlecSpeaks.com

ERIK SWANSON ~ 13 Time #1 International Best-Selling Author, Award Winning Speaker, Featured on Tedx Talks and Amazon Prime TV. Founder & CEO of the Habitude Warrior Brand
~ www.SpeakerErikSwanson.com

LORAL LANGEMEIER ~ 5 Time N.Y. Times Best-Selling Author, Featured in *The Secret*, Author of *The Millionaire Maker* and *YES! Energy - The Equation to Do Less, Make More* ~ www.LoralLangemeier.com

DORIA CORDOVA ~ CEO of Money & You, Excellerated Business School, Global Business Developer, Ambassador of New Education
~ www.FridaysWithDoria.com

JOHN ASSARAF ~ Chairman & CEO NeuroGym, MrNeuroGym.com, N. Y. Times best-selling author of *Having It All, Innercise*, and *The Answer*. Also featured in *The Secret* ~ www.JohnAssaraf.com

KEVIN HARRINGTON ~ Original "Shark" on the hit TV show *Shark Tank*, Creator of the Infomercial, Pioneer of the *As Seen on TV* brand, Co-Author of *Mentor to Millions* ~ www.KevinHarrington.TV

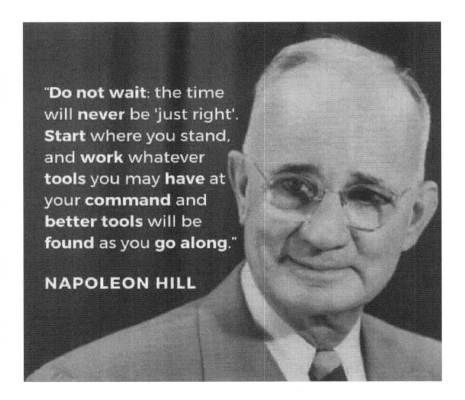

"**Do not wait**: the time will **never** be 'just right'. **Start** where you stand, and **work** whatever **tools** you may **have** at your **command** and **better tools** will be **found** as you **go along**."

NAPOLEON HILL

CONTENTS

Testimonials	What Others Are Saying	5
Acknowledgment	To Napoleon Hill	13
Dedication	To CPL. Daegan W. Page	15
Celebrity Authors	The 13 Featured Celebrity Authors	17
Introduction	By Don Green	23
Foreword	By Scott McKain	25
Glenn Lundy	Just Imagine	37
Erik Swanson	Imagine This	50
Jon Kovach Jr.	Your Disbelief Is My Fuel	55
Amado Hernandez	Imagination	62
Angelika Ullsperger	Imagination Will Find The How	68
Anthony M. Criniti	Great Thoughts Become Great Things	74
Barry Bevier	Imagine - Visualize - Manifest	81
Bonnie Lierse	Imagination Runs Wild	87
Brian Schulman	Believe What Can Happen If You Just Imagine	93
Candace & David Rose	A World Of Pure Imagination	100
Collier Landry	Where Creativity Begins	105
Corey Poirier	Imagine	111
Deb Scott	The Workshop Of The Mind	118
Dori Ray	Decisions, Decisions, Decisions!	123
Elaine Sugimura	Imagination Equals Infinite Possibilities	128
Elizabeth Walker	7 Steps To A Great Imagination	133
Erin Ley	Enjoy The Playground Of Your Mind	140
Fatima Hurd	Imagination With Purpose And Direction	146
Frankie Fegurgur	Can We Imagine The Future?	151
Fred Moskowitz	Curiosity And Imagination - Powerful Human Faculties That Work Hand In Hand	157
Freeman Witherspoon	Just My Imagination	162
Gina Bacalski	Hallyu To The Rescue	168
Griselda Beck	Imagination Gone Wild!	173
Jason Curtis	3 Steps To Daily Imagination Maximization	179

Jeffrey Levine	Imagination Is The Workshop Of Your Mind	183
Lacey & Adam Platt	The 2 Types Of Imagination & Can I Do It?	188
Louisa Jovanovich	Imagine Your Future	194
Lynda Sunshine West	Imagination Unlimited	200
Maris Segal & Ken Ashby	Imagination: The Power Tool Of Life	205
Mel Mason	Imagining The Possibilities	212
Miatta Hampton	The Power To Create	219
Michael D. Butler	Imagination	224
Michelle Cameron Coulter & Al Coulter	Imagination … The Seed To All Creation!	230
Michelle Mras	Imagine The Outcome	237
Mickey Stewart	The Swinging Doors Of Imagination	243
Natalie Susi	Imagination. Meditation. Manifestation.	249
Nita Patel	Positive Possibilities	254
Olga Geidane	What Are You Going To Draw On Your Canvas Tonight?	258
Paul Andrés	The 6 Powers Of Genius	266
Paul Capozio	What's For Lunch?	273
Phillip McClure	Imagination Turbo Speed	279
Robyn Scott	The Power To Create Something From A Thought In Your Head!	285
Shannon Whittington	The Subconscious Road To Dreams	290
Soraiya Vasanji	Permission To Imagine	296
Stacey Ross Cohen	Let Your Imagination Run Wild	302
Teresa Cundiff	Imagination Now & Then	309
Vera Thomas	Just Imagine!!!!	315
Yuri Choi	Meditation Is The Portal To The Realm Of Infinite Possibilities	323

INTRODUCTION

by Don Green

ERIK SWANSON & DON GREEN

Once you give yourself the gift of reading Erik Swanson's newest book series, **The 13 Steps to Riches**, you are sure to realize why he has earned his nickname, *"Mr. Awesome."* Readers usually read books for two reasons – they want to be entertained or they want to improve their knowledge in a certain subject. Mr. Awesome's new book series will help you do both.

I urge you to not only read this great book series in its entirety, but also apply the principles held within into your our life. Use the experience Erik Swanson has gained to reach your own level of success. I highly encourage you to invest in yourself by reading self-help materials, such as *The 13 Steps to Riches*, and I truly know you will discover that it will be one of the best investments you could ever make.

Don Green
Executive Director and CEO
The Napoleon Hill Foundation

FOREWORD

by Scott McKain

People want you to "wow" them. They want to believe that what keeps you awake at night is how to re-imagine your leadership style, approach, service, or product in a manner that knocks it out of the park for them. They crave your IMAGINATION.

Here's the problem: They're getting the status quo. Most want to continue doing it the way it has always been done.

That's why this book is critically important!

There are innovators in small businesses in almost every community. How do we know? They have survived both the Walmart and Amazon onslaughts in their towns. Whether it was the local grocery store that continues to exist because of innovating custom-cut meats and home delivery, or a sporting goods store that led with the novelty of letting you try out the equipment and get a feel for what you're buying, innovation is found in many places.

Unfortunately, many of us fail to get saved by the "religion of IMAGINATION" until it's too late.

The classic opening line of the bestselling business book by Jim Collins, *Good to Great*, is: "Good is the enemy of great." When we devote all our efforts to mere incremental improvements -- maintaining the status quo and disregarding IMAGINATION -- we are merely accepting the good and choosing not to take a shot at becoming great.

The modern challenge, though, is obvious. Innovation is expensive, difficult, potentially unrewarding, and more than a little scary. Even the businesses that used creativity to introduce new products are looking forward to the time they can merely focus upon improvements, rather than growing their imaginative approaches.

The problem that many entrepreneurs and leaders have with innovation is pretty basic: IMAGINATION is a messy thing.

Give me a billion dollars and five years, and I still cannot promise you that I'll come up with the next big thing. Yet, two young guys in a garage with practically no money can create the personal computer!

Constant improvement of a mediocre and non-compelling product or service is like the old cliché about rearranging the deck chairs on the Titanic. Be bold! Show customers you deserve their loyalty, because you're willing to innovate for their benefit.

Customers do not need another imitation of what's already available. As the saying goes, "Been there. Done that." We want IMAGINATION! We want compelling products and services that amaze, astound, and inspire us.

Please don't misunderstand the point – you must always strive to improve what you're currently doing. It's just that incremental improvements do not inspire customer loyalty. To provide what customers REALLY want, you must foster the improvement process – and be wildly passionate about IMAGINATION!

IMAGINATION VS. IMITATION

Let's examine the dangers of imitation as another way to propose that innovation is the strategy to overcome customer disconnections. Here are just three of the pitfalls encountered by imitating organizations:

You can only be as good as what you imitate

You fail to create customer loyalty

You're at the mercy of the competition's innovations

You can only be as good as what you imitate

First, let's be clear – by "imitation" I don't mean an activity as extreme as crafting a "knockoff" Louis Vuitton purse. That's copying…and that's illegal.

The meaning of "imitation" for our discussion here is "something made to be as much as possible like something else." And, like most innovators, I don't believe imitation is the "sincerest form of flattery." It's a competitive maneuver – and one that provides few long-term rewards.

Research reported in Harvard Business Journal stated that less successful companies take imitation – and their imitating added to the relevance of the competition and products or services that they were mimicking.

When I first started in the field of professional speaking, my mentor and hero was a humorist named Grady Nutt.

Grady had been a minister at a small church in Kentucky. He began his career by entertaining youth groups with humorous stories about experiences from his early life in Texas, especially his growing up in a small Southern Baptist church. He had gained a national reputation as a speaker because of the insight his stories provided and the laughter his monologues provoked. He appeared numerous times on the "Mike Douglas Show" in its heyday and had become a regular on the classic country comedy show, "Hee Haw."

Grady was a great dichotomy. He gained fame through his stories of small-town preachers and church-related bloopers, yet he was one of the most profound thinkers and discerning men I've ever known. Grady's way of writing and telling a story had a deep impact on me – so much so that I tried to sound like him…I wanted to be him!

One day Grady called me and asked to take me out to lunch – an honor I quickly accepted. In his kind and gentle manner over the table, he told me that he was flattered that I appreciated his talent to such a significant extent.

Then, he dropped the bomb that was the reason for lunch – and a pivotal moment in my life. "Scott," he said, "there's something else you must consider."

"As long as you keep trying to be the next Grady Nutt, then second place is the best you can conceivably hope for."

"My advice to you is to seek to become the best Scott McKain you can possibly be."

I sat there stunned, and a little embarrassed. Yet, I also had what I like to call the "blinding flash of the obvious." Unless you're someone like Frank Caliendo or Rich Little, no one has ever imitated his or her way to success and greatness. (And, in fact, the impersonator, by definition, will never be as famous as those he parodies.)

Whether it's in show business or your business, the imitators are never perceived as good as the original.

I realized I needed to follow a different route than my mentor, or else I would always find myself in the same classification as he. I had a natural interest in the way business works and leadership functions -- so I changed direction and pursued a career in business. Now, thirty years later, I can look back and be happy about that decision.

You can never be as good as what you imitate. If you decide to follow the strategy of replication or simulation, the absolute best you can hope for is to come in second.

You fail to create customer loyalty

Without IMAGINATION, your best customers aren't being inspired to remain loyal. Many of them are instead inspired to take their business elsewhere.

Likewise, imitation does not inspire customers to become your fans.

No one ever recommended to a friend that they should be doing business with an organization because they are "exactly like" an original. Recommendations are based on what makes you distinctive – not what makes you a copy.

You're at the mercy of the competition's innovations

Imitators are always playing "catch up" with their imaginative competition. They always must be on guard for the next new thing, so they can find some way to replicate it.

Take razors, for example. For many years, Gillette was the innovator. However, two guys having a conversation at a party changed the razor business.

When Mike Dubin and Mark Levine met, by chance, their conversation somehow steered toward something men have complained about for decades -- their frustration with buying razors. Razors cost too much, they were kept under lock and key at many drugstores, making purchasing a pain.

Companies would announce great breakthroughs in technology that no customer was clamoring

for – yet increased the price of blades again. When a guy tried to save money and use an older blade, he often got hurt from a cut or nick.

Rather than being at the mercy of Gillette – as most men were – Dubin and Levine decided to do something about it.

Notice that others in the shaving industry played the same game as Gillette -- and were perceived as imitators. Even though it was Schick that introduced the first four-blade razor blade, they were viewed by many as imitating Gillette's "more blades" approach to shave technology by the marketplace.

Dubin and Levine decided there was a market for lower priced, lower technology blades delivered without the hassle of the typical retail purchase.

So, from Mike Dubin's living room as the office – and a garage in Venice, California, as company headquarters – Dollar Shave Club was born in July 2011, from the spirit of innovation, not imitation. By June 2015, Dollar Shave Club had about 2,000,000 subscribers. And on July 19, 2016, Unilever acquired Dollar Shave Club for a reported $1 billion in cash.

All because they didn't put themselves at the mercy of the competitor's innovations. They used their IMAGINATION to create a billion-dollar business.

By definition, an innovation is something that isn't currently in the marketplace. So, in most cases, your employees and customers haven't thought of it yet.

There's no reason why the company that gave us the Walkman failed to give us the iPod. Sony had already innovated in portable music.

There's no excuse why the company that had the good sense to create Sports Illustrated couldn't come up with ESPN. SI had already innovated in sports reporting.

Why couldn't Maxwell House or Folger's – with such an amazing head start – develop what we now know as Starbucks? Those companies had already innovated in coffee.

Don't just consider the current state of your organization – think about the future. Ask yourself these questions:

How are my products and services different today than they were a year ago? Five years ago?

Ten years ago?

If your answer is, "not very," how are you keeping pace with the changes happening? You're not. And you're missing the intellectual growth that occurs when our minds are challenged by alternative ways of thinking.

The bottom line on Imagination

Not only do your customers want you to be imaginative, but it is also necessary for your organization, no matter what you do!

Innovation must have a means of transference within the organization. By that, I mean that you must not only conceive of a creative idea and plan its execution, but also focus on how your IMAGINATION and practice will be transferred throughout your business.

Do you have educational sessions?

Do you create a video on it to share and review? Do you provide a manual for all employees?

No matter what action you take, you must act.

Consider an "internal advertising campaign" to sell your imaginative ideas internally prior to its external exposure.

As my friend, the brilliant author and speaker Stephen Shapiro, says, "Maybe instead of thinking outside the box – we need to create a new box!"

The bottom line is that IMAGINATION is good for the bottom line.

It enhances customer excitement and loyalty towards your organization. It helps inspire employees to deliver at a higher level and builds their organizational loyalty. It generates recognition within your industry and community. It provides a differentiating factor from that horde of business that, through their action or inaction, merely advances the status quo of which the customer is so tired.

As you'll discover on these pages, some of the best thought leaders, authors, and speakers will provide you with both insights and instruction on how you can become more imaginative – and leverage that into enhanced success in business and in life.

It's one of the most critical in the *13 Steps to Riches!*

SCOTT MCKAIN

About Scott McKain: Scott's matchless experiences have continued throughout his life. They range from playing the villain in a Werner Herzog film that Roger Ebert called one of the 50 "great movies" in cinema history to being booked to speak by Arnold Schwarzenegger for an event on the White House lawn with the President in the audience; from being the author of business books named among the "year's ten best" to membership of multiple Boards of Directors.

The tapestry of Scott McKain's distinctive experiences have blended to create the inimitable content that makes him one of the world's most in-demand business experts and speakers.

Scott first became interested in business — and creating Ultimate Customer Experiences® — while helping in the family business, the grocery store in his hometown of Crothersville, Indiana.

After high school graduation, Scott was elected as the Indiana President, then as a National Officer of a half-million-member student leadership organization. By the end of his terms, Scott had presented over 1,000 speeches on platforms ranging from high school cafeterias to arenas with audiences of 20,000+ in attendance. By age 21, Scott had chatted with the President in the Oval Office, lunched with the President of Brazil, had a private meeting with the Chairman of General Motors, and dined with the real-life Colonel Sanders of KFC fame.

These unique experiences as a youth inspired both a passion for the platform and a fascination with business and leadership that continues to this day.

Scott has delivered over 2,000 presentations in 36 countries across six of the seven continents helping audiences create more compelling connections, provide ultimate customer experiences and stand out personally and professionally.

Scott shares his distinctive ideas and iconic speaking style to the most important events in the world and has been honored with the following:

- Currently "Corporate Educator in Residence" at High Point University, named by *U.S. News & World Report* as the nation's "most innovative" university.
- He has been honored with induction into the "Professional Speakers Hall of Fame."
- He was selected to join Seth Godin, Zig Ziglar, and Dale Carnegie as one of about 25 members of the "Sales and Marketing Hall of Fame."
- He is a member of "Speakers Roundtable" — an elite, invitation-only group of twenty business speakers considered by many to be among the best in the world.

Scott currently lives with his wife Tammy in Las Vegas where they are involved in several charitable organizations.

Scott is the author of four #1 business bestsellers on Amazon; all teaching how to expand profits, increase sales, and engage customers. To name a few of his books, Scott has written:

- *ICONIC: How Organizations and Leaders Attain, Sustain, and Regain the Ultimate Level of Distinction*
- *Create Distinction: What to Do When "GREAT" Isn't Good Enough to Grow Your Business*
- *7 Tenets of Taxi Terry: How Every Employee Can Create and Deliver the Ultimate Customer Experience*
- *Digging Wells and Building Fences: Discover the Steps to Combat Showrooming, Converge Physical & Digital Retailing, and Create Customers for Life*
- *All Business is STILL Show Business: Create Distinction and Earn Standing Ovations from Customers in a Hyper-Competitive Marketplace*
- *What Customers REALLY Want: How to Bridge the Gap Between What Your Organization Offers and What Your Clients Crave*

Glenn Lundy

JUST IMAGINE

Once upon a time, in a land far, far away…There was a princess…and a Villain! A hero and his trusty steed! There was turmoil, epic battles, and moments where all was thought to be lost. There was magic! Excitement! Adventure! And nail-biting triumphs! And in the end, they all lived… Happily Ever After.

Just imagine if all stories were like that. Fiction and Non-Fiction. Imagine what humanity would look like if the villains of the world were exaggerated to the point that they were blatantly obvious. Like they wore a cape and had a huge hunchback, or they carried a living, shape-shifting staff. Their teeth were all gnarled, and their noses and feet were, for some reason, oddly out of proportion, things like that.

And the heroes! They, of course, were chiseled and perfectly symmetrical. They would strut around with quiet confidence, poised and positioned to come to the rescue at any given moment. Easily identifiable by their colorful one-piece suit and the undeniable sense of humility that they carry themselves with.

Can you imagine it? A world where bad guys are easy to see coming, and good guys are always there to save the day? A world where it always ends up "Happily Ever After. My guess is probably not. What a far stretch from the world we live in today, right? I mean, sheesh, nowadays, half the time, you don't even know what country the bad guy lives in. With internet scams, trillions of dollars stolen and exchanged, politicians on the take, fake news, misinformation, agendas, pandemics, etc., I mean, crime is just a part of life nowadays, right? Everything from shoplifting to insurance scams to the outright taking of someone's life, we have come to live in this world with an understanding that both good AND evil do exist, and it can be quite tricky distinguishing between who is who—both externally and internally.

My name is Glenn Lundy. I am a husband to one, a father to eight, a 23-year automotive professional, and the proud owner of three companies. I am also an author, a motivational speaker, a leadership business consultant, and the host of the #1 Online Morning Show in the world, "#RiseandGrind." Oh yeah, and did I mention I am the founder of "Breakfast with Champions" on the Clubhouse app? Well then, there is that too.

I have also been to jail 17 times. I have stolen a vehicle from a rental company before, drained my girlfriend's bank account when she wasn't looking, fallen behind on years' worth of child support, done most drugs you can think of, took full advantage of women when the opportunity knocked, and traveled around the United States lying to and cheating just about every person I came in contact with. I have been homeless. I have been depressed. I have, at one point in my life, tried to kill myself. I have been labeled by many as a villain and a villain I was.

So, which one am I? A good guy? Or a bad guy?

Tough question, right? I mean, I've done many of the things that you would associate with a bad guy, and yet I've also used my life to make a positive impact on millions of people's lives worldwide. There are people who know me that would tell you I changed their life for the good, and more than a handful of people will tell you I changed their life in a negative direction. Both exist. There is no denying it. What's interesting, though, is you'll find that how someone responds to the name "Glenn Lundy" will relate to one thing and one thing only. Time.

People that knew me 15 years ago and before will likely describe me as the villain. People that have met me or had an opportunity to connect with me in the last 15 years will likely say the opposite. There is a clear and definite line. A line that I will share with you in detail. A line that if you are looking to create lasting and positive change in your life, you too can cross. When you do, the person you are today will become just as unrecognizable as the real-life, modern-day heroes that exist in our world today.

A Story of Death.

When I received the phone call, I was floored. Grandpa's surgery had caused the cancer to spread all throughout his body. He only had minutes left to live, hours at best. I instantly began searching for flights out of Lexington, KY. I had to get to Phoenix, AZ, and I had to get there fast.

After booking my flights, I began to reflect on Grandpa's life. A military man through and through, he had dedicated his entire life to three things: The Army, the Republican Party, and his family. He was an average-sized man physically, but a giant in my mind. A loyal man, a hard-working man, a lifelong member of the middle class, and a man who ALWAYS, and I mean ALWAYS, wore a tie.

He and my grandmother were married for 49 years. Forty-nine loving, caring, tremendous years they had been together, and through that entire time, not once had my grandmother held a job, carried a driver's license, or ever wanted for anything. They loved each other so much that even the fact that my grandmother was a die-hard Democrat couldn't keep my grandfather away. Can you imagine? My grandfather was the president of the men's republican society for the American Legion, and my grandmother was the president of the women's Democratic society for the American Legion. Yet, they spent forty-nine years together blissfully married! I wouldn't have believed it if I didn't witness it myself. These two were inseparable.

They had five kids together, four girls and one boy. All five of their children joined the military at one point in their lives, and most carried their Army fatigues long into their lives. They lived in a small apartment in Chandler, AZ, and were both hometown heroes and legends at the local American Legion. But none of that mattered now. Grandpa was going to die in a hospital bed from Agent Orange he had breathed in during the war. It had taken years to set in, but ultimately emerged as the cancer that would take his life.

I had to get there to say goodbye. I needed him to hold on.

It took me a while to get out of Kentucky and over to Arizona, but thankfully when I arrived at the hospital a day and a half later, Grandpa was still alive. Most of the other family members had arrived, but a few were still on their way. I guess that's the negative side of a military family. We were spread out all over the country. Everyone was scrambling to get by his side before he passed, but the odds were stacked against us. If only he could hold on just a little bit longer.

Two days after the initial phone call, the last family member, my aunt Julie, arrived. Everyone was a bit confused, of course, and many questions were being asked. They all were tired from travel, from sleeping in the hospital, or maybe just the emotional drain that comes with knowing a loved one is on his way out, but we were all there—every last one of us.

As a complete family, we all waited, talked, laughed, and cried, and then at one point, they allowed us all to go into his room. He lay there sunken, hollow, A shell of the man I remembered. His eyes were hallowed in, he had lost tons of weight, and his skin color was off and looked translucent. I barely recognized him. He had tubes attached in every orifice, and his breathing was labored. It was awful. Absolutely awful.

We all stood in a semi-circle a few steps away from his bed. Tears were leaking out of all of our eyes, and then suddenly, he spoke. It was raspy and clearly difficult for him to get the words out, but after a few stutters and gasps for air, a surprising request could be heard.

"Everett, can you please come and tell me my favorite joke?"

Everett was my stepdad, and you must understand something. As well as being a soldier, a veteran, a husband, a father, and an admirable man, my grandfather was also a fan of dirty jokes. He always had one for every occasion. Grandpa always had a dirty joke to set the tone for the evening, whether it be a speech he was giving at the legion or a family gathering for the holidays. (He also had a tie for every occasion, from St. Paddy's Day to Jesus on the Cross, to Santa doing naughty things with Mrs. Clause, but that's a different story.) So, though the request was a surprising one considering the situation, it was fitting considering Grandpa's personality.

My stepdad hesitated but then walked towards my grandfather and leaned in. "Al…" He looked back at all of us. "What do you call Moby Dick's father?" Grandpa cracked a short grin. "What, Everett?"

"Poppa Boner." Whispered Everett, just audible enough for all of us in the room to begin to laugh as the tears rolled down our faces.

Grandpa chuckled as well, and then he began to cough and wheeze a bit, and then his voice could be heard again.

"Bring me my wife." He said, with the command and authority I had always remembered. Kind, but clear, this wasn't a request. This was an order.

My grandma walked over to the bed.

Standing at 4 feet 6 inches, she was one of the tiniest of women, but her presence filled every room she had ever stepped into. Betty Smith was a force to be reckoned with. Kind, intelligent, and spirited. She was a woman who likened herself to Betty Boop. Classy, memorable, and just a little bit of sass. At this moment, she was no different. All eyes were on her as she walked confidently over to her husband and climbed into the hospital bed next to him. He then wrapped his arms around her tightly, squeezed her for one last embrace, and at that moment, he passed away.

It's been fifteen years since that day, but I remember it like it was yesterday or even this morning, for that matter. I remember it so vividly and so clearly because I learned two powerful things from that experience.

The first one might be expected. I learned that we ARE spiritual beings.

Unarguably, undoubtedly, it is a FACT. Science cannot explain to me how this deathly ill man was able to hold on for TWO DAYS while our entire family made their way to the hospital. Science cannot explain to me how he waited for the very last family member to arrive. Then after being told his favorite joke, getting in a small chuckle, he was then able to wrap his arms around his lifelong wife and pass away peacefully.

He got to choose his last moments on this earth, he had control, and science had nothing to do with it. His soul, his spirit, the spiritual side of my grandfather, choreographed his ascension into heaven. No man or woman on this planet can convince me differently, and that one fact, the fact that WE, you and me, ARE spiritual beings, is an absolute game-changer.

As spiritual beings, we have the power to create. To create the visions and the dreams of our wildest imaginations. To be able to create life, create wealth, and create machines, technology, books, poems, tables, chairs, parachutes, rockets, basketballs, and even blankets with sleeves. As spiritual beings, we can connect differently and see the world through new eyes. We can breathe inspiration into people all around the world and spark the spirits of mankind through a story, a production, a musical experience.

As spiritual beings, we transcend all that is of this earth and can connect directly with the God of the universe and all things within it.

As spiritual beings, we are no longer "just" humans, but more importantly, we are children of God, and that, my friends, means two things; A: We are loved. B: We have the DNA of the Creator in us.

You.

You are loved.

Your hair, your skin, your body shape—all of it. Exactly as you are, YOU are uniquely, urgently, and powerfully loved. Loved and protected, in a very fatherly way, God is there protecting you from the storms. He is watching over your every move and all along the way cheering you on so that you never, and I mean you never, will be alone.

Secondly, I learned that we are most comfortable in life, right before death.

There was a moment right before my grandfather passed away. A moment that came just as his last family member arrived to tell him goodbye and while he was listening and laughing to his favorite joke. It was brief, but it was there. It was just before wrapping his arms around his wife and saying his last goodbye that my grandfather was surprisingly comfortable. I mean, it was literally visible. The color had come back in his skin; the brightness in his eyes had come back as well. It was as if his cancer had gone away, along with the pain and fatigue it brought with it.

Suddenly he was recognizable. He looked, acted, and WAS the Grandfather I had known my whole life. The strong, pain-free, military man who had provided for his wife and kids his whole life while serving our country in the process. For just a moment, just before he passed on, he was Alfred Smith, honorable and strong, and I will never forget the way it sent shivers up my spine to witness him come back to the way that he did.

I had never experienced anything like this before. As a matter of fact, I had never experienced death of any kind before. Watching this man I loved die was my first ever experience in what the end of life looks like, and surprising as it sounds, his manner of death was the spark that has impacted me (and will continue to) for a lifetime.

That experience has led me to look at things differently in my life and ultimately was the catalyst of change for me. Before my grandpa's death, I was homeless, in and out of jail, on drugs, and known as a con artist and a thief. Since then, I've gotten married, raised eight babies, built two successful nationwide businesses, traveled the world, and have dedicated my life to bringing motivation, education, and inspiration to millions of people worldwide. Along the way, I've heard so many wonderful people say these words; "I just want enough to be COMFORTABLE." And every time, I can't help but correlate comfort with death. You're most comfortable in life, right before death. Now I don't know about you, but I am not ready to die yet.

Seeking comfort is the single most detrimental thing you can do as human beings to limit your true potential. All lessons, all growth, all fulfilling aspects of life can be attributed to situations where there is change, and wherever there is change, there is struggle. The struggle is where the growth occurs, and success is always just on the other side of growth. You see, in life, the path to living a purpose-filled, impactful existence is always going to follow that same cycle. Change, struggle, grow, succeed. Change, struggle, grow, succeed. Change, struggle, grow, succeed. Over and over, repeatedly, until one day you look up, and you've got your arms wrapped about your wife of 49 years saying your last goodbyes.

Seeking comfort is like seeking death. Simply put, IF YOU'RE NOT GROWING, YOU'RE DEAD already. Even though your physical body hasn't made that decision yet, that's neither here nor there. No growth = no life. No life = Death.

Comfort is a killer.

Whether you lose your job because you got comfortable in the position and quit performing, or you got divorced because you got comfortable in the relationship. It could be a loss of connection with your child because you were comfortable with the idea that they would be around forever and never truly appreciated them. Or maybe it's your spirituality. It's not uncommon for people's love for a higher power to lead to comfortable belief systems and behaviors. Sitting in the same chair every week, going to church weekly more to socialize than anything else. All these things are feeding into the comfort narrative and truly will keep you from your greatness.

Maybe you make enough money to be "Comfortable" but don't have enough to help others. Maybe you're comfortable with average, and it's killing your soul, a little bit at a time.

Maybe you're comfortable with the performance of your business, and you're missing out on the destiny God truly as planned for you.

Whatever it is for you, comfort is a killer.

This is the line. Learning these two things about myself and about you changes everything. Actions have consequences—both in this life and the next. Negative consequences, or positive, you choose.

It all starts in your imagination. Whom do you believe you are? A child of God? Or a child of flesh? A Villain? Or a Hero? A human living in lack and through trials? Or a spiritual being living in a world of abundance and triumph? What you imagine to be true for you becomes your reality. You have the power to create the life of your dreams, to draw the line, to choose to stay uncomfortable, and step into your greatness. This we know to be true, so what's it going to be?

How are you going to be remembered?

GLENN LUNDY

Glenn Lundy is a husband to 1, a father to 8. He is the host of the wildly popular Facebook Live show #RiseAndGrind and top Clubhouse group Breakfast with Champions. He's been seen at places like Hustle and Grind Con, Grow Your Business For God's Sake! and many more stages across the country. Glenn has been spotlighted on ABC, NBC, and CBS, and is an expert in dealership culture development, and leadership training. With 20 years of experience in the automotive industry, Glenn led a dealership from 120 cars a month to an 800% increase in sales in five years, becoming the 2nd largest used car franchise in the country. His unique style makes him one of the most coveted GM's in the business. Glenn has the unique ability to help identify the areas for growth in your store, and teach creative ways to invoke your dealership's spirit. With a background in sales, and finance, he uses his skill sets to create growth, as well as tapping into the mental side of human development.

Who Glenn was is no longer who he is, however, who he was has made him the man he is today. From behind bars and homeless, God managed to lift him out of the depths and has given him an opportunity to make an impact on this planet. It's an opportunity Glenn take seriously.

HUSBAND TO 1

Glenn's wife's skin has healing powers. From the first time his hand touched hers she transformed him from a broken and discouraged man, into the man he is today. Married since 2011 Glenn's wife is his best friend, his rock, his shoulder to cry on, and his biggest supporter. Before Glenn's wife came into his life, he had all but given up on his dreams, now he doesn't believe there is one that can't be achieved. With her in his corner they can take on the world in a powerful way, and God willing, be able to make a tremendous impact in other people's lives.

FATHER TO 8

Each of Glenn's kids have a unique and creative soul. Constantly learning, failing, growing, and achieving. He has learned more from them than he ever could've imagined. They are by far the most powerful teachers he's ever had in his life. From teaching to live a life filled with magic, to teaching that with sheer will and determination you can get through anything. Glenn's children are the blood in his veins, the beat of his heart, and the greatest gift God has ever given him in this lifetime.

AUTOMOTIVE INDUSTRY EXPERT

20 years of automotive industry experience has taught Glenn a lot. The first 7 he spent in Arizona learning how not to do things, and the last 9 he spent in Kentucky, leading a dealership in a small town, population 9,600, through a process of developing a winning culture. They experienced 800% growth in 5 years and ultimately grew from 120 cars a month, to a record 1,043 cars sold in March of 2018. Glenn now gets the honor and

the privilege to work with over 40 dealerships nationwide to help them achieve similar results!

HOST OF THE #RISEANDGRIND FACEBOOK MORNING SHOW AND BREAKFAST WITH CHAMPIONS ON CLUBHOUSE!

With over 500 episodes in less than two years, the #RiseandGrind daily morning show is filled with Motivation, Education, and Inspiration. Live from the #RiseandGrind studios, Glenn is sure to help you kick your day off on the right foot! The Breakfast With Champions Clubhouse room has housed some of the biggest names in the world, from Grant Cardone to Brian Benstock and beyond!

Author's Website: *www.GlennLundy.com*
Book series website & author's bio: *www.The13StepsToRiches.com*

Erik "Mr. Awesome" Swanson

IMAGINE THIS

"Man's only limitation, within reason, lies in his development and use of his imagination." – Napoleon Hill, *Think and Grow Rich*

Imagination is the beautiful creation of a mental image in our minds so powerful and astonishing that it is believed to be real. It truly is what makes the world go around in my eyes. Without Imagination, the world simply would be stagnant and at a standstill.

Napoleon Hill teaches us that there are two types of Imagination - the Synthetic and the Creative. Although both are so vitally important to our success, I would like to focus on the Creative Imagination with you today.

In fact, I have created a new concept in which I use Imagination along with three other important components; when combined, literally transforms anyone's success quotient into a fantastic proven result!

"VICI"

The concept is called "VICI," which implements four critical components: Visualization - Imagination - Creation - Implementation.

When I started working in the personal development world in my late twenties, I used to travel around the United States and Canada, training corporations and sales teams in various industries. It was a grueling job, to be honest. But it did give me the awesome opportunity to see the world, experience different cities and cultures, and meet so many individuals. It opened my eyes to so many lessons throughout those years.

One part of my job back then would be to conduct training workshops in front of strangers whom I had never met before and motivate them to take action on our company's offer for further training systems and seminars. So, if you think about it, I was a young guy in my twenties, just out of college, expected to go and train professionals who were older than me and most likely making twice the income I was at the time. To say that I was nervous at times would be an understatement.

I had to figure out a way to calm my nerves. I had to figure out a way to be the amazing and awesome individual I am and still get the fear out of the equation, at least pretend that the fear was not there. I had to do all of this without the strangers in front of me knowing what was truly going on in my mind while I stood in front of them. I was hoping they would not see the perspiration dripping from under my suit and tie.

I started to notice there was a direct correlation between my perspiration and my income. The more my fear showed to these strangers, the more my results and my income would take a dive. You know that saying, "Sweat and Tears?" Well, I started calling it my "Sweat and Fears!"

I really needed to change this around in my favor. If I didn't figure something out and quickly, I would have to reconsider what my career choice should truly be.

The fear was even creeping into my dreams the night before. If I knew I had an appointment with a team the next morning, that night before would be a rough ride in the brain of Erik Swanson while he slept.

Then one day, it hit me! I figured it out! I decided that if I was going to dream about these strangers every night before I met them the next morning in reality, then I would start to work on my dreams and win them over there!

Why not talk to them while I'm dreaming and get to know them there so that I would not be as nervous when I meet them the next day. I started to visualize them smiling and being very welcoming to me. I began to visualize them not judging me but actually enjoying my training and embracing my techniques. I started to visualize what types of objections they would have and actually visualize myself handling those objections perfectly in my dreams. This was such a game- changer!

Then I took it to the next level and imagined them applauding my speech and training. I imagined each one of these strangers signing up for our future trainings. I imagined that I already knew each of their names. I imagined they were great friends of mine already. Imagination worked in my favor in presenting to my mind something that felt like it was already in reality.

Once I had these two components all set in my dreams the night before each and every meeting, I took it to the next level. This would be the level of consciousness. It's also what I called the Level of Creation. In the morning, when I awoke, I would walk over to the mirror while brushing my teeth and start to Create the reality by repeating some amazing affirmations to myself about how this meeting will actually go.

I would say to myself things like: They love you! They respond to you in such a favorable way! They need you! They want you there with them!

I kept repeating great affirmations like this, and I would speak these words of affirmations out loud to myself. I would even thank them back out loud... even using common names. At first, it was hilarious. You could hear me saying my affirmations and then saying, "Thank you, John," "I appreciate that, Kathy," "You are so right, David!"

Once I had these three components down, it was time to suit up and conquer! Time for Implementation! I was so pumped up during my drive over to their offices that nothing could stop me— not even fear!

I would march right into their offices with a certain aura about me. People noticed that I was in such a great mood. People would start to smile at me for no reason. Everything just seemed to start flowing in such a positive way for me, no matter where I turned. Then, I started to notice that people wanted to surround themselves with this feeling and with ME!

Perfect! I'm ready! VICI was working! I started implementing all of the components while standing in front of these perfect strangers. And, wouldn't you know it, there would actually be a John, Kathy, and a David in the room somehow. Wow! Image that. I literally used the power of Imagination to create such a wonderful and beautiful environment. An environment in which I call your "PME," which stands for Positive Mental Environment. This is the environment in which we all strive to be in, yet many fail to achieve. You must subconsciously and consciously seek and create this environment.

Napoleon Hill was once asked if the art of Imagination can be learned as a skill. I am here to say it can. So, practice my VICI method and watch your results and your Imagination bring you to new successes in reality. In fact, let your Imagination go wild!

ERIK SWANSON

About Erik "Mr. Awesome" Swanson: As an Award-Winning International Keynote Speaker and 13 Time #1 Best-Selling Author, Erik "Mr. Awesome" Swanson is in great demand around the world! He speaks to an average of more than one million people per year. He can be seen on Amazon Prime TV in the very popular show SpeakUP TV. Mr. Swanson has the honor to have been invited to speak to many universities such as the University of California (UCSD), Cal State University, University of Southern California (USC), Grand Canyon University (GCU), and the Business and Entrepreneurial School of Harvard University. He is also a Faculty Member of CEO Space International and is a recurring keynoter at Vistage Executive Coaching. Erik also joins the Ted Talk Family with his latest TEDx speech called "A Dose of Awesome."

Erik got his start in the self-development world by mentoring directly under the infamous Brian Tracy. Quickly climbing to become the top trainer around the world from a group of over 250 hand-picked trainers, Erik started to surround himself with the best of the best and soon started to be invited to speak on stages alongside such greats as Jim Rohn, Bob Proctor, Les Brown, Sharon Lechter, Jack Canfield, and Joe Dispenza... just to name a few. Erik has created and developed the super-popular Habitude Warrior Conference, which has a two-year waiting list and includes 33 top-named speakers from around the world. It is a 'Ted Talk' style event that has quickly climbed to one of the top 10 events not to miss in the United States! He is the creator, founder, and CEO of the Habitude Warrior Mastermind and Global Speakers Mastermind. His motto is clear... "NDSO!": No Drama – Serve Others!

Author's Website: *www.SpeakerErikSwanson.com*
Book Series Website & Author's Bio: *www.The13StepstoRiches.com*

Jon Kovach Jr.

YOUR DISBELIEF IS MY FUEL

"Whether you believe you can or can't, you are right." - Henry Ford

Just like the scripture suggests, "Faith without works is dead," IMAGINATION without ACTION is merely a daydream."

I've heard it time and time again, "Jon, you need to be more realistic…, get your head out of the clouds…, that's a nice dream, but do you know how long it will take or how much it will cost…." Even though these responses to my dreams, visions, and aspirations often come from someone's hope to be helpful, their criticism has always led me to think bigger. I believe that the influence and expectations from others limit our thoughts and beliefs.

"It has been said that anything can be created that a human being can imagine." ~Napoleon Hill, *Think and Grow Rich*

My principal sat us down to debrief the 2007-2008 Student Council leaders. He informed us that the budget was about $5,000 in the hole. He advised us to do a fundraiser to save the senior prom planning. Instantly, after he said we did not have a budget, my brain immediately raced through ideas to solve this problem with non-costly ideas and creativity. They say it takes money to make money, but I was about to prove that statement incorrect.

I knew I could pull the student body, the faculty, the community, and even students from other schools with a Battle of the Bands concert, a live dance party, and complimentary concessions, which were every adolescent's trigger words in 2008. I called it BOB (Battle of Bands)! I began reaching out to all my friends and connections to book ten local bands for our battle concert. I used some of my birthday money and sound equipment to create an iPod-operated DJ system for the event. We marketed that DJ Jet was emceeing the event (that's me, Jon the Jet, known for his track and field speed). I knew people would come no matter the cost because of the hype, so we charged $20 per person.

I had the student council then create ambiguous marketing publicity and place them on every door and window of the high school, asking questions such as, 'Who is performing at BOB?, What should I wear to BOB? I hope DJ Jet plays my song,' to name a few. We needed everyone to talk about BOB without knowing precisely what BOB was to stir up interest and curiosity. I also knew that this would be our school's first band battle event.

On the evening of the event, my team and I finalized our preparations, said a prayer, and then walked out to greet the guests. We figured there'd be at least a couple of people waiting outside. I was so nervous. But I knew that we had fulfilled all the plans that had built up in my imagination. I opened the doors to let people in, shocked by what I saw—a long line of students wrapped around the building and the block.

Before we even planned this event and thought we could solve our deficit problem, I didn't know we would experience fire code issues with the capacity of the concert hall. All I knew was if we could fill the open commons space at the school, we would have enough room for bands and dancing and make a lot of money.

After 20 minutes of taking ticket sales at the door, we surpassed our goal of raising $5,000 and bringing our budget out of the hole. After two hours of ticketing, we had made over $15,000 in profits. We gave a $300 check to the winning band and a $150 check to the second-place band. The BOB event was a huge hit! We broke school records, spent zero funds setting up the event, and we started a tradition that outmatched all of the annual student council fundraisers for years to come!

I had never thought it was impossible. But when our principal broke the news of the significant deficit in our funds, I thought to myself, "Why are we getting so hung up about things that are keeping us down? Instead, let's create something that will be amazing and bring us back on top." I guess that's just how my mind works.

Your imagination can create solutions for anything in this world. I believe that four significant attributes of imagination lead to creating ideas, implementing plans, and bringing ideas to full fruition. Those attributes are:

- Problem-solving heart
- Inquisitiveness mindset
- Optimistic beliefs
- Solution-oriented

These attributes have served many of my clients and me for years as we strive to achieve high- performance outcomes in all things. My imaginative brain didn't stop nor pique in high school. I've managed to harness this belief system for many years. As crazy as it may sound, though I lack balance in them daily, these attributes have guided me to live multiple lives in my few short decades of existence in this life.

To list a few: I built a DJ business at age 16, evangelized Christianity to hundreds of people throughout the world, learned three foreign languages, lived in two countries, moonlighted in an English-Filipino cover band, competed in five 200-mile Ragnar relay races, worked with multiple non-profits, coached over one-thousand professionals on their goals and habits, and much more.

I am proud of two recent accomplishments within the last five years: building a networking company that helped professionals make profitable connections that led to $20 million of connection-to-connection transactions between my members. The other achievement is my devoted study, application, and implementation of the mastermind methodology defined by Napoleon Hill in *Think and Grow Rich*, dedicating over 7,000 hours of learning and honing my understanding and craft in the mastermind art. I'm blessed to have a great friend and mentor in Erik "Mr. Awesome" Swanson take me under his wing to learn this trade and service through the application of facilitating and leading many of the Habitude Warrior Mastermind Groups founded by him.

Imagination + Action = Anything You Can Dream

I've done this in almost every aspect of my life. However, if a young kid with ADHD from a farm town in Colorado can do all of this in such a short amount of time, imagine what you can achieve with your most extraordinary talents and strengths.

I imagined competing in the decathlon against top Division I athletes.

I imagined getting a college degree and ranking as one of the top student leaders in the country. I was elected as the Public Relations Student Society of America's Vice President, received multiple awards, and led my university's chapter to be number one in the nation in 2016.

- I imagined being happily married to the love of my life. That came true.

- I imagined being an international motivational speaker.

- I imagined making a six-figure income.

- I imagined traveling to unique countries around the world.

- I imagined building my own company. I've created four of them.

- I imagined creating a drop-shipping company that would pay for all of my apparel through my sales. It took me 30 minutes to complete that one.

- I imagined filling a room of people to hear me give a speech. That was easier than I thought.

- I imaged building friendly relationships with top motivators and personal development masters throughout the world. Each person I connect with feels natural.

I think you get the point. If you can dream it, you can build it. No questions asked. Every time I dream it, it comes true. I believe the same is in store for you.

I invite you to imagine what you will achieve next. Then, instead of creating a goal of what you want, start phrasing your goals using words that describe you as already being in possession of those goals. Then, the power of infinite intelligence, desire, and human nature will automatically begin to put the results of those imaginations into works.

"The view you adopt for yourself profoundly affects the way you lead your life. It can determine whether you become the person you want to be and whether you accomplish the things you value." ~ Carol Dweck, Mindset: Changing The Way You think To Fulfill Your Potential

IMAGINATION is the birthright of all living, functioning beings. Ideas, thoughts, and actions all stem from creating this infinite source. In and of itself, life is the accumulative odds and outcomes of ideas followed by measures taken from the entire existence of humanity.

If it weren't for the world's attempts at convincing me of having more "realistic expectations," I might not have gone above and beyond the norm. Now that you've eliminated your limitations, what will you imagine next?

Thank you for fueling my fire of desire and helping me dream bigger.

JON KOVACH JR.

About Jon Kovach Jr.: Jon is an award-winning and international motivational speaker and global mastermind leader. Jon has helped multi-billion-dollar corporations, including Coldwell Banker Commercial, Outdoor Retailer Cotopaxi, and the Public Relations Student Society of America, exceed their annual sales goals. In his work as an accountability coach and mastermind facilitator, Jon has helped thousands of professionals overcome their challenges and achieve their goals by implementing his accountability strategies and Irrefutable Laws of High Performance.

Jon is the Founder and Chairman of Champion Circle, a networking association that combines high-performance-based networking activities and recreational fun to create connection capital and increase prosperity for professionals.

Jon is the Mastermind Facilitator and Team Lead of the Habitude Warrior Mastermind and the Global Speakers Mastermind & Masterclass founded by Speaker Erik "Mr. Awesome" Swanson.

Jon speaks on a number of topics, including accountability, The 4 Irrefutable Laws of High Performance, and The Power of Mastermind Methodologies. He is a #1 Best-Selling Author and was recently featured on SpeakUp TV, an Amazon Prime TV series. He stars in over 100 speaking stages, podcasts, and live international summits on an annual basis.

Author's website: *www.JonKovachJr.com*
Book Series Website & Author's Bio: *www.The13StepsToRiches.com*

Amado Hernandez

IMAGINATION

He stood at the beginning of Main Street, watching a crowd of 28,000 people rushing toward him. To his right was a Hollywood movie star. To his left was the product of his IMAGINATION — a five-foot mouse with giant ears. A little nervous and a lot excited, Walt Disney turned to Ronald Reagan and said, "I only hope that we never lose sight of one thing — that it was all started by a mouse." It was July 17, 1955. After a lifetime of IMAGINATION, the gates of "The Happiest Place on Earth" opened for the first time.

Four months later and 1,600 miles to the south, I was born in Villamar, Michoacan. My *Wonder Years* were as different from Kevin Arnold's as Frontierland was from Tomorrowland. Like many other people around the world, my father struggled to support our family and took his entrepreneurial IMAGINATION to America. I was six years old when my father left to make his fortune in Los Angeles. For the next five years, my father returned to Mexico for a month each year and promised me that one day we would all move to America where I could be anyone I wanted to be and have anything I wanted to have.

I was eleven years old when my father arranged to legally bring our family to America. So one day, my mother, my little sister Lupita and my baby brother Roberto, and I jumped on a giant bus with three gold stars on its side. That ride was about to change my life and was more exciting than any ride at Disneyland ever could have been. Finally, we were coming to America! The land of IMAGINATION and opportunity; la tierra de leche y miel.

IMAGINATION is the process of creating new mental images. "New" means just that - things we have not yet experienced. It is a magical process. And IMAGINATION may be the most personal, powerful, and priceless gift that God has given us, beyond the basic gift of life itself. Private? Who knows what technology might have in store for us? For now, nobody can know what we are thinking unless we choose to share it. Powerful? Because it empowers us to take the actions needed to change our lives and our society. Priceless? The ability to imagine provides more value to our lives than virtually any other thought process.

IMAGINATION comes from a combination, or combinations, of the faces, places, things, thoughts, and words that we have experienced. That includes what we have seen, heard, smelled, tasted, or especially felt in the past. These are the raw elements of our imaginations. Our minds then reshuffle and deal cards with infinite possibilities. For some people, it may be like a game of Old Maid or Crazy Eights. For others, it might be a more complex card game. For me, it's a lot like 52-Card Pickup. It's an exercise of forming and evaluating many different possibilities and impossibilities.

The process of IMAGINATION can also be like the experience of putting together a jigsaw puzzle. With elementary imaginative skills, one might only be able to assemble a puzzle of a few pieces like those little puzzles in kindergarten. You know the ones made from wood or cardboard with simple red, blue, yellow, green, and orange shapes. So, you look at the pieces and then at the frame and imagine where each piece fits. There is only one possibility. Either the pieces fit into their own space, or they don't.

It's important to note that we're probably all born with imaginations but that developing our personal imaginative skills comes from our unique life experiences. That's why some people have what is often called a "lively IMAGINATION" while others can't imagine their lives ever changing for the better. But unfortunately, those same people often waste their limited imaginative talent by only imagining a worse version of themselves rather than the best possible versions.

So back to puzzles. If you only try to put together simple five-piece puzzles, you will only have simple dreams — ones that are limited rather than unlimited. On the other hand (de otra manera), putting together, or even attempting to put together, more complex puzzles yield infinite possibilities. Think of the term "in my wildest IMAGINATION."

Obviously, none of us started out by dumping out a 1,000-piece puzzle of the Milky Way onto our dining room table or living room floor. But think of your IMAGINATION as a virtual and dynamic jigsaw puzzle with unlimited configurations that are made up of everything you have consciously or subconsciously experienced. That means, up to any given moment in your life (situations and sensations, the good, bad, and ugly of your life)—everything from your tears and fears to your happiest and most triumphant times.

As the little Mexican boy (me) sat on the bus heading for the border at Tijuana, my excitement and hope over-rode my IMAGINATION. But that all changed as we all jumped in the car with our father in San Ysidro. We were in America heading for someplace called Los Angeles. It was then that my IMAGINATION went to work. Looking out of the window of my dad's car was strikingly different than looking out of the window of the bus in Mexico. I thought about Alicia en el País de las Maravillas (Alice in Wonderland) and imagined myself falling down the rabbit hole into a magical new place.

The whole trip, I kept thinking about my father's yearly promises that I could be anyone I wanted to be and have anything I wanted to have in America. I still didn't know what that meant. Overwhelmed, I looked around inside the car at my family and thought, "I already have everything I want." And looked at my father's face in the rear-view mirror, smiled to myself, and thought, "I am already who I want to be; my father's oldest son."

My father taught me to dream. I come from a long line of Mexican emprendedores. But the most important thing that my father taught about dreaming is that IMAGINATION without action is entirely worthless. His formula was: IMAGINATION + action = success. Without action, dreams are just dreams!

IMAGINATION is knowing there's something out there and being able to visualize it even if you can't see it. It's kind of like looking up into a cloudy sky at night and not being able to see the stars even though you know they are there. We all see something different when we look up at a cloudy sky at night. The tycoons that Napoleon Hill interviewed and wrote about all had great imaginations. When Andrew Carnegie looked up into the sky, he imagined selling more steel than anyone else in the world. Henry Ford imagined revolutionizing the way automobiles were assembled. Harvey Firestone imagined putting tires on as many "horseless carriages" as possible. And Thomas Edison imagined lighting up the world.

Our modern entrepreneurs are like Steve Jobs, who imagined "putting a dent in the universe" with a personal computer. He recruited Pepsi's hottest vice president by asking him, "Do you want to sell sugar water for the rest of your life or come with me and change the world?" Elon Musk is the *NOW* entrepreneur who seems to have an unlimited IMAGINATION that will take us to those stars that are hidden from us on cloudy nights.

The iconic American Dreamer? Walter Mitty, who had an enormous IMAGINATION in The Secret Life of Walter Mitty (2013), quoted the Life magazine motto, which pretty much says it all: "To see the world, things dangerous to come to, to see behind walls, draw closer, to find each other and to feel." Now that takes an IMAGINATION!

Some people are naturally capable of making their own dreams come true. Others need help, guidance, inspiration, and empowerment. I envision myself continuing to help others realize their dreams, change their lives, and impact the world. Whether that's as a Latino entrepreneur, mentor, coach, friend, author, or speaker doesn't matter. That's what my father meant when he told me I could be anyone I wanted to be.

AMADO HERNANDEZ

About Amado Hernandez: Amado was born in Mexico of humble beginnings and raised in Los Angeles, California. As an avid reader, Amado always focused on self-development. He coaches sales professionals to make six and seven figures in real estate.

Amado believes in a progressive culture, one people-centric where clients' dreams come true and salespeople thrive; at the end of the day, we all want to be respected and pursue our happiness.

My goal is to leave a legacy-making a difference in people's lives.

With 33 years of Real Estate experience, Mr. ABC Amado Hernandez successfully operates and grows his Excellence Empire Real Estate Moreno Valley office. Broker/Owner Amado first opened his doors in 1995, and Excellence currently has over 60 offices in Southern California, Las Vegas, Merida Yucatan, Mexico, and over 1,000 Agents. He is also part owner of a highly successful Mortgage company Excellence Mortgage and owner of Empire Escrow Services. Mr. Amado is also involved with his community and currently serves as Director at Inland Valley Association of Realtors and will be the President-Elect for 2023.

Author's Website: *www.ExcellenceEmpireRE.com*
Book Series Website & Author's Bio: *www.The13StepstoRiches.com*

Angelika Ullsperger

IMAGINATION WILL FIND THE HOW

"If you want to do it. YOU CAN. Where there is a will there is a way and IMAGINATION is the how." -Angelika Ullsperger

Every solution to every problem started in the mind and was fueled by IMAGINATION. Every creation created, every invention invented, and every step taken forward was powered by IMAGINATION.

So, as I write, I'm going to be honest because there's no point in pretending I've ever had trouble with being creative. Throughout my entire life I've had an expansive IMAGINATION. Instead, let's talk about how I got to that point. Because everyone, regardless of who you are, has the power to imagine. I think that's the beauty of it; you can imagine anything and no one can stop you. The world in your mind is as big as you want it to be.

The best part is there are no bad ideas. Edison had to imagine 999 different ideas for a lightbulb before he found one that worked. IMAGINATION isn't about being perfect, it's about having fun exploring the corners of your mind. Your ideas don't need to be perfect. Every idea can be fuel for another, better concept. Over time, you can use your IMAGINATION to build on to your previous ideas. IMAGINATION is the fuel that will empower your ideas to come fully to fruition.

Where does IMAGINATION come from?

To make it simple, what you put in will form and create what comes out. It may not be the same, but without the ability to take in information, we wouldn't be able to imagine anything.

It can come back out into your IMAGINATION. For example, when babies are first born, they don't dream. This is because they actually can't see anything, and because they can't see anything, they can't dream. That sounds weird, doesn't it? Well, it's because there's nothing for them to see, so there's nothing to fuel their IMAGINATION. Their brains have no record of anything to refer to. Once they can see and their brains begin to absorb information, they can finally dream. Therefore, the more you can take in, explore, try new things, read new books, or watch new movies, the wider your IMAGINATION can be. Stay open and observant so you can take in as much as possible and use it to fuel your IMAGINATION. There are so many ways to do this. I wish I could list every way in this book, but by practicing some of the techniques (listed at the end of the chapter) you'll be able to imagine more

You CAN!

I'm sure you've heard someone say they aren't an artist. Maybe you are that person. But why? An artist is defined as "a person who engages in an activity related to creating." No part of the definition says you have to be amazing, perfect, or a professional. The only requirement is creating.

This might mean that the only barrier between you and creating is you.

I've always loved the quote by Henry Ford, "Whether you think you can, or you think you can't, you're right." Don't let your IMAGINATION create boundaries and hurdles for you that don't actually exist. You CAN create, you CAN solve your problems and find answers to your questions.

You CAN. If you want to do it, YOU CAN. Where there is a will there is a way and IMAGINATION is the how.

Have fun!

I'm saying this one more time to make sure you know IMAGINATION is NOT about being perfect; it's about having fun exploring the corners of your mind. Your ideas don't need to be perfect. Sometimes they don't even need to be good! They can be trash and that's okay because every idea can be fuel for another, better concept. Over time, you can use your IMAGINATION to build on to your earlier ideas. IMAGINATION is the fuel that will empower your ideas to come into being.

Improving IMAGINATION.

As we discussed in *Volume 4: Specialized Knowledge,* the power in your mind is potential and it will stay as potential until you put it to use. This next step is particularly important if you want to widen your IMAGINATION's potential.

Let go and let yourself flow. Have fun.

Now, we need to get your brain moving and your ideas flowing. Go outside and seek adventure. You can walk, drive, or fly. But find something new to you. Our brains and our senses get used to what is around us, but when we go somewhere new, our senses are put on high alert. In an unfamiliar environment, you look around and your brain tries to take in everything in its surroundings. Your mind becomes stimulated and creates new neural connections and forms memories. All of this helps create divergent thinking, cognitive flexibility, critical thinking skills, and much more. All by fueling your mind with new stimuli.

Well, what if you can't travel?

No problem! There are plenty of ways to introduce new stimuli to our brains. The brain is a muscle. Just as there isn't only one way to gain arm muscles, there isn't only one way to improve your IMAGINATION.

Reading is a powerful tool. Books expand your knowledge and expose you to new ways of thinking. Fiction books use descriptive words to paint a picture in your mind.

If books aren't your thing, movies can help too. Even video games have been proven to increase creativity. Find creative media that's different from your usual and challenge your perception. Be diverse in the content you take in and the ways the content is presented to you.

Some of you are like me and are much more hands-on, but lucky for us there are plenty of ways to use your IMAGINATION to create something new. Activities like painting, wood working, or sculpting not only help you tune in to your IMAGINATION, but they can also let you achieve a state of flow.

The best way to access your IMAGINATION is to be with yourself. Put your phone away, turn the TV off, and sit somewhere where you are alone. Give yourself time to let your mind wander. You'll be surprised by how many ideas jump into your mind.

Now for a favorite of mine: Napping! When all else fails and you feel frustrated, relax, get comfortable, and take a nap.

And yes, this is a thing.

When you sleep, your brain creates new connections and solves problems which in turn fuels your creativity. It is believed the brain is most active somewhere between being awake and being unconscious. This state is referred to as hypnagogia or the hypnagogic state One usage of this is the "slumber with a key" method which Salvador Dali wrote about in his book, *50 Secrets of Magic Craftsmanship*. As we fall asleep, we enter a different brain stage. During this stage, the brain becomes more creative. Dali, Einstein, Edison, and others used this to their advantages. You sit in a chair and get comfortable with a key in your hand with a plate under that hand. Let yourself drift off to sleep. The key then slips from your hand and falls onto the plate, thus awakening you, refreshed with new ideas.

Inspiring IMAGINATION Action List

- Plan an Adventure!
- Attend a mastermind
- Take a trip to a new city, state, or country
- Take a creative class (free or paid)
- Practice Visualization
- Get Crafty (paint, scrapbook, woodwork, dance)
- Learn something new
- Try a new recipe
- Teach yourself a new skill
- Take a walk
- Observe your surroundings
- Go cloud watching. Try to see images where there are none
- Ask Questions: STAY CURIOUS
- Talk to others about ideas
- Create art, create anything
- Daydream
- Take a nap. Or Use the Slumber Key Method
- Look at the ideas and creations of others
- Read a book
- Play a video game or board game

ANGELIKA ULLSPERGER

About Angelika Ullsperger: Angelika is a serial entrepreneur from Baltimore, Maryland. She is a fashion designer, model, artist, photographer, and musician. Angelika has extensive and well-rounded professional experience having worked as a business owner, carpenter, chef, graphic designer, manager, event planner, sales and product specialist, marketer, and coach. Angelika is now a #1 Best-Selling Author in the historic book series, The 13 Steps To Riches. She is a life- long learner with a sincere and genuine interest in all things of the world with a major interest in the formal subject of abnormal psychology, neuroscience, and quantum physics.

Angelika prides herself as someone who has saved lives as a friend, first responder, EMT, and knowledgeable suicide prevention advocate. With a vast knowledge and experience in multiple professions, Angelika is also a proud honorable member of Phi Theta Kappa, The APA, the AAAS, and an FBLA (Future Business Leaders Association) Business Competition Finalist. She is Certified in basic coding and blockchain technology. Amongst the careers and vast experience, Angelika is an adventurer and avid dog lover.

Her ultimate goals and dreams are to make a lasting positive impact in people's lives through her wealth of knowledge and skillsets.

Author's Website: *www.Angelika.world*
Book Series Website & Author's Bio: *www.The13StepstoRiches.com*

Dr. Anthony M. Criniti IV

GREAT THOUGHTS
BECOME GREAT THINGS

Think and Grow Rich by Napoleon Hill is one of the best classic books to teach someone about how to become a financial success (as well as a success in other areas of life). In there, you will find his thirteen steps to riches; each one has its own separate chapter and analysis. The subject of our book is to interpret his fifth step to riches: IMAGINATION. But, first, let's review some of the significant highlights of this chapter.

First, Hill arranged the imaginative faculties of the human mind into two major forms: "synthetic IMAGINATION" and "creative IMAGINATION." For synthetic IMAGINATION, Hill says: "Through this faculty, one may arrange old concepts, ideas, or plans into new combinations. This faculty creates nothing. It merely works with the material of experience, education, and observation with which it is fed. It is the faculty used most by the inventor, with the exception of the "genius" who draws upon the creative IMAGINATION, when he cannot solve his problem through synthetic IMAGINATION." For creative IMAGINATION, Hill elaborates, "Through the faculty of creative IMAGINATION, the finite mind of man has direct communication with Infinite Intelligence. It is the faculty through which "hunches" and "inspirations" are received. All basic or new ideas are handed over to man by this faculty. It is through this faculty that thought vibrations from the minds of others are received. It is through this faculty that one individual may "tune in," or communicate with the subconscious minds of other men." (Hill, 2011, p. 136-138).

The above statements from Hill set the tone for this chapter on IMAGINATION by describing the foundation of his concepts. As I was reading his description of the above two forms of imaginative faculties of the human mind, I thought of a similar (yet slightly different) conclusion that I had reached in my last major book on the creative process of all life forms (not just human) that leads to individual evolution. Two out of the three major processes of my explanation of unique evolutionary selection in individual evolution used creativity; absolute creativity evolutionary selection and hybrid creativity evolutionary selection.

From *The Survival of the Richest*: "First, the individual can create a new inheritable evolution that is completely unrelated to any of the previous evolutions that ever occurred in its ancestral line. This evolution will be called absolute creativity evolutionary selection to reflect the pure creativity of the individual. Future descendants might be able to choose later if they want to keep this unique change as part of their inherited genetic wealth. This is one of the most important evolutionary changes and certainly one of the rarest. The second major process of unique evolutionary selection in individual evolution can be called hybrid creativity evolutionary selection. With this process, the individual learns how to create a new evolution by combining what it was taught to evolve by its ancestors. In other words, a person can combine her genes to create a unique pattern that has never been seen before." (Criniti, 2016, pp. 319-320). Indeed, IMAGINATION is a powerful force in humans and all life forms.

The conclusions of using the IMAGINATION to attain riches can also be applied to the abstract. In my field, my IMAGINATION has always been one of the strongest tools that I have used to derive many unique conclusions, which have helped to shift the paradigm of how economics and finance are viewed in academia. I delved very deep into Hill's "Infinite Intelligence" to derive the title and the arguments for my first book, *The Necessity of Finance*. I concluded that money and wealth are inescapable in modern civilization using my creative faculties. "The science of finance is necessary for everyone. In modern civilization, every individual, group, organization, and country (in the case of economics) needs money, and consequently wealth, to survive. Thinking of a situation where money would be irrelevant to function today takes much IMAGINATION." (Criniti, 2013, p. 45). And I did take much of it. I imagined many different scenarios, some mentioned in the same book, where money and wealth would not be necessary. This exercise only led me to open more and more doors to more profound conclusions. Hill was correct.

Another key highlight of Chapter 6 was Hill's admittance of his intention to reveal "The Secret": "Through repetition, and by approaching the description of these principles from every conceivable angle, the author hopes to reveal to you the secret through which every great fortune has been accumulated. Yet, strange and paradoxical as it may seem, the "secret" is not a secret." (Hill, 2011, p. 140-141). Here was another example of Hill demonstrating the marketing skills that he had acquired to hook the reader into wanting to know more. This "secret" being advertised throughout this book probably was the foundation of the major modern film produced with the same title.

Speaking of secrets, Hill gives a clue where he possibly came up with such a great concept. He highlighted one of the biggest brand names in history, Coca-Cola, as an example of the success of the thirteen steps to riches in his book. "Whoever you are, wherever you may live, whatever occupation you may be engaged in, just remember in the future, every time you see the words "Coca-Cola," that its vast empire of wealth and influence grew out of a single idea, and that the mysterious ingredient the drug clerk—Asa Candler—mixed with the secret formula was IMAGINATION! Stop and think of that for a moment. Remember, also, that the thirteen steps to riches described in this book were the media through which the influence of Coca-Cola has been extended to every city, town, village, and crossroads of the world, and that any idea you may create, as sound and meritorious as Coca-Cola, has the possibility of duplicating the stupendous record of this world-wide thirst-killer. Truly, thoughts are things, and their scope of operation is the world itself." (Hill, 2011, p. 145).

It is important to note that the last sentence in the above quote, although it later became famous, is inaccurate. Several years ago, Bob Proctor and Greg S. Reid authored a book titled Thoughts Are Things modeled after Hill's words. However, as Reid admitted in my interview of him on The Dr. Finance® Live Podcast in 2021, their work indicated that thoughts are not things but "become things." Greg said, "If thoughts were things, then I would be a pizza." Either way, Hill's point is made on how powerful a thought truly is. Using IMAGINATION, a thought can lead to the next major company that rivals the greatness of Coca-Cola.

The following phrase that I will mention from Hill highlights the monetary value of a great idea when properly put into action. The underlying lesson behind it is so powerful that it was stated in Principle 4 of *The Most Important Lessons in Economics and Finance*: "Almost every idea can transform into a successful business if applied correctly." (Criniti, 2014, p. 35). Hill states, "The story of practically every great fortune starts with the day when a creator of ideas and a seller of ideas got together and worked in harmony. Carnegie surrounded himself with men who could do all that he could not do. Men who created ideas, and men who put ideas into operation, and made himself and the others fabulously rich." (Hill, 2011, p. 153). The world is filled with countless examples of failed business ideas, but the ones that worked well were those that were applied properly by the right people.

One of my favorite quotes from this chapter and this book indicated the pain that Napoleon Hill had to go through to become a success. This quote is not only important from a historical perspective on the life of Hill and the *Think and Grow Rich* book that we have dedicated 13 books in this series to discuss, but also as a testimony to the difficulty of becoming a successful entrepreneur. Hill states, "The favorable break came through Carnegie, but what about the determination, definiteness of purpose, and the desire to attain the goal, and the persistent effort of twenty-five years? It was no ordinary desire that survived disappointment, discouragement, temporary defeat, criticism, and the constant reminding of "waste of time." It was a burning desire! An obsession!" (Hill, 2011, p. 153-154).

When reading this passage, the most striking part for me was about the "constant reminder" that what he was doing was a "waste of time" — imagine (excuse the pun) 25 years of this abuse that he had to face to become successful. I have noticed this was indeed a major part of my climb as well. This is an extremely frustrating process, especially when those words are heard by some of the closest people in your life. However, through interviewing many successful entrepreneurs, I have found it even more striking that Hill and I were far from alone. Actually, it was such a common theme in the stories of successful people who I have spoken to that I now view "naysayers" and "dream killers" as expected obstacles to navigate around on the right road to success.

To conclude, this chapter might seem odd to a novice. It is tempting for someone to ask, "Why would we need to discuss IMAGINATION in a book about becoming wealthier?" But as you read on and reflect, it is not difficult to discover its accuracy and necessity. All the objects that are displayed in front of us at this very moment represent a former idea that dangled in the mind of some "genius." Although children have a heightened use of their IMAGINATION, ironically, many adults seem to have diminished, or even lost, this great asset. If only they actually understood the message of this chapter, many more inventions (and millionaires) could be made. Our imaginative spirit, when used properly, can truly help to make great thoughts become great things.

Bibliography

Criniti, Anthony M., IV. 2013. *The Necessity of Finance: An Overview of the Science of Management of Wealth for an Individual, a Group, or an Organization.* Philadelphia: Criniti Publishing.

Criniti, Anthony M., IV. 2014. *The Most Important Lessons in Economics and Finance: A Comprehensive Collection of Time-Tested Principles of Wealth Management.* Philadelphia: Criniti Publishing.

Criniti, Anthony M., IV. 2016. *The Survival of the Richest: An Analysis of the Relationship between the Sciences of Biology, Economics, Finance, and Survivalism.* Philadelphia: Criniti Publishing.

Hill, Napoleon. 2011. *Think and Grow Rich.* United Kingdom: Capstone Publishing Ltd.

DR. ANTHONY M. CRINITI

About Dr. Anthony M. Criniti IV: Dr. Anthony (aka "Dr. Finance®") is the world's leading financial scientist and survivalist. A fifth generation native of Philadelphia, Dr. Criniti is a former finance professor at several universities, a former financial planner, an active investor in diverse marketplaces, an explorer, an international keynote speaker, and has traveled around the world studying various aspects of finance. He is an award winning author of three #1 international best-selling finance books: The Necessity of Finance (2013), The Most Important Lessons in Economics and Finance (2014), and The Survival of the Richest (2016). As a prolific writer, he also frequently contributes articles to Entrepreneur, Medium, and Thrive Global. Dr. Criniti's work has started a grassroots movement that is changing the way that we think about economics and finance.

Author's website: *www.DrFinance.info*
Book Series Website & Author's Bio: *www.The13StepsToRiches.com*

Barry Bevier

IMAGINE - VISUALIZE - MANIFEST

I'm extremely grateful to be a part of *The 13 Steps to Riches* project with an amazing group of brilliant, heart-centered entrepreneurs. Less than a year ago, I did not imagine being an author, let alone a multi-time bestselling author, collaborating with such an inspiring group of people.

In *Think and Grow Rich*, Napoleon Hill describes two types of IMAGINATION. Synthetic IMAGINATION, where existing ideas or things are brought together in a new and different way to produce an original concept or product, and Original IMAGINATION, where an entirely new concept or product is born of hunches and inspiration. Throughout my life, I've experienced mostly Synthetic IMAGINATION. Although until recently, I was imagining and creating subconsciously, not with intention.

In his teaching of *Think and Grow Rich*, Paul Martinelli discusses the concept of training our IMAGINATION by simply putting it into use by thinking about something we desire, to the smallest detail, and visualizing that we already have it. Now that I'm a student of personal development and *Think and Grow Rich*, I am becoming more intentional with my IMAGINATION and using it to create the life I desire.

As I continue to read and study *Think and Grow Rich*, I've gained a better grasp of the principles and an understanding of just how much they must work together. As I look back on my life, I never felt that I was an imaginative person and did not consider myself creative. Yet, during my engineering career, I was creating all the time. It took intentional IMAGINATION to be able to design the projects we worked on in our engineering business. As I get deeper into the philosophies of *Think and Grow Rich*, I've discovered that throughout my life, I have used the principles in *Think and Grow Rich* unknowingly. Sometimes to my benefit, and sometimes to my detriment. Fortunately, I think I have always benefitted from using my IMAGINATION.

As a homeowner, whether in a new home or an older home, I can imagine and visualize the changes I would make as if they were completed. I could see in my mind what the finished project would look like and how excited I would be with the result. Where I haven't used my IMAGINATION and vision was in planning my career or my finances. Through my personal development experience, I've learned, especially with studying *Think and Grow Rich*, that my life may have been very different had I intentionally trained my IMAGINATION, and used my IMAGINATION to dream and visualize what I would desire my life to be. So I'm doing that now.

I have no regrets about not knowing about these principles and putting them into play earlier in my life. Everything has been a lesson, molding me into who I am today. Because of the life I have lived, I'm excited and blessed that I now have these new tools and knowledge to be able to use my IMAGINATION and visualization skills to a higher level to manifest what I now desire in my life. As I think back where IMAGINATION, visualization, and manifestation have come into my life, I can think of a few experiences where, although I did not realize I was using these principles, I was, and the outcome was amazing.

One of the greatest and most memorable events in my life was an adventure I experienced with my dad not long before he passed away. In the early 1980s, The Great Race was conceived in the IMAGINATION of Tom McRae, a Texas entrepreneur, and his friend, Norm Miller, then

CEO of Interstate Batteries. They imagined, visualized, and brought into reality a cross-country adventure for antique and classic car lovers. The Great Race is a time-speed-distance precision driving rally for, at the time, 1937 and older cars and trucks. A coast-to-coast course is laid out on the back roads across America, through over 40 towns and cities. Up to 100 teams, consisting of a least a driver, navigator, and two crew or mechanics, trekked across the country over a two-week period, competing for over $250,000 in prize money. Each daily route has a perfect time based on the route instructions, and the goal is to have the perfect time. Any second too fast or too slow is a penalty point. The event itself was a feat of IMAGINATION, visualization, and the hard work of McRae and everyone he collaborated with.

I learned of the event in 1989 when there was an overnight stop in San Diego on its way from Norfolk, Virginia, to Disneyland. When I saw the event, I immediately imagined being an entrant with my dad. The variety of cars, the stories behind the teams, and their experiences on the race intrigued me. Dad had recently retired from farming and was pursuing his life-long dream of restoring antique cars. I imagined him building a car for us to compete in this event. He had completed his first restoration and was starting on the second one when I implanted my idea into his mind that we must do this event. He was as excited as I was about the idea. We applied and were accepted to the 1991 event, which was set to run from Norfolk, Virginia, to Seattle, Washington. Dad embarked on building and preparing a 60-year-old car to travel 500 miles a day and to endure a 4500-mile cross-country trip in two weeks. My task was to learn how to calibrate the car and navigate this type of rally, which I had never done.

The motto of the event is "To Finish is to Win." Meaning the daily goal is to get these old cars through each day without breaking down and having to be towed in. Having never done anything like this, we both imagined three goals: Getting the car ready, learning how to be competitive in the event, and never being towed in. Our goal was just to finish the adventure in one piece and have some fun along the way! As we loaded the car he had built on the trailer for the trip to Norfolk (and just about any spare part we could imagine, even an extra engine), it had been driven less than 500 miles since the total frame-off rebuild. It wasn't even broken-in and certainly not proof tested for endurance.

As we started with the event, our scores were awful. The teams experienced with the event would finish the day with a few seconds error off the perfect time. The first few days, our scores were way over a minute. Yet, we finished without a breakdown! Then on day four, the clutch gave out. We were still able to limp in without being towed and avoided a dreaded DNF. With the help of our and other crews, we were able to get the car repaired overnight and ready for our 6 am start the next day.

We imagined finishing every day and just enjoying the trip and our time together. But each day, we improved. Dad's driving skills got more accurate. My navigating skills became more precise. We started to feel "one" with each other and the car. About halfway through the race in Colorado, we broke a 1-minute score. We were ecstatic! I knew we were getting this, and I started imagining being in the winner's circle. We continued to work on our skills, improving our scores every day. And that vision of being in the winner's circle in Seattle got stronger and stronger. The days got long, hot, and tiring. Yet we persevered and continued to improve every day. As we would cross the finish line each evening and hear our score for the day, we got more excited and had a stronger visualization about being good enough to win. We became consistent with scores less than 20 seconds in the last few days and placed in the top few of our class.

While your score each day counts throughout the event, the last three days of the event, the Trophy Run, determines the winners of the awards and prize money.

We had a great first day of the Trophy Run. We scored with less than a 10-second error which put us in the running for placing in our class. I envisioned us doing even better the next two days and saw us crossing that finish line in Seattle as a winner! Placing in the top three, and bringing home some prize money was something we had never imagined when we embarked on this adventure a year earlier. Day two started out great. We had a rhythm and knew that we were doing well.

However, Murphy's Law came into play in the afternoon. I missed an instruction for a turn, and we were off course for several excruciating minutes, destroying our score for the day and the Trophy Run. I lost hope. Dad had worked so hard; we were doing so well. As we crossed the finish line that afternoon, we were surprised that we had a very low score. The instruction for the turn I missed was confusing, and many teams missed the same turn. Our bad-scoring leg was thrown out! That inadvertent success created an even stronger vision of us winning in our class.

The next morning as we prepared for the day, I knew we had a chance at it. The ESPN and event camera crews were filming us. As we came through the last checkpoint and headed toward Seattle, we were directed to a staging area just outside of town where the cars were lined up in a specific order to cross the finish line. This had never been done on any of the other days of the race. So, when we were motioned forward, I knew that we had manifested success. We placed third in our class and brought home a really cool trophy and over $6,000 in prize winnings. I was so proud of dad! As it turns out, he was the oldest rookie driver to participate in the race that year.

While it was tiring and at times stressful, it was the most amazing thing I could have ever imagined doing with my father. We had a wonderful time and learned how to work through the difficulties and problems as well as celebrate the daily successes. And I had my first lesson in using my IMAGINATION to consciously visualize and manifest a result that we both desired yet had never imagined we would be able to accomplish. The power of *Think and Grow Rich*!

BARRY BEVIER

About Barry Bevier: Barry Bevier is a proud father of two amazing daughters in their mid-twenties, who are pursuing their passions in psychology and architecture in Southern California. He was raised on a family farm near Ann Arbor, Michigan. Growing up, he developed his faith in God, a strong work ethic, a love for nature, and a passion to help others. After completing his master's degree in civil engineering at the University of Michigan, he pursued a career in engineering, which eventually brought him to Southern California.

In 2000, he married the love of his life, Linda. They shared a beautiful life for ten years, until she succumbed to the effects of lupus and 20 years of treatment with prescription medications. Since then, Barry pivoted his career path into educating and helping others. Barry has educated himself in alternative, natural modalities in wellness and became a Licensed Brain Health Trainer through Amen Clinics. He also works with a new technology in stem cell supplementation that releases your own stem cells.

Author's Website: *www.BRBevier.Stemtech.com*
Book Series Website & Author's Bio: *www.The13StepstoRiches.com*

Bonnie Lierse

IMAGINATION RUNS WILD

IMAGINATION is definitely one of my favorite Napoleon Hill principles! It makes me think about distinct, unusual colors, styles, sparkles, glitter, bling, and anything shiny! It's ok to laugh! Don't ever lose the child within you! To me, that's where the IMAGINATION all begins.

It started when I was very little! I definitely wasn't a predictable child. I loved using my IMAGINATION even at a very young age, my mother let me be me. Building tents or rooms out of cardboard boxes, that was an incredible high to me at that age. I loved collages and doing anything out of the ordinary.

Wouldn't you agree that the Magic Kingdom is the all-time magical place? Every kid and grownup's fairy tale! I know it is ours. "IMAGINATION runs wild!"

Have you ever been to Disney, EPCOT, MGM, Universal, and other magical places?

I have been to these places many times over with my family! These places brought out a side of me and made us THINK BIG!!

I can live in a fantasy at any time, of course! Can you? Genius and creating financial freedom can come out of one's IMAGINATION.

Being around that magical Disney environment always made me reach my potential. My son, Brandon, did an internship there! That was the spread of IMAGINATION on steroids!

You can be anyone and do anything you dream of if you imagine. I loved the figment character from Disney. It's all about IMAGINATION!

Time to manifest what you truly want! It just takes some beliefs! I watch my daughter, Cassi, constantly creating through her extensive IMAGINATION for herself and her children. My son in-law Jared is working on projects that began with imagination and an idea. Whether for events, decorating the house, or projects for the toddlers, her IMAGINATION runs wild!

Cassi, my daughter, inspires people to learn how to trust and heal their own bodies through whole foods low-tox living and mindfulness. All started with an idea that pops in one's head, belief and imagination.

My son and daughter-in-law have three boys, aged from 3 to 10. Each on their own levels, especially the 7 yr old, lives for IMAGINATION and is always encouraged by their parents. My ten-year-old grandson discovered music and keyboard on the computer. The sounds he's creating are off the charts. It started with his IMAGINATION and is still growing strong! That is an ear for music! Constant encouragement is vital! My daughter in law Viktoria, started her own business as a Reiki specialist. As she explains you are vibrations of light. Began with imagination and belief.

Even as a young girl, my teachers always said to me, "You're daydreaming again! You're not listening."

Truth be told, that's where my IMAGINATION started. But, especially sitting in a class I was not excited about!

As an artist, you have to have the IMAGINATION to create! That's my background from Pratt Institute. I was always challenged there to be imaginative. Even in subjects I never thought I would have taken. In Pratt, they want you to try many media and be well-rounded.

One of my favorite projects was a children's book I created and wrote in college. Definitely an imaginative story! IMAGINATION can start with an idea that pops into your head.

I created art in every type of media and texture all my life!

Even in the film industry, doing the front and back credits for movies, I did for years! You have to be imaginative in those careers. But, there are times on our journey life gets in the way, can be stress, challenges, and so we shut down our imaginary side of the brain! Been there, done that!

The best news is, you can get it back! It's a choice! (You can look at the glass half empty or half full).

Like what I am going through now, as we speak! You just need the right association of individuals that encourage you and help you bring out the best you!! Sometimes, it's a voice in your head from the other side. In my case, probably my husband or my mom.

I very, very recently lost my dear husband, best friend, and soulmate Tom Lierse and one of our sweet puppies, Diamond, in just one month. I can go two ways: I can crawl in a little ball and sulk indefinitely, or I can bring out my imaginative and magical qualities, use my creative brilliance I know is there, and let Tom from heaven see the best of myself surface! My dream would be to make him and my family proud and to honor them seeing the creative, imaginative genus surface! IMAGINATION can help you overcome any challenge and obstacle, as I am going through right now with the losses.

Everything is possible with concentration and a positive attitude, especially if you want to use your peak IMAGINATION! It might take a clear head, focus, mediation, and some breathing exercises.

Many years ago, I had the opportunity to work with mentally and physically challenged adults through an art program.

My purpose was to develop extraordinary projects and creative ideas that the individual could connect with and inspire and challenge them. It still starts with IMAGINATION running amuck.

E.g., One young man must have spent half his life in an attic (I was told his family couldn't handle his mental challenges most likely, and so he lived in the attic). He would draw things without picking up his pencil from the paper in one continuous line—things like fire hydrants, bugs, telephones. I'm guessing things he might have even seen out the window. His drawings were so creative. Have some saved, to this day.

Watching his IMAGINATION run wild inspired me daily. He barely spoke, but his communication was his IMAGINATION and through his drawings.

Another fellow was deaf, but his creative side exploded. He often painted from his IMAGINATION, even with his subtle mental challenges. IMAGINATION lets you release some enormous ideas inside, ideas you didn't even know you had!

Another way I loved how my IMAGINATION ran wild was doing event planning for my kids' huge events, like their Bar and Bat Mitzvahs. The sky was the limit! My daughter's event was Disney-based; my son's was limousine-based! Creating centerpieces to beautiful posters and signs, just to name a few, especially doing it with the kids together. It starts with everyone's IMAGINATION.

You can do anything you want when you let your IMAGINATION run wild!

People use their IMAGINATION in so many different ways! That's the beauty of it. Some use imagination through writing, like the extraordinary poems my husband wrote to me over the years, or the kids (some I even wrote to him with a lot more effort, didn't come easy for me). People do blogs, websites, etc., others through various and diversified art forms. You can use your IMAGINATION when starting a business or writing a book, like this one. It comes in so many forms. I have had multiple businesses in my life. It all started with imagining them or an idea that popped in my head, from an Interior Accessory design business, making jewelry, painting on clothes and rocks. The list goes on. Each can create cash flow.

Even creating a greeting card line, called "Prose and Condoms," totally started from my friend & partner Bob Shapiro and myself bringing our genius gifts together! It was based on safe sex in the '90s. It definitely took incredible IMAGINATION first!

Staging was another area I excelled in, in the early years. I used my IMAGINATION to help others create beautiful environments residentially or commercially with items they had or new ones they brought in (today called "Staging"). It ties in nicely with my real estate career these days.

Photography was a focus and passion in my college days when they had developing rooms. I am aging myself! This was way before instant pictures like today. So whether on the developing side of photos or taking the picture side, it starts with the creative IMAGINATION.

For a short time, I did children's birthday parties. It took being very imaginative to come up with ideas to stimulate the children. There were times I would just close my eyes and just let my IMAGINATION run wild!

IMAGINATION comes in so many various forms… the importance of it is that you don't forget to use it. Don't bury it. I promise it's there. Just take quiet time and maybe meditate. It will surface! Guaranteed.

BONNIE LIERSE

About Bonnie Lierse: Bonnie Zaruches Lierse is extremely artistic and creative, with an entrepreneurial bent. Besides that, she is a seasoned agent with more than twenty years' experience in real estate in the New York/Long Island area. She relocated to Northern Virginia in 2012 and continued her real estate career there.

Another passion is creating leaders by working in business leadership development with Leadership Team Development (LTD), marketing products supplied by Amway. She was also a member of The Screen Cartoonist Guild of Motion Pictures for many years. Also, she did freelance for Sesame Street in New York City. In addition, she was a District Director for an interior accessory design company, as her own business.

Bonnie is blessed with five beautiful grandchildren and is very close with her children and family, some of whom are also in Virginia. Her missions, are leadership, mentorship, paying it forward, and changing lives one at a time. Her motto is "You be the difference!"

Author's Website: *www.amway.com/myshop/SplashFXEnterprises*
Book Series Website & Author's Bio: *www.The13StepstoRiches.com*

Brian Schulman

BELIEVE WHAT CAN HAPPEN IF YOU JUST IMAGINE

"The ones who are crazy enough to think they can change the world are the ones that do. It will surface, guaranteed!"
- Steve Jobs

It is the willingness to believe.

If you allow yourself to imagine something, the door is open to anything.

I didn't exactly imagine what was happening now, but it didn't mean it couldn't happen because I already believed. I was open, ready, dreaming, manifesting, and already doing! The universe delivered what I was asking for. It may not have looked exactly like the picture in my head, but it delivered!

If you can imagine it, it can happen.

IMAGINATION doesn't always start with a clear vision. I remember sitting down with a dear friend, client, and mentor. I was at a transition point, and I was doing the same things that I always did when facing a change. However, something was different this time. I had achieved what I set out to accomplish, but this was the first time I found myself wondering, "Do I want to do it again?"

Sitting with him in his office, he poses the million-dollar question, "What do you want to be doing?" It was, essentially, the same question I have asked everyone I work with in this position: "Putting money aside if you could wake up tomorrow and do absolutely anything, forget if you have the experience you think you need or not, and LOVE what you're doing - what would it be?" Surprisingly, I had never asked myself this question because, for me, it was always about taking care of my family. It was the first time I permitted myself to believe the two were not mutually exclusive!

In the conversation, he pointed out that I had been working behind the scenes with Fortune 500 executives for years, reminded me that I am the only one that does what I do on LinkedIn, and challenged me by questioning, "What are you waiting for?" After a few retorts from me and his asking me repeatedly, "So what are you waiting for?" I found myself buying a couple of domains right there in that office, and when I came home, I filed for my LLC.

There was no guarantee that Voice Your Vibe would succeed like other businesses I had built. Desire and faith are what led me to start, but IMAGINATION is what propelled me forward. Not only did I have the vision of a successful company, I continually imagined the positive impact I could have by manifesting my vision.

As T. F. Hodge said, "The sky is not my limit, I am," which is true. However, the converse is also true! There is no limit if I refuse to limit myself and allow my IMAGINATION to envision well beyond what I can see.

"People may forget what you said, but they will never forget how you made them feel." - Maya Angelou

I remember seeing the Radiate Positive Vibes and Voice Your Vibe logos. I looked at them and instantly fell in love. They inspired emotion. Voice Your Vibe is all about the feel and IMAGINATION. My IMAGINATION inspired the logo, and when I saw it, I imagined it on hats, sweatshirts, t-shirts, stickers, water bottles — on everything. I imagined people wearing it because of how the brand made them feel. That is the most important thing because we fall in love with how it makes us feel a sense of belonging and connection to the brand.

The Voice Your Vibe swag line is one of the IMAGINATION manifestations I am most proud of. It came from building my brand and imagining how Voice Your Vibe and the positivity it brought to so many could become tangible. Finally, there was a way that people could hold it in their hands and share it with strangers.

> *"If you can dream it, you can do it."*
> *- Walt Disney*

IMAGINATION is a powerful thing. Look at The Walt Disney Company - Imagineers! They created a job title with IMAGINATION in it. An Imagineer is someone who creates and imagines. They're in charge of dreaming, designing, and creating! They bring out and tap into the inner child within ALL of us and the belief that anything is possible.

How many times have you heard:

"Imagine this… Imagine when…"

"Imagine if you created something that was all about radiating positive vibes and having fun!"

Through the global award-winning LIVE shows, Shout Out Saturday and What's Good Wednesday, we are always helping others remember, recognize, and bring out their inner child because that is where the love of creativity is born. The true unfiltered, unbridled, brilliant IMAGINATION comes from the notion that you CAN.

We do that by showing up through music, comedy, and dancing, which happen to be natural calming mechanisms I discovered in childhood to cope with my neurological disorder, Tourette's Syndrome (TS), and became part of the shows.

> *"Music is the great uniter. An incredible force. Something that people who differ on everything and anything else can have in common."*
> *- Sarah Dessen*

Music is a universal language that we all speak. It's an incredible tool for creating, imagining, and communicating. As a kid, I used to sit for hours, in the dark, in front of the piano, feeling the music and letting the keys guide me. I always felt it. Music was an outlet for what was in my mind. It was about creation and giving life to my IMAGINATION. Just as it did for me as a kid, and still does, music plays a vital role in both shows as it stirs the IMAGINATION and evokes emotions. You feel as if you are a part of the shows, and we all understand each other because of the power of music.

We imagine the vibe we want for each show and find music that matches that vision and feel. Because of that, we use songs on every episode so that people know them and become a conduit to that feeling of belonging. (Autosuggestion).

> *"Allow yourself to laugh and when you do, share your laughter with others." - Catherine Pulsifer*

Laughter is created by IMAGINATION. Laughter is a mighty healer and connector. We need it. It can change our lives and turn our day around in an instant. When we are laughing, we are radiating positive vibes. Growing up with Tourette's, I was the weird kid everyone laughed at.

Comedy and my IMAGINATION gave me a way to connect and switch the script such that people were laughing with me and no longer at me.

One way we use IMAGINATION to create laughter on the shows is through the use of filters. I was introduced to Snapcam and learned how to integrate it LIVE, which ignited my IMAGINATION. My mind was swirling with ideas. I was five years old again! I asked myself, "How can I make this more fun"? "How wacky can I make this?" because the world had become total chaos, and we needed to laugh, now more than ever. I was finding ways to incorporate the filters and my love of impressions. Every time I discovered a new filter, my IMAGINATION would pop, and it would spark new ways to bring positivity and laughter to Shout Out Saturday and What's Good Wednesday!

"Dance brings us all together." - Kreesha Turner

Much like music and comedy (laughter), dancing evokes an emotion and makes you feel a certain way. Dancing had a profound impact on me. In a sea of people, feeling uncomfortable, bodies moving, arms flailing, making faces and noises - I could be me. I could blend in. I didn't look weird or stand out in a bad way because of my Tourette's. What was my everyday reality, which usually made me stand out, helped me fit in. Knowing how dancing, especially together, helps us to have a sense of belonging, I imagined making it part of the shows.

During the pandemic, 'social distancing' emerged. Physically separated from one another, yes, but did we have to be socially? We needed a way to be together while being apart. SocialdisDANCING was hatched from my IMAGINATION. It brought together the power of music, dancing, and laughter. Perhaps most importantly, socialdisDANCING allows us to be together in a positive way in a time when being together has become taboo. Similarly, LinkedIn Lip Sync Battle came from inspiration and IMAGINATION. No karaoke at the club, no problem! We got you covered!

Until later, I did not even realize that all three calming mechanisms had become intertwined with and woven into the shows. Music, comedy, and dancing, which had always been sources of joy and belonging in my life, were now being shared with others, and they were experiencing the same.

> *"Laughter is timeless, IMAGINATION has no age, and dreams are forever." - Walt Disney*

IMAGINATION is not limited by age, race, ethnicity, where you come from, who you love. It is free to all. We all have access to it.

IMAGINATION makes things more fun.

IMAGINATION transports us from the burdens of the 'adult world' and reminds us of the delight and wonder that each of us is capable of experiencing!

IMAGINATION is a priceless gift. When you take that leap of faith and believe anything is possible, that's when the magic happens.

BRIAN SCHULMAN

About Brian Schulman: A 4X #1 Best-Selling Author and internationally known Keynote Speaker, Brian Schulman is known as the Godfather, and Pioneer, of LinkedIn Video and one of the world's premiere live streaming & video marketing experts who's insights have been featured on NASDAQ, ROKU and a #1 Best-selling live-streaming book.

With 20+ years of proven Digital Marketing experience strategizing with Fortune 500 brands across the globe, Brian founded & is the CEO of Voice Your Vibe, which brings his wealth of knowledge, as an advisor and mentor to Founders & C-Suite Executives by providing workshops and 1-on-1 Mastery Coaching on how to voice their vibe, attract their tribe, and tell a story that people will fall in love with through the power and impact of live & pre-recorded video.

Named "2020 Best LIVE Festive Show of The Year" at the IBM TV Awards, his global award- winning weekly LIVE shows #ShoutOutSaturday & #WhatsGoodWednesday have been featured in Forbes, Thrive Global, Yahoo Finance, an Amazon best-selling book and syndicated on a Smart TV Network. Among his many awards and honors, Brian has been named a 'LinkedIn Top Voice', 'LinkedIn Video Creator Of The Year', one of the 'Top 50 Most Impactful People of LinkedIn' out of 800 Million people for three consecutive years and a 'LinkedIn Global Leader of The Year' for two consecutive years.

Beyond all the achievements and accolades, Brian is most proud of his two children and the connections and relationships he's made along the way.

Author's Website: *www.VoiceYourVibe.com*
Book Series Website & Author's Bio: *www.The13StepstoRiches.com*

Candace & David Rose

A WORLD OF PURE IMAGINATION

Anthony Newley and Leslie Bricusse said it best in Willie Wonka and the Chocolate Factory with their song, "Pure Imagination."

Come with me, and you'll be
In a world of pure imagination
Take a look, and you'll see
Into your imagination

We'll begin with a spin
Traveling in the world of my creation
What we'll see will defy
Explanation

If you want to view paradise
Simply look around and view it
Anything you want to, do it
Want to change the world?
There's nothing to it

There is no life I know
To compare with pure imagination
Living there, you'll be free
If you truly wish to be

In book three of this series, I bring up that ALL things are literally in your head. That there is nothing in this world that exists without having first been a thought that existed in your head. In our minds, we create, and destroy. We see, and we move things into place.

How many songs are written about seeing a future that could exist, but doesn't currently? We envision it. We see it as though it is. And then we can create it into reality.

But as a society, we are losing that power of creation. So instead, we allow the "tried-and-true" experts to do it for us.

We are currently trying to move to another state. In the process of selling our home to move, we have had to remove much of the personal touches we have added to the house and return it to the "stock pictures" look with a very select few pieces of furniture and paintings placed strategically. This is because people who look at our house to purchase it need someone to paint the picture for them. So instead of being able to look at the space and imagine what they can do with it, they need it to look that way already.

Society has taken creating models to a whole new level, and now it's become a crutch. Movies and video games have come a long, long way. The things technology can do are spectacular. They enhance our lives and make things easier. Not to mention exciting. Sims and virtual realities copy IMAGINATION but leave very little up to the users' imaginations.

We go for car rides with portable movie and game systems. No more looking at clouds, trees, scenery, and creating our own picture.

But what if?

The fact is that those who are making money are those who can still imagine. Or those who can pay someone to do it for them. Those are the ones holding our personal power and gaining control of our lives.

But if we could do that for ourselves, we take back the power to create reality and wealth for ourselves.

All the steps so far: Desire, Faith, Auto Suggestion, and Specialized Knowledge come together in your mind as you master each one. And by taking those skills and adding IMAGINATION, you can create a reality that fulfills you on a deeper level than before experienced.

Just imagine! Wouldn't that fulfillment be amazing?!

So, close your eyes. Make a wish. Count to three. Let your mind wander. What do you see? Add a desire. Create a vision.

Imagine. Create. Repeat. Enjoy!

~ Candace Rose

We have a five-year-old daughter. One day we went to a store, and while looking at the toys, she asked for one of everything on the shelf in genuine child manner. As her little legs carried her through the store, she carefully selected items and put them in her cart. As she presented her treasures, we told her that she could only pick one. So began the difficult task of elimination. She sorted and tried to negotiate for additional items. When all was said and done, she had settled on a toy microwave. I wasn't sure that was the best choice, and I tried to guide her to something else. But she was set. So, we purchased the microwave and brought it home. She was ecstatic to get home and play with her microwave. Once we got home, she opened her new toy. She instantly started making something for everyone using nothing but her IMAGINATION. I learned that day that my new favorite meal is the "Super Daddy Special."

As adults, I think we forget or grow out of using our IMAGINATION. We start worrying about "grown-up" things like our weight, the report our boss has been nagging us for, mortgages, and car payments. We start thinking, "I don't have time for imaginary things." The truth is you need imaginary things to brighten up the "adult" things we must deal with.

Here are a few ideas on how to "Work out" the IMAGINATION muscle. Copy or watch kids. Kids obviously have good strong imaginations. So they can find joy and fun using the simplest of things. A cardboard tube, for example, can be a telescope or a trumpet.

Video Games. Many games have been created to help strengthen your IMAGINATION. Fantasy games like Dragon Age or The Elder Scrolls can allow you to enter a magical world full of dragons and magic. Letting your IMAGINATION run wild on what you can do with those skills. Games like Minecraft allow your creative juices to flow and build large castles in the sky or a small cottage by the sea. With the large number of games available, you can find almost anything to work your IMAGINATION.

Draw. Draw anything. A good drawing exercise is to draw something without looking at the paper. Instead, close your eyes or look away and just let your creative side express itself.

Take a shower. This might seem strange, but in the book Wired to Create by Scott Barry Kaufman, he says that 72% of people have creative insights in the shower. We usually shower alone, and there are few distractions. It is creating a perfect relaxing environment for opening our IMAGINATION to new ideas. Meditate on the sound of the water and breath in the warm, humid air. Smell the fresh scents of the soap and relax because a relaxed mind is a creative mind.

~ David Rose

CANDACE & DAVID ROSE

About Candace and David Rose: Candace and David Rose, are #1 Best-Selling Authors of the book The 13 Steps to Riches series. They grew up together and currently live in South Jordan Utah with their 6 Children, 6 Chickens, 2 Dogs, 4 Cats and a rabbit. They both are veterans of the US Army. David served as a mechanic and Candace as a Legal NCO. David is currently a Product Release Specialist, delivering Liquid Oxygen and Nitrogen to various manufacturing plants and hospitals throughout Utah, Colorado, Idaho and Nevada. Candace is the owner of Changing Your Box Organization. She specializes in helping people organize their space, both physically and mentally, with the ultimate goal to help you change your box and find more joy in your life. Both Candace and David are proud members of the elite Champion Circle Networking Association in Salt Lake City, Utah, founded by one of our Co-Authors of The 13 Steps To Riches book series, Jon Kovach Jr.

Author's Website: *www.ChangeYourBox.com*

Book Series Website & Author's Bio: *www.The13StepstoRiches.com*

Collier Landry

WHERE CREATIVITY BEGINS

"Imagination is the beginning of creation. You imagine what you desire, you will what you imagine, and at last, you create what you will." - George Bernard Shaw.

In *Think and Grow Rich*, Napoleon Hill asserts that the imaginative faculty of the mind is where "The impulse, the desire, is given shape, form, and action."

This leads to two distinct forms of imagination: Synthetic and Creative. Hill concludes that man's only limitation, within reason, is his development and ability to use his imagination. In general, most only realize that they have an imagination, and very few know how to use it.

As a creative entrepreneur, I would argue that I spend most of my time navigating the delicate balance between both, albeit while trying not to lose my mind.

Man can create anything that he can imagine, written in the annals of history. Through the use of the imagination, man has harnessed the use of the sky to create planes and rockets that fly at supersonic speeds, submarines to plunge the depths of the sea, or genetic sequencing into unraveling your DNA to lay out the blueprint which is you; 23andMe anyone?

All joking aside, man has conquered much through the use of his imagination. Combine that with an army to do your bidding, and I think an argument can be made this is the very heart of developing civilization.

Synthetic imagination is where you take your existing concepts, then integrate and rearrange them into a new combination. This creates nothing; it simply works with ideas and materials already present. It is the essential faculty that most entrepreneurs use to get stuff done.

The vast majority of people in the world are endowed with plenty of synthetic imagination. Want to design a website? It's a breeze if you already have experience creating a website of the same kind. It's where synthetic imagination kicks in as soon as you begin to find a solution. Kind of like turning on auto-pilot

Synthetic Imagination joins your pre-existing ideas, your concepts, and your products. It transforms them into something completely different, into a completely new form or a new, unanticipated solution to a problem. Very little of what is created today is absolutely original.

Having worked the entirety of my career in the film business, I love this quote from fêted director Jean-Luc Godard.

"It's not where you take things from, it's where you take them to."

A perfect example is Hollywood's latest obsession over reinventing superhero comics and fairy tales ad nauseam. Love it or hate it, I think everyone can agree that the Walt Disney Company is the very definition of imagination-fueled success.

Creative imagination is when we create something completely new and out of the ether. It is where the finite mind of man has direct communication with infinite intelligence. Where we "tune in" or communicate with the subconscious mind of others and the infinite source. This creative faculty becomes more polished as you develop it and use it. The greatest leaders of business, science, physics, finance, music, art, and literature become geniuses because they have learned how to develop and harness this faculty of creative Imagination.

A good way to look at this is to think of creative vision as dialing directly into your creative source. This is what Napoleon Hill called your "infinite intelligence." You might refer to this as God.

In essence, it's your intuition. It's the way the infinite intelligence or God gives us our hunches and our "inspirations." Hill had a great story involving Thomas Edison in which the famous inventor, known for his relentless pursuit of the light bulb, uses both creative vision and synthetic imagination. Edison was well known for the many cat naps he took throughout the day. What is not so well known is how he utilized these to his creative advantage.

When Edison was tired and frustrated by the day's "failures" at not discovering the best method of creating this invention, he would nap. Before falling asleep, he formed a clear view of the problem he was currently facing in his mind. Then, as he wakes from his nap, in that limbo-like peaceful state before he's fully awake, he realizes the solution to the problem. In order to function, the light bulb must be placed in a vacuum.

The vacuum was indeed the only environment that would prevent the quick burnout of the wire and prevent any electrocution. Edison's thoughts immediately jumped to charcoal. He recalled images of charcoal covered with dirt and subconsciously realized they burned much more slowly than the rest. It was that realization – coming out of his nap which his subconscious was trying to share with him. Limit the oxygen, and the filament that illuminates the lightbulb will not burn out so quickly! Personally, I'm a big fan of the twenty-minute power nap.

You don't always need to use your creative vision and bring something as meaningful as the light bulb to the world. But, more often than not, synthetic imagination becomes the vehicle to success.

All you really need to do is combine two ideas that are already pretty darn good on their own. Take the Reese's Peanut Butter Cup. If you're old enough, you may even remember the initial commercial introducing the product to us. One person walked along the street, totally absorbed in his chocolate candy bar. Another individual, equally absorbed in his peanut butter, walked in the opposite direction.

BAM! They walked right into each other, and a new tasty treat was born!

When compared, fewer people are gifted with creative imagination. Where synthetic imagination cannot rescue you, creative imagination is what you can rely on. That's because it comes in the form of a hunch, inspiration, intuition, or what we commonly call gut feeling.

I can attribute every significant failure in my personal or professional life to my refusal to follow that intuition, that gut feeling.

The creative imagination has produced the telephone, the automobile, the airplane, the light bulb, the internet, and pretty much any device carrying the " i " prefix.

Like any muscle or organ, your creative and synthetic imaginations become stronger with use. To achieve the lifestyle and wealth they desire, an entrepreneur must create something to fill the void in the marketplace or create something better than the competition.

If we are looking specifically at generating material wealth, entrepreneurs require a plan to turn the intangible impulse of thought into actual money. The imagination will assist in that. If you have the white-hot burning desire for wealth but lack a plan or a truly genius idea to get you there, tap into the imagination to develop that plan for you.

And when it does, reduce that plan to writing. The moment you do so, you take the first of a series of steps that empower you to take your thoughts and imagination and turn them into the riches you so desire.

When you combine that with doing what you love for a living, you create far more than what material wealth could ever provide. You create the life you always IMAGINED.

COLLIER LANDRY

About Collier Landry: While most hosts of true crime podcasts simply discuss murders that fascinate them, he has actually lived through one.

As a formally trained musician and photographer, Collier segued into filmmaking and podcasting as a means to creatively express and deal with his own traumatic childhood story - the premeditated murder of his mother Noreen by his father, Dr. John Boyle - and to give a narrative voice to others in similar circumstances.

Subsequently, Collier is the host of the Moving Past Murder Podcast, and the subject of Investigation Discovery's documentary A Murder in Mansfield. Collier's work has been featured in The New York Times, Variety, Esquire, USA Today, The Daily Mail, and The New York Post. Collier is a TEDx Speaker and a featured guest on the Dr. Phil show. He resides in Santa Monica, CA.

Author's Website: *www.CollierLandry.com*
Book Series Website & Author's Bio: *www.The13StepstoRiches.com*

Corey Poirier

IMAGINE

I have so many different takes on using our IMAGINATION to accomplish great things I hardly know where to begin.

In fact, ironically, this is the first contribution to this book series that I have found hard to start because there are so many paths I could take. It's almost as if my creative IMAGINATION is flowing at such a rate that there are 'almost' limitless options; almost like when we have too many options on a menu at a restaurant, it's tough to choose just one.

I have decided to cover a few aspects of IMAGINATION in relation to how I perceive, how they seem to work in my life, and how I use them. Let's jump in.

First, I'd like to tackle how I attempt to tap into my IMAGINATION to create things.

Vision Board:

This past New Year, my girlfriend and I created our own vision boards on the living-room floor. The last time we did our vision boards, we left them up for 3+ years without making new ones. So they just sat there on the wall, and we almost became desensitized to them as we walked past them each day.

Interestingly, even though we didn't actively look at them daily, when we finally took some time to take stock of the things on our vision boards, we realized that we had accomplished over 90% of what was on our boards without even actively trying to do so.

And these weren't small goals. We had things on our vision board like buying our dream house, making a bestseller's list like the USA / Wall Street Journal Bestsellers list, becoming debt free, having a family, speaking on prestigious stages (I spoke at Harvard before we took the board down), and so on.

Realizing that we had achieved so much without even knowing it, we knew what we had to do. First, we had to create the new vision boards I mentioned us creating this past New Year.

What we also did, though, was take a new approach to what we had done before. For instance,

We went through a vision board workshop together:

- We designed our vision boards so they would become a part of our house rather than Bristol boards simply hanging on the wall (in this case, using Victorian style frames)

- We dug deeper into what we wanted to achieve as a result and used that vision versus what we wanted to attain

The resulting vision board, in my opinion, is next level.

Just weeks after we put it up, I had achieved a big vision on the board. I had said I wanted a best- selling book, and shortly after, one of our books made a prestigious must-read list.

And how does this relate to IMAGINATION? Well, without the power of IMAGINATION, how could our vision board exist in the first place?

Invisible Imagination

Now, I totally understand that the words invisible IMAGINATION are like an oxymoron, but stay with me on this one. What I mean by invisible IMAGINATION is the IMAGINATION that I'm not seeing before creating it.

Here's what I mean.

Over the years, I have written multiple books and many songs. I have released 4 CDs / Albums, and I have had songs on the radio and have released videos. My last CD / Album was nominated for Rock Recording of the Year.

I don't say this to impress you or from an ego perspective but simply to demonstrate that the songs are at least listenable, and yet, when I wrote them, I didn't sit down and map out where the songs would go.

Instead, I felt the urge to write. So I sat down with guitar and pen in hand and wrote coherent songs without planning ANY of the words in the song. Meaning I didn't say, "What rhymes with Orange?" (Hint: Nothing really rhymes with Orange).

I sat down, and these songs came to me—complete songs.

Now, some may say the songs were gifted to me from somewhere else and that I was simply channeling the songs, but I instead like to think that I was tapping into my invisible IMAGINATION.

Now, I may be correct, and they may be correct. But, either way, this is what I believe is tapping into our invisible IMAGINATION by constantly working our IMAGINATION in the first place.

Reframing

The last aspect of IMAGINATION I want to cover, at least concerning how I use my IMAGINATION, is reframing.

Now, some may call this self-brainwashing, or re-conditioning, or even question whether this is simply related to thoughts and not necessarily IMAGINATION.

To me, this one is a mix between thoughts and IMAGINATION and using both to create what you want the moment to be about vs. what it may really be about.

If you do this enough, you ultimately create the future you want to see and the you that you want to become in that future.

I believe reframing will allow you to imagine a positive-oriented future vs. a negative one, which alone changes the core of who you are.

I also believe reframing relates to IMAGINATION because it all starts with you first seeing and then believing. After that, the circumstance is one way vs. another, which takes IMAGINATION for most.

Oh, and if you're curious about the actual meaning of the word, reframing involves (according to the APA Dictionary of Psychology) a process of reconceptualizing a problem by seeing it from a different perspective.

Again, I believe you need to use your IMAGINATION if you want to see something from the other perspective than your initial thoughts around the situation.

To help explain further, here's a real-world example of reframing from my life.

A few years ago, my mother and I were in a coffee shop drive-through, and a man behind us was yelling obscenities at us. My mother didn't hear him, and I waited until we drove away to ask her what she thought of him yelling at us and calling us names.

She was immediately angry and suggested we drive back there so she could tell him what she thought of him.

I reframed the situation and explained that maybe he was having a bad day and it wasn't even about us. Perhaps he saw a mother and son in the car and wasn't close to, or didn't know, his mother, and was therefore mad that he didn't have that relationship in his life.

Without skipping a beat, my mother's entire energy changed when she was able to see with her IMAGINATION a different image of the man and the situation. And she said that "instead of going back to yell at him, perhaps we should go back and pay for his coffee."

Notice, nothing else about the situation changed. I simply used my IMAGINATION to tap into her IMAGINATION to reframe how she looked at the situation.

The result would mean a completely different outcome had we driven back to that coffee shop.

Now, imagine if you do this daily and reframe, using your IMAGINATION, the way you look at every negative situation and imagine instead that the positive situation is indeed true.

Do you think this could change who you are and the future you see, and the future you experience over time?

It has for me, and all thanks to using my IMAGINATION (and thoughts) to create what I'd like to believe is happening vs. what the negative part of my mind could otherwise believe.

I use these three forms of IMAGINATION regularly, and the results over time have been staggering.

I also know this list isn't all-inclusive. For example, I didn't even discuss the difference between Synthetic and Creative IMAGINATION. Still, I decided that rather than dive into what Napoleon already did so well in his chapter on IMAGINATION, I would simply share how I try to tap into my IMAGINATION regularly to offer you perhaps a unique perspective.

I'd like to end this chapter with a very simple question:

Are you truly making the most use of your IMAGINATION, and if not, how could you begin to use yours differently?

Until that time, here's to your greater success.

COREY POIRIER

About Corey Poirier: Corey is a multiple-time TEDx Speaker. He is also the host of the top-rated Let's Do Influencing radio show, founder of The Speaking Program, founder of bLU Talks, and has been featured in multiple television specials. He is also a Barnes & Noble, Amazon, Apple Books, and Kobo Bestselling Author and the co-author of the *Wall Street Journal* and *USA Today* bestseller, *Quitless*.

A columnist with *Entrepreneur* and *Forbes* magazine, he has been featured in/on various mediums and is one of the few leaders featured twice on the popular *Entrepreneur on Fire* show.

Also appearing on the popular Evan Carmichael YouTube Channel, he is a New Media Summit Icon of Influence, was recently listed as the # 5 influencer in entrepreneurship by Thinkers 360, and he is an Entrepreneur of the Year Nominee—and, to demonstrate his versatility, a Rock Recording of the Year nominee who has performed stand-up comedy more than 700 times, including an appearance at the famed Second City.

Author's Website: *www.TheInfluencerVault.com*
Book Series Website & Author's Bio: *www.The13StepstoRiches.com*

Deb Scott

THE WORKSHOP OF THE MIND

I must admit this is my favorite chapter in Napoleon Hill's book *Think and Grow Rich*.

Imagine all the possibilities! An endless sea of ideas that can manifest into reality for you and the world around you. This is powerful. You are only limited by NOT putting your ideas from your thoughts of IMAGINATION into tangible action. Grace builds on nature, a biblical truth for everything. This means you have to create something in the physical world for the spiritual world to grab onto it and grow into whatever you desire.

Napoleon Hill states there are two types of IMAGINATION. The first is synthetic the second is creative.

Hill states that synthetic IMAGINATION is based on "old concepts, ideas or plans into new combinations." This type of IMAGINATION doesn't create anything new but is valuable for accomplishing your goal.

Creative IMAGINATION is where the real power exists. This is known as your "hunches" or "intuition," which automatically inspires you. This type of IMAGINATION can only be catalyzed when "the conscious mind is vibrating at an exceedingly rapid rate." The more aware and alert you are to divine downloads, the more your IMAGINATION can gather them into an idea to manifest. Make vibrating at a high rate a priority, and you will be increasing your odds of getting clear ideas in your IMAGINATION.

Can you see how each chapter and step is integral to the next? You can't have one without the other and having the other catapults you into a new level of achievement by practicing all. It's like going to the gym and using your muscles. The more muscle you have, the more fat you burn. Use it or lose it, as the old saying goes.

I remember when I had the inspiration to start a radio show. I knew nothing about creating an internet radio show other than having been a guest to promote my bestselling book "The Sky is Green and The Grass is Blue – Turning Your Upside-Down World Right Side Up!"

I wanted to learn from other people who had what I wanted. It could be spiritual, business success, a new way of thinking. I wanted to learn the character traits of winners and how they achieved their dreams. But would anyone famous want to chat with Deb Scott? Of course not! But would these people be interested in promoting their ideas if I created a positive platform to share their success with the world? Yes, now I am helping myself to learn from these masters in the process of letting the population learn at the same time and promoting the guest who has accomplished the goal. Everyone wins! It was just an idea, and I had no formal training, just a genuine desire to share the "Best People We Know" tools in any industry with anyone who wanted to listen and learn. I was attached to the desire of what I imagined would be a positive outcome from deep within my heart. I marinated in the thought for a bit and then decided just to do it. My first show had three listeners; by the end of 500 podcasts, I had over 2 million downloads. The podcast winning a Shorty Award in New York City was an unexpected bonus of validation my dream needed to come true. IMAGINATION is the most priceless gift you can never buy.

Sometimes we have these ideas that linger and almost become an obsession. We want to do something, but we get stuck because we don't understand or believe how it will happen, so we stop. Yet God continues to push us; we can't get the idea out of our minds. We feel it in our gut that something we desire in our IMAGINATION must see come to life. We believe on one level but not enough to pull the trigger and risk putting ourselves out there for some reason we made up in our own heads. Stop stopping yourself and take the first step into your greatness. Stop denying the world of your gifts and the help you can offer to let others achieve their goals and dreams too. It almost feels selfish to hide this inspired gem from the world, doesn't it?

Hill gives an example of himself and how he came to write *Think and Grow Rich* through the inspiration of Dale Carnegie. For decades Hill was nurturing this idea in his IMAGINATION, but he never took the steps to manifest them into a tangible reality. "Gradually, the idea became a giant under its own power, and it coaxed, nursed, and drove me."

It's like the story where the person hits the block 99 times before it breaks on the 100th. Don't give up five minutes before the miracle. If you continue to get an inspiration and imagine a reality, that is all the evidence and proof you need to move forward and make it happen.

An exercise I find very helpful when I am in that dreamy IMAGINATION mode is to do some automatic writing or simply write down words, thoughts, and ideas on paper that come to you. Do this without judgment or understanding; just write it down. Scientifically there is power in writing something down to make it happen; we are wired this way as human beings. Let the process unfold naturally, and you will discover a pattern to the words to create an action to manifest a result when you review the words you wrote down without understanding. I promise you an "ah-ha" moment is waiting just around the corner for you.

Hill gives an example of a preacher who had an idea for years to start a vocational school to learn by doing. The preacher knew he needed a million dollars to build the school and was stuck for years on making his dream come true because he did not understand how to get the million dollars. Finally, his burning desire became so overpowering he just decided to share his dream and preach a sermon, "What I would do if I had a million dollars." He described to his congregation his vision of what he would do with the money in his next sermon. Without any expectation, a man after the sermon approached him, loved his idea, and provided him the million dollars he needed to create the school. The preacher was Young Gunsaulus and the million-dollar man Philip D Armour. As a result, the Armour Institute of Technology was founded. He got the money within 36 hours after he reached a definitive decision in his mind to get it and decided upon a definitive plan for getting it!

Build it in your mind, have trust and confidence to risk getting your vision out into the world, and they will come. Build it, and they will come.

"For man, it is impossible, but with God, all things are possible." Matthew 19:26

I have imagined everyone on earth is the best person God created them to be. I have imagined a world of kindness, love, healing, and hope. I have imagined a world where we are all spiritual self-loving spiritual billionaires. I am committed to making, to taking this chance on change. Just one letter in a word makes all the difference. What a metaphor for life!

There are many roads to get to the same destination. There are many leaves to create the shade we enjoy under a tree. I am willing to put what I imagine on paper with you here today. I put it out to the world in my writing, real estate career, and talks; maybe you have an idea of another road to my destination. Perhaps I have an idea for you to get to your destination. We all help each other. This is what I have imagined.

"All glory comes from daring to begin." Eugene F. Ware

DEB SCOTT

About Deb Scott: Deb Scott, BA, CPC, and Realtor was a high honors biology major at Regis College in Weston, Massachusetts, and spent over two decades as an award-winning cardio-thoracic sales specialist in the New England area. She is a best-selling author of *The Sky is Green & The Grass is Blue: Turning Your Upside Down World Right Side Up*. She is an award-winning podcaster of The Best People We Know Show. Following in her family's footsteps, she is a third generation Realtor in Venice, Florida. As a certified life coach, Deb speaks and teaches on how to turn bad situations into positive, successful results. As a top sales specialist, she enjoys teaching people "sales without selling," believing that integrity, good communication, and respect are the winning equation to all outstanding success and happiness in life.

Author's Website: *www.DebScott.com*
Book Series Website & Author's Bio: *www.The13StepstoRiches.com*

Dori "On Purpose" Ray

DECISIONS, DECISIONS, DECISIONS!

I decided to take a break from my story to re-engage with PURPOSE in this chapter! I want to begin by saying my manuscript was late. This is important to know, and you will understand later in the chapter. Although I was given grace, I could not understand why I could not find the inspiration or the energy to write this chapter. It wasn't because I had waited until the last minute, that's what I've always done, and it worked before. Why was this time so difficult? I wasn't super busy, just laying around most of the time wondering why lately I'm so uninspired about EVERYTHING. I am Ms. EXCITEMENT! I am the girl everyone turns to to light their candle, and I could not even manage a flicker of hope for myself, my purpose, and my future. I had managed to fool everyone. Facebook, Instagram & TikTok were utterly unaware that a ghost was entertaining them and that Dori On Purpose had "left the building." I was so good that I was even fooling REAL LIFE people I encountered every day, including friends and family. No one knew the lights were out! Some are learning for the 1st time while reading this chapter! The only reason the words even made it to the pages of this volume is pure principle. I had committed to 12 chapters, and I was determined to honor that commitment. I would be damned if my legacy would be "the one who quit at the halfway point!"

At this point, five days after the manuscript was due, sitting on an airplane to Atlanta on my way to a business trip, I decided to get it done (just on principle). I MUST HONOR MY COMMITMENT is the mantra I repeated every time I started a text to Mr. Awesome and Jon, saying, "I have to sit this one out." Thank God for principle! I could not find the nerve to send the text! Instead, I decided to listen to the chapter one more time and pray for inspiration. In doing so, I heard the story of What Would I Do With A Million Dollars for the umpteenth time. I, at that moment, had a revelation! Not only were the lights out, but so was the fire. I mean, I was really sitting in a cold space with no lights and no heat. The craziest part is in listening to the story I heard many times before, I realized that the key to unlocking my passion once again was to go back to the things that set my soul on fire. That was indeed the ticket. I can't explain what physically happened but all

I know is that my fingers instantly started typing as if someone had come in and flicked on the lights and thrown me a book of matches for safekeeping. I instantly started to remember the feeling of no more than six months ago when I was walking on cloud 9. When ideas were flowing, all of the ideas fit perfectly into the BIG PICTURE God had placed in my heart. I remember feeling invincible. I remembered feeling so close to the prize that I could touch & taste it. It did not matter whether the money was there or my credit was shot. I was so on fire for the things I believe aligned with my purpose that none of that mattered. And guess what, looking back, NONE OF IT DID!

The best way to share my emotions is to share how I became a part of this amazing project. I guess I should begin by saying that the closer I get to God, the less I believe in coincidences.

I have been a Network Marketer for the past 22 years. I was in the process of changing companies and encountered a bit of controversy with my move. The lady who was my sponsor was unhappy that I had called a few of her recruits to see if they were interested in joining me on my new venture. I hadn't broken any rules, I was fully separated from my old company, but I broke her trust. Regardless of who was right, she was my friend, and her feelings mattered to me. It was causing additional strain in our relationship that was already under attack because I decided to part ways from our company. One day, heavy with the burden of all that was going on, I jumped on the CLUBHOUSE platform. On the platform that day was a gentleman named Paul Capozio. That night after asking my controversial question, Paul was the only one on the platform willing to challenge my reasoning. He gave me feedback that night that made me respect him very highly and admire his honesty. I decided to follow him and check him out. I was intrigued. The next time I saw Paul was on the same platform (I *HAD HIM ON NOTIFICATION*). This time along with him was Erik, Mr. Awesome, Swanson. Before starting the session, Mr. Awesome announced the upcoming project and was clear that "There were only two spots left!" Somehow I knew he wasn't blowing smoke! One of the gentlemen on the live that night said, "I'm in," instantly, and did too!

What you must understand, before this "encounter," I had already written a book. However, I ALWAYS declared I would write 100 books before I die! I would say it with confidence and believe it. Here was my opportunity to knock out 12 at one time! I had always believed and said it from my CHEST! "I AM FULL OF BOOKS" was my constant declaration. I had no idea how it would happen and didn't care. I believed and would get excited about it. You can imagine that when on that night on clubhouse, when Mr. Awesome announced this opportunity to join the project, I felt my heart leap. I knew God was at work. There was not a doubt in sight! I FELT THE FIRE! There was one problem. I was unprepared for the financial commitment. Guess what, you're right, that didn't matter either. The fact that I'm currently writing Volume 5 is proof that this was a vision that was part of my purpose.

My own burning desire generated the creativity I needed to attract and find the financial commitment to be a part of history. Before that night, I had never heard of either of the two gentlemen. That night I could feel myself closer to the goal! I used to literally imagine myself traveling the world, meeting people like Sharon Lechter, and eventually hitting my ultimate goal of speaking in large auditoriums on massive stages. In the short time between desire and the closed deal in my mind, I had graced stages, attended book-signings where the lines wrapped the corners. I was featured on news stations and even had a chance to meet Oprah Winfrey and Tyler Perry! It was real, and nobody could tell me otherwise. I was excited, and everyone knew it. Just like fire does, it began to ignite more dreams I had tucked away, like starting my sweatshirt line, opening my online academy, and starting my talk show podcast. If you were to scroll back six months on my social media, you could feel the energy floating from the pages! And I never once thought about how it was going to all happen. I simply believed! All of it was happening.

But then here comes life, getting in my way! Money became very tight, so I decided to focus on what brings me money but DOES NOT set my soul ablaze! It's no wonder the icicles in my IMAGINATION almost snuffed out God's purpose and plan, at least for a season.

I share this as we consider why some of us may not be reaching the goals that we set. Have you let money or the lack of money steal your dream? With purpose comes provision, not the other way around. I learned that the hard way. It has cost me dearly in the past, and I thank God that principle stepped in the way so that I would not be fooled once again!

DORI RAY

About Dori Ray: Dori "On Purpose" Ray is a native Philadelphian. As a businesswoman, her mission is to help people transform their minds, bodies, and bank accounts!

Dori was educated in the Philadelphia Public School System. She graduated from the Philadelphia High School for Girls in 1982 and Howard University School of Business in 1986 with a BBA in Marketing. Dori is a member of Delta Sigma Pi Business Fraternity and Delta Sigma Theta Sorority, Inc.

Dori leads teams around the world. She is a sought-after Speaker and Trainer within her industry and beyond. She is an experienced Re-Entry Coach as she has helped hundreds of Returning Citizens get back on track after incarceration.

Having suffered from depression for 20 years, she always reaches back to share her story and help break the cycle of silence. Her audience loves her authenticity!

Book Dori for speaking engagements www.linktr.ee/dorionpurpose

Author's Website: *www.linktr.ee/DoriOnPurpose*
Book Series Website & Author's Bio: *www.The13StepstoRiches.com*

Elaine Sugimura

IMAGINATION EQUALS INFINITE POSSIBILITIES

Wow! This is an exciting topic for me as I think about what IMAGINATION really means to ME. Most of us relate to the webster dictionary for its true meaning. IMAGINATION: the act or power of forming a mental image of something not present to the senses or never before wholly perceived in reality. Is this the only perspective we get to have on such a powerful word? For me, it represents possibilities; it's when magic and miracles are created and anything the heart and mind desire. That is what we get to explore today as you read through my experience with my IMAGINATION. Napoleon Hill stated that your IMAGINATION is divided into two parts, synthetic IMAGINATION, and creative IMAGINATION. Each serves a purpose, but success is driven by your ability to explore your creative IMAGINATION at its highest level. By exercising your mind and combining your infinite intelligence, magic is created.

I can remember as a child wondering how my crazy IMAGINATION might get me what I truly wanted in life. Having grown up in, at times, a challenging home life, I remember allowing my mind to wander and imagine what life would be like IF...If only I had a "normal" life, if only I had the control to fix all the broken things, if only I could make all my dreams come true! I had a big IMAGINATION, one that my teachers stated was not reality—telling me that what I dreamt of may not be possible. Who were they to crush my dreams, my wishes, my desires to be the best I could be so I could create the life I imagined was possible? I continued to imagine a life where the grass was greener; roses were in full bloom; whatever my mind imagined was the picture I painted. Of course, it was easy to take Napoleon Hill's thoughts on synthetic IMAGINATION and expand upon them. Borrowing ideas and solutions was never a comfortable path for me. I challenged myself to think out of the box and create the inspiration I needed from scratch to bring key thoughts and ideas to *LIFE.*

I knew that to manifest what I wanted in life, I had to work hard, harder than the person next to me, to drive myself to be the best at whatever I was willing to work for. Of course, I veered off course from time to time, and I failed as much as I succeeded. I began to imagine how I would affect others, as well as myself, by providing the best opportunities for financial and career growth. To create a life of possibility, I had to allow my IMAGINATION to run free, free of ridicule, free of other's opinions, free of negativity. As I matured, my willingness to broaden my IMAGINATION was key to the successes I began to experience in my life.

As my career in fashion continued to grow, I began to imagine what it would take to be a powerhouse fashion executive in New York City. As an Asian American Woman, reaching the glass ceiling was thought impossible. I asked myself, "What would it take to reach the ultimate seat in any company I chose to be a part of?" Running into obstacles along the way, I relied heavily on my intuition and joined companies that powerful women ran. I wanted to be mentored by the best and chose to be a student at any cost. You see, we can all choose to play inside the box we are comfortable with. Still, I always knew in order to succeed, you need to challenge yourself to step beyond the boundaries of the original box; in other words, be uncomfortable. Every experience from that point on was expanding the box, so there was no boundary.

Imagining what my days would look like, from days at the office to days abroad, I kept dreaming about where my experience would take me. Closing my eyes and imagining what LIFE would be like if I could create the possibility of traveling the world fulfilling a personal wish and in alignment with the brands I represented. Every step that landed me closer to the corner office inspired a more imaginative approach to run each of the brands I was hired to manage to lead. The creativity from design, marketing, operations, and sales was integral to my journey to the top. One does not achieve the top step without pushing the boundaries and creating beyond expectation. From the design room to the sales floor, to see and experience the success of the designs the team created proved that magic happens when you stretch beyond your norm. For me, to imagine a life as a CEO for many top fashion accessories brands was beyond reach, but what I realized when you create from a place of possibility, magic happens. Do you recognize the theme here? I will share an analogy that really excites me to the core of my being. I always believed that my life was like a puzzle (one of my favorite hobbies too). I would build the frame and create the picture that supported my current IMAGINATION of what I envisioned. But, just like the box I played in early on, I knew I needed to break the boundary in order to explore and imagine the impossible. I blew out my puzzle's edges and allowed my creativity and IMAGINATION to expand to infinity. What does that allow me to create as I move forward in life?

Well, I will share it with you now. By blowing out the edges of my life's puzzle, I can expand beyond the arcs of what is expected. I am allowing myself to explore what it means to be in 100% possibility. As I enter into the next phase of my life, I know that there is so much more to learn and be a part of. Expansion requires an IMAGINATION that will take you beyond what you believe you are capable of. What does it mean to level up and improve YOU? It means you get to stretch yourself to the point of getting ill. It is when you reach that pinnacle that something beautiful and magical happens. Many of us believe life begins to slow down when you have gone past your prime years, but it is the contrary. Allow your IMAGINATION to run freely and see what you can create based on the possibilities before you; the growth never ends!

IMAGINATION represents infinite possibilities! Possibilities that life gets to be full of the unknown and thus adding to my endless puzzle that is shaped from day-to-day. Isn't life wonderful when we allow ourselves to be free of judgment, our own and of others, so we can continue to think big thoughts and create what we feel is not possible? Allow your IMAGINATION to take up space wherever you go. When you think *BIG*, big things happen. Be committed, courageous, passionate, loving, joyful, and inspiring, and let your IMAGINATION run wild. Go for it, never stop, pursue all the dreams you have imagined and know everything is possible if you put your mind, heart, and soul into it. Life gets to be fun, creative, magical so live it NOW.

What's next? Well, I am not exactly sure of what that will be. Still, I know I am playing the GAME of LIFE. Whatever the outcome, I will enjoy each and every day as every part of my life is coming up roses because of my willingness to imagine *BIG* thoughts that create infinite possibilities. We get to keep expanding by understanding what limits us from thinking *BIG*. If we learn how to move past synthetic IMAGINATION and live our lives in creative IMAGINATION, again, what are the possibilities? If we all set our belief system on this compass, this would be a pretty impressive world to live in. I am clear that I get to continue expanding in this space.

I leave you with this quote and let your IMAGINATION take you to a place of infinite possibilities.

> In Every Little Thing Lies Infinite Possibilities.
> Don't Limit your IMAGINATION.
> Create Beauty from the Little Things in Life!
> - Unknown

ELAINE SUGIMURA

About Elaine R. Sugimura: Elaine is an accomplished CEO turned Business Consultant / Life Strategist who has a passion to create Leaders amongst Leaders. With over 35+ years in the fashion and food and beverage industry, she has a passion to not only lead but support those who are seeking to reinvent who they are no matter where they are in life. She is a two-time breast cancer survivor and she knows a thing or two about surviving to thriving. Fun fact: she is an adrenaline junkie—the higher, the faster, the better. Her love for adventure has led her to travel to many parts of the world by plane, train and automobile. She and her husband, Hiro, share their home in Northern California. They have raised two extraordinary sons, Bryce and Cole and have added two beautiful daughters-in-law, Erica and Giselle to their growing family. Her legacy is to share what is possible when we open ourselves up to the issues that hold us back. Her life's mission is to move those who are just surviving into Thrivers!

Author's Website: *www.ElaineRSugimura.com*
Book Series Website & Author's Bio: *www.The13StepstoRiches.com*

Elizabeth Walker

7 STEPS TO A GREAT IMAGINATION

IMAGINATION: [Imag: a picture | in: inside my mind | ation: the experience of] IMAGINATION: the experience of a picture in my mind

Can you see where I'm going with this? Just imagine, what would happen if you experienced the images in my mind in your mind? What would we create?

What have you created? What is the current picture in your mind? Is it what you want or what you don't want? What is the picture asking you to do? Is it asking you to create something like it, or is it showing you to ensure that this particular picture never happens?

I don't know. It's your creation.

Let me take you back to an old ancient dream. The IMAGINATION of a culture, a people, a tribe, your ancestors….

How far back does your IMAGINATION go?

Ask yourself: "If I dreamed it, can I do it?" The answer is yes. The question is, have you?

Have you ever truly followed your dreams? Have you allowed yourself to run away with your IMAGINATION? Have you allowed yourself to be worthy of your dreams?

So many questions!

Imagine if questions were the way to answers through creating and developing your IMAGINATION....

How many times have you imagined something and hoped it was real? How many times have you told yourself that it's not possible? What would happen if you allowed your imaginings to be possible for 24 hours?

And if you're someone to who IMAGINATION doesn't come easily too, I wonder if there's a question that would create something, an idea perhaps, in your IMAGINATION too?

For example, have you ever wondered what it would be like to be a pencil?

- What color would you be?
- What would you draw?
- Where would you live?
- What colors would you be friends with?
- What colors would you not associate with?
- If you and your pencil friends all drew a picture, what would it look like? Sometimes the joy in IMAGINATION is creating a joyous or fun state from where we can create something spectacular.

See, we have IMAGINATION that can rearrange our past knowing's, for example, "imagine if that had have gone differently," and we have creative IMAGINATIONs where we make the whole thing up!

I remember as a child wanting to get a medal for something. I didn't care what I got the medal in. I just wanted a medal. Olympians got the kind of medals, a big coin on a material necklace. So, I did sport in my quest to get a medal. The first medal I won was in tennis, an iron medal. Grey in color and more like a little badge I could wear. Not really my idea of a medal. I kept going creating the IMAGINATION of what it would feel like as I did multiple different sports. I became a champion at netball, trampolining, pistol shooting, and ballroom dancing; however, none of them gave me the medal I had imagined. I kept imagining the day I would receive a medal; however, even though I was an Australian Champion Trampolinist, they didn't add trampolining into the Olympics until the year after I retired.

The funny thing was the amount of time I'd spent on that IMAGINATION had set in motion the wheels to something quite remarkable. I was 35 years old, and I went on a holiday to a place where they had a flying trapeze. One of my other childhood imaginations was that I would fall into a trapeze net and do that elegant bounce that trapeze artists do from the net to the ground. Something I'd imagined since I was a small girl going to the circus.

So, I spent the holiday learning how to do flying trapeze. I got great at it! Lo and behold, there was a sports awards night on the last day of our holiday. Guess what I got? A medal!

I finally did it! I finally got the medal that I'd imagined more than 30 years before! And funnily enough, it meant more than it would have done when I was a child.

What have you been imagining?

The above is more about utilizing the IMAGINATION in manifestation. Have you ever thought about the fact that your ideas come from your IMAGINATION 99% of the time?

And have you wondered why some people have great ideas while others never seem to have a good idea?

IMAGINATION is the precursor to ideas. Think about the last few ideas you've had for your life. Did they come from reality, or did they come from your IMAGINATION?

Ideas are the building blocks of society and how all significant world changes are created.

When I was a young girl, I would imagine being on the stage! My parents took me to all the musicals, and I would imagine myself growing up and being the leading singer or dancer and bowing to the crowd giving me a standing ovation. I took dancing lessons as I grew up and was in many performances; however, I imagined something much bigger. Now at 48, I speak on global stages and my own stage regularly and receive those standing ovations every time! I followed the formula.

I was inspired as a child. I made a picture of me being famous and impacting millions. I acted by taking any speaking gigs from the age of 14. I gained more and more information from everyone I met. I met them with curiosity and a thirst for knowledge. I told many people about my ideas, and I still do, and people have supported me greatly along the way. Finally, I found the necessary learnings and tools required for what I wanted to do. And then I expanded my ideas, and now I'm here writing this book!

Now I wonder if you thought about the process of taking something you imagine to create it in reality?

Let me share it with you.

- I – Inspiration from your internal or external environment
- M – Make a picture of what that would look like, and apply it to you
- A – take one action towards your goal
- G – Get more information on your imagining from other sources
- I – Impress upon others your IMAGINATION or idea
- N – Find the necessary people, things, or places
- E – Expand your ideas

So, to create a good imagining. First, take inspiration from your internal or external environment. This may be an idea you've had; it may be something in nature; it may be something someone says to you. Start with that inspiration.

Secondly, make a picture of what that would look like. If your IMAGINATION ran to full fruition, what would it look like? Now apply that to you. What will it do for you? How will it make you feel?

Thirdly take action! This is the step that most people miss. They get impressed, make a picture in their minds, and never take any action. So, start small. Take one action every day towards your goal that appeared to you in your IMAGINATION.

Fourthly Get more information! The more information you can get, the more resources you have, and the more effectively you can take your IMAGINATION and make it a reality!

Fifth: Impress upon others your IMAGINATION or idea. The more people you convince about the validity of your vision, the more successful it will be.

Sixth: find the necessary people, places, tools, and resources you need. The more you collect each individual piece of the IMAGINATION, the easier it is to put together as time goes on.

Seventh: expand your ideas. Perhaps what you started with has had further IMAGINATION added to it along the way. Allow your thoughts to grow to give you the next IMAGINATION and the bigger idea.

Some of you have done this many times before, and some of you reading this will be the first time you've really understood how powerful your IMAGINATION is.

I wonder what would happen if you just got out in nature more, took some breaths, breathed in the green of the ocean, and allowed inspiration to spark IMAGINATION?

Imagine if your imaginings allowed someone else to imagine something that sparked an idea that changed the world?

What will you imagine next?

ELIZABETH WALKER

About Elizabeth Walker: Elizabeth is Australia's leading Female Integrated NLP Trainer, an international speaker with Real Success, and the host of Success Resources' (Australia's largest and most successful events promoter, including speakers such as Tony Robbins and Sir Richard Branson) inaugural Australian Women's Program "The Seed." Elizabeth has guided many people to achieve complete personal breakthroughs and phenomenal personal and business growth. With over 25 years of experience transforming the lives of hundreds of thousands of people, Elizabeth's goal is to assist leaders to create the reality they choose to live, impacting millions on a global scale.

A thought leader who has worked alongside people like Gary Vaynerchuck, Kerwin Rae, Jeffery Slayter, and Kate Gray, Elizabeth has an outstanding method of delivering heart with business.

As a former lecturer in medicine at the University of Sydney and lecturer in nursing at Western Sydney University, Elizabeth was instrumental in the research and development of the stillbirth and neonatal death pathways, ensuring each family in Australia went home knowing what happened to their child, and felt understood, heard, and seen.

A former Australian Champion in Trampolining and Australian Dancesport, Elizabeth has always been passionate about the mindset and skills required to create the results you are seeking.

Author's website: *www.ElizabethAnneWalker.com*
Book Series Website & Author's Bio: *www.The13StepsToRiches.com*

Erin Ley

ENJOY THE PLAYGROUND OF YOUR MIND

In his book, *THINK AND GROW RICH*, Napoleon Hill said, "Man's only limitation, within reason, lies in his development and use of his IMAGINATION. He has not yet reached the apex of development in the use of his imaginative faculty. He merely discovered that he has an IMAGINATION and has commenced to use it in a very elementary way."

Napoleon Hill describes the difference between synthetic IMAGINATION, where we use past experiences to create what we want, and the creative IMAGINATION, where we experience hunches and inspiration. I call the creative IMAGINATION the Divine Download.

Much of what I've created in life has come from the synthetic IMAGINATION; however, the many miracles I've experienced have come about because of the creative IMAGINATION. One example of this was when I followed my gut when I was living with cancer, non-Hodgkins lymphoblastic lymphoma, in 1991. Instead of relying solely on what the doctors had to say, I listened to my intuition and read the many personal development books I was divinely guided to read. I credit those books for me living every time the doctors said I'd die and for going on to have three miracle children when the doctors swore it would never happen. I love my doctors. They did their best and treated me with their greatest care. I just knew there was more I could do for myself utilizing the power of the IMAGINATION and the intentional heartfelt feelings of gratitude. It was imperative I allowed myself to focus on gratitude and appreciation. Many people thought I "wasn't facing reality," and that was alright. Personalizing anything at that point was a waste of valuable time.

When I was a child, I used to look out the window for hours, daydreaming about all the things I wanted to accomplish in life. I spent just as much time thinking about all the reasons why I could not achieve those big dreams. As a child, I had no idea there were so many self-limiting beliefs and so much self-doubt in place in my subconscious mind. It was the limiting beliefs and doubt that stifled my creative IMAGINATION. When I look back on what I did accomplish up until I was twenty-five years old and diagnosed with the cancer diagnosis described above, it amazes me how much more I could have done. At that time, I wanted to work on Wall Street in New York City as a licensed Account Executive in a big-name brokerage house. And that is precisely what I went on to do. When I wanted summer homes in the Hamptons or winter homes in Hunter Mountain, I did that too. But if I wanted something and thought there was no way for me to achieve that end goal, I stopped trying immediately. I had no idea how powerful the IMAGINATION is. When we have a burning desire of any kind and we couple it with faith, the creative IMAGINATION kicks into high gear and begins to send the roadmap to our ultimate goal in the form of gut feelings, hunches, and ideas out of the blue. When we experience doubt, though, it stops everything in its tracks. Doubt is a dream-crusher. It is the nemesis of the creative IMAGINATION. When we can negate all doubt and fear-based thoughts, we become unstoppable.

Life is always throwing us obstacles to see how we handle them and who we are in the process. Another example of when I slipped temporarily into self-doubt and fear was when I was going through a tumultuous divorce that went on from 2014 to 2016. I was shocked and heartbroken. When I was experiencing all the negativity, so many negative things continued to happen, such as my hot-water heater flooding my basement and getting hit from behind in a car accident that sent me to the hospital, followed by a few surgeries. During one of the surgeries, I realized what was going on. My IMAGINATION was no longer the playground for creating amazing things in my life. Instead, it became the breeding ground for everything I did not want.

I knew at that moment that I had to shift my energy into being intentional about staying in the mindset of gratitude and appreciation. I knew I had to put pen to paper and write a crystal-clear vision of what I wanted for my life, beyond my wildest dreams. I knew I had to have the feeling that my goals had already been achieved. I knew I had to have the feelings of excitement, enthusiasm, and optimism to attract the right people, places, and things into my life. I had to remember that everything happens in divine order and divine timing. Finally, I had to have faith.

Most importantly, I had to shift out of the self-doubt and shift into the self-confidence I once had. The funny thing is that when I shifted into the self-confidence, after having the courage to take massive action, my self-confidence rose to a level I had never experienced. As a result, the inner peace I feel is the deepest I've ever experienced.

I stopped my Empowerment Coaching business for a couple of years to focus on the family at that time. When I started back up again, I started with nothing and grew my business to six figures in a year and a half utilizing what I'm sharing with you here. I hired coaches and mentors to help me scale to seven figures. What started off as a tragedy brought me to new heights because I understood the power of the IMAGINATION.

Imagine how much more amazing your life could be once you release your self-limiting beliefs and self-doubt. You get to create a vision for your life beyond your wildest dreams. You get to allow yourself to have the white-hot burning desire to make those goals a reality. You get to utilize your gift of faith. You get to use autosuggestion to reprogram your subconscious to allow you to do, be, and have anything you want as the direct result of knowing how to redirect doubt and fear very quickly if and when they come up.

When I interviewed NY Times bestselling author Sharon Lechter, she summed up something I understood for decades but couldn't put into words. Sharon brilliantly said, "Worrying is just a prayer for what we do not want." That is one of the most powerful statements I have ever heard, and I share it with anyone and everyone, crediting Sharon for the quote.

What is it that you want to do, be, or have? Take the time to write it all down, personally and professionally. Think big. We are here to live an abundant life, not a mediocre life. Utilize the most untapped gift we have, the gift of the IMAGINATION. It's where it all starts. When we write our imagined goals down, they take form and become what we desire. Let the momentum build with the right mindset and the feeling of knowing beyond the shadow of a doubt that it will become your reality. The only way the momentum will stop is if you introduce self-doubt. Self-doubt always leads to some form of fear, and then all of what you've imagined dissipates. The only way to get back on track is to shift into gratitude and faith and feel the self-confidence. Autosuggestion is the greatest strategy for achieving the self-confidence you are looking for.

In *THINK AND GROW RICH*, Napoleon Hill also said, "Ideas are intangible forces, but they have more power than the physical brains that give birth to them. They have the power to live on after the brain that created them has returned to dust."

After overcoming the cancer diagnosis at age twenty-five in 1991, as an Empowerment and Success Coach, I've taken my personal survival journey to create a step-by-step process for realizing true peace of mind, synergy, and success, personally and professionally. I've shown thousands upon thousands of business leaders globally how to become victorious by utilizing the power of the IMAGINATION to become focused, fearless, and excited. My mission in life is to introduce the idea of love in the workplace to encourage team building, loyalty, and leadership. This all stems from imagining what life and your business will look like when this is in place.

How are you utilizing your IMAGINATION? It's like a muscle. It gets stronger with use. What is your mission in life? What do you want to be remembered for in generations to come? Start to work your IMAGINATION more and more every day. Be committed to allowing your IMAGINATION to grow. This is the playground of the mind. Have fun with it. Utilize it for the greater good and always move onward and upward. You deserve a great life filled with an abundance of health, wealth, and happiness. Imagine that.

ERIN LEY

About Erin Ley: As Founder and CEO of Onward Productions, Inc., Erin Ley has spent the last 30 years as an Author, Professional Speaker, Personal and Professional Empowerment and Success Coach predominantly around mindset, Vision and Decision. Founder of many influential summits, including "Life On Track," Erin is also the host of the upcoming online streaming T.V. Show "*Life On Track with Erin Ley,*" which is all about helping you get into the driver's seat of your own life.

They call Erin "The Miracle Maker!" As a cancer survivor at age twenty-five, single mom of three at age forty-seven, successful Entrepreneur at age fifty, Erin has shown thousands upon thousands across the globe how to become victorious by being focused, fearless, and excited about life and your future! Erin says, "Celebrate life and you'll have a life worth celebrating!"

To see more about Erin and the release of her 4th book "*WorkLuv: A Love Story*" along with her "Life On Track" Course & Coaching Programs, please visit her website.

Author's website: *www.ErinLey.com*
Book Series Website & Author's Bio: *www.The13StepsToRiches.com*

Fatima Hurd

IMAGINATION WITH PURPOSE AND DIRECTION

IMAGINATION is crucial and instrumental in our evolution as humankind. Without it, we would not be where we are, and life would be very primitive. IMAGINATION draws from our prior experiences and knowledge of what we are familiar with to help us explore the unknown and all that is possible.

"IMAGINATION is more important than knowledge. For knowledge is limited, whereas IMAGINATION embraces the entire world, stimulating progress, giving birth to evolution." ~Albert Einstein

In this quote, Albert Einstein is referring to Creative Knowledge vs. Synthetic Knowledge.

When we align with our higher power, we are in a receiving state of mind that stimulates conscious minds with the five senses and strong desires that help us form new ideas creating room for new possibilities!

Now imagine all that we can create if we were always tuned into from our Creative IMAGINATION faculty for one moment?

A great example of being tapped into creative IMAGINATION was back in 2008. As you might recall from previous chapters, I was laid off from my job due to the 2008 recession. That experience, although not the best, was a blessing in disguise. I see now how that layoff shifted my life in a new direction. Reading self-help books and shifting my mindset led me to be open to all the possibilities. I had accessed my vortex, and things were falling in place for everything I wanted in life. Life was finally going in an upward direction after a tough year. I had met and moved in with my now-husband. Found a job that paid well.

Then one day, I got a call from a friend I met in college. She was eager to connect, and we decided to meet for lunch. We hadn't connected in a long time, so as you can imagine, I was excited. When we met for lunch, she was excited to tell me she had started her photography business. She showed some examples of her work, and she was genuinely talented. However, the purpose of the visit was to ask me for money; she needed a loan to open a studio. She had been renting space from another photographer, but it didn't work out. So, she needed a studio fast and was looking for someone to lend her some money.

Instantly I was inspired and driven to make a decision. I did not lend her the money; I chose to invest in the business as a partner. I had no idea what I was doing; I was just doing, following my intuition. Using my Creative IMAGINATION, I was able to see that opportunity was knocking at my door. My mind began to bring to reality my desire to be an entrepreneur. I knew that I wanted to start my business, but I wasn't sure what I wanted to do until that precise moment. We went into business together, and photography became my vision, my passion! I enjoy serving others with the gift of my photography. When we sat there and talked, my heart was inspired, and then the desire to serve others in such a creative way was painting the picture. I could feel it, I sense it; we had the idea, and now we just needed a plan. Two weeks later, we had a studio, and we were in business. Not only was I able to visualize my intention, but I was in the moment, and that emotion was intense. I knew that it was my reality, and I brought it to fruition.

Since then, I have learned so much, and I continue to grow and expand my knowledge in combination with my creative IMAGINATION, and the ideas have facilitated many incredible opportunities.

The more you use your Creative IMAGINATION faculty, the more alert and receptive you become to the vibrations around you. I use mediation to help me build up the muscle of the creative IMAGINATION faculty.

Another example of how my creative IMAGINATION has served me is when I joined Habitude Warrior masterminds. Being a member of the amazing mastermind, I have developed some incredible ideas through what Mr. Awesome "Erik Swanson" calls borrowed benefits. Another opportunity that being a member of Habitude Warrior has brought me is being a contributing co- author in this amazing Book Series, *The 13 Steps to Riches*! When I was young, I was such a bookworm; even then, I enjoyed nourishing my brain reading and expanding on ideas with an endless pool of possibilities of what I wanted to do and be when I grew up. To be an author was definitely one of them. So here we are years later, and it's happening, but here's the thing, not just an author, I am a 4x Best Selling Author alongside some incredible co-authors and celebrity authors! This opportunity still has me on cloud nine. It still seems surreal to me that this is happening, but it is, and I am enjoying every moment with a heart filled with gratitude for this incredible blessing!

I am so grateful to have met Erik Swanson, and because of him, I also met Jon Kovach Jr. I have learned so much from them, such a gift! When I am present at the meetings, the creative flow goes nuts with an abundance of great ideas—the IMAGINATION faculty muscle on steroids.

I also find it interesting how when we come together and pour into each other in a high frequency of love, people share similar ideas, as though we have tapped into each other's minds. I guess this is why they say to act on an idea; otherwise, someone else will.

I truly believe in my heart that this is the secret sauce, the magic that Napoleon Hill experienced in his masterminds. Now imagine tapping into the creative and great minds of leaders such as Erik Swanson, Jon Kovach Jr., and the amazing members of the Habitude Warrior Mastermind.

I've always had a great IMAGINATION, but now I have IMAGINATION with purpose and direction in joining the mastermind. Through these borrowed benefits, my creative IMAGINATION has expanded ten folds driving me to take inspired action to transform my desires into money with a plan and inspired action. IMAGINATION is a gift that creates a mental image in your head of that desire before you can see it in your reality. The saying "I have to see it to believe it" makes no sense because the creative process doesn't work that way. We must first create it in our mind, feel it in our hearts and bring it into form through inspired action.

And this is the part that people don't get when it comes to manifesting what you want; IMAGINATION is key, visualizing it, feeling it "emotion," and then following through with action. Unfortunately, people fail to act on their ideas.

This past year has been a year of expansion and action! My IMAGINATION and ideas are expanding to a new level as I continue to surround myself with incredible leaders. I am looking forward to what the new year will bring as I continue to up-level and develop my Creative IMAGINATION.

FATIMA HURD

About Fatima Hurd: Fatima is a personal brand photographer and was featured in the special edition of Beauty & Lifestyle's mommy magazine. Fatima specializes in personal branding photography dedicated to helping influencers and entrepreneurs expand their reach online with strategic, creative, inspiring, and visual content. Owner of a digital consulting agency, Social Branding Photography, Fatima helps professionals with all their digital needs.

Fatima holds ten years of photography experience. An expert in her field, she helps teach photography to middle school students and she hosts workshops to teach anyone who wants to learn how to use and improve their skills with DSLR and on manual mode. Hurd is also a mother of three, wife, certified Reiki master, and certified crystal healer. She loves being out in nature, enjoys taking road trips with her family, and loves meditation and yoga on the beach.

Author's website: *www.FatimaHurd.com*
Book Series Website & Author's Bio: *www.The13StepsToRiches.com*

Frankie Fegurgur

CAN WE IMAGINE THE FUTURE?

We are all born creative. Humans have long utilized spoken, written, and illustrated stories to explain our origin, how the world works, and our place in the universe. Think back to when you played as a child. A cardboard box became a rocket ship, pots and pans from the kitchen became the drums for your astronaut rock band, and the mud on a rainy day became the surface of the moon, or maybe even alien slime. There was no limit to the fun, no judgment on how 'realistic' any of your ideas were. But then you had to grow up, and your IMAGINATION turned into a doom and gloom machine. Suddenly you could only predict the worst. Traffic on the way to work was going to be heavy, work especially draining, and don't think about finally getting ahead in life, because any moment now, the other shoe will drop. "This can't be it!" you exclaim. What if you could imagine a better future? Not a dystopian life full of regret, but one where you embrace financial freedom and a long life well-lived?

IMAGINATION doesn't have an age limit. Although children experience reality in a very different way than the average adult, this doesn't mean we can't tap into our inner Imagineer. You can reinvigorate your IMAGINATION whenever you choose. That's because it exists outside of time and location. Sure, we can measure what happens in the brain when we have creative thoughts. But can you point to your IMAGINATION like you can your kneecap? Reality as we know it is vast. And yet, so much of our universe is unknown or nonexistent. IMAGINATION resides somewhere in between what is real and what is nonexistent. Our creative process is driven by our desire, turning thoughts into metaphors and metaphors into images. We can build and integrate something new into our reality from an image.

Developing your IMAGINATION is critical to financial freedom. If you can't imagine a better life for yourself and your family, you won't see the incredible emerging opportunities throughout our new economy, particularly Web 3.0. Unfortunately, not everyone will rise to the occasion. The wealth disparity will largely be dictated by who can adapt to the new way of business versus who succumbs to distraction and resistance to change. Before I discuss being at the forefront of change by acquiring both tangible and digital assets, we'll need to address managing distractions while cultivating our IMAGINATION. There are two types of IMAGINATION, Synthetic and Creative.

Synthetic IMAGINATION combines old ideas with our experiences, beliefs, and environment to create something slightly different. A modern example is found in meme culture. Someone feeling clever will take a photo of something funny and add an unrelated but potentially funnier caption. They created nothing new or revolutionary, but memes take on a life of their own, with countless people rushing to create their version. This type of IMAGINATION is what we use in our day-to- day lives, and while not our strongest, it is the easiest to develop. Our current cultural experience offers more than enough material in the form of music, books, movies, and food for you to determine what variations you want to launch.

Creative IMAGINATION is less common yet more powerful than Synthetic IMAGINATION. It is like the Eureka Effect, where an amazing idea appears out of thin air. Napoleon Hill described these moments as "direct communication with Infinite Intelligence." Such ideas are often taken for granted now but were revolutionary at inception. Think about hand soap and how many countless lives have been saved. I bet you can't believe that there was a time not too long ago that people didn't wash their hands. Another is the number zero. We didn't always use zero, but it forever changed math and science, making many other ideas possible. Your 'zero' is ready for you to bring to fruition and create the riches you desire. Although there will be obstacles, the good news is you won't have to work through them alone. The power of a mastermind group will support you and provide access to collective insight.

The greatest obstacle to a robust IMAGINATION is Digital Distraction. We are flooded with information, especially online. You probably aren't intentionally contributing to the noise, but we've all heard the "publish content daily" mantra. Anyone with a social media account knows that you can scroll for hours and not even scratch the surface. Most of it is synthetic, hastily constructed for cheap entertainment. These days you don't need to know anything. You just need to know how to Google it. A plethora of resources at your fingertips is great but makes your brain lazy. Why would you ever need to formulate your own opinion when a talking head or a YouTube star can give you theirs? This reduces our critical thinking ability because we outsource our problem-solving to technology. Don't believe me? Without checking your cell phone, recite the phone numbers of the five most important people in your life.

To beat Digital Distraction, you need to spend time in your movie theater. Our IMAGINATION allows us to preview an idea to determine its effect on our future. Most people preview based on their current limitations, but your limitations no longer serve you. Here is a simple exercise you can do every day to release those beliefs and strengthen your IMAGINATION:

1. Set aside 5-10 minutes and sit or lie down in a quiet place.

2. Imagine you are enjoying your very own movie theater. It can be modern, with recliners and a huge surround sound system, or retro with ornate decorations and gaudy curtains. It can be in your dream house or even underwater.

3. The screen lights up, and you realize that it's a preview of your future. Take notice of what you're wearing, how you're behaving, and who you're with. What idea have you launched? Who helped you along the way? Who is enjoying your idea, and how have they compensated you? How has this idea changed your life? Is it what you expected? The more details, the better.

4. Write down whatever is noteworthy, along with immediate action steps.

5. Take a breath and start the next preview. Assess the outcome in comparison to your first idea.

6. Reference this book every week.

Technology and IMAGINATION are inseparable. Now that you have a tool to harness your IMAGINATION in this rapidly changing economy let's discuss the tremendous opportunities in Web 3.0. The internet has evolved, with the basic premise that Web 1.0 was read-only. The news and corporate entities posted articles or other information, with little to no interaction between consumers. In Web 2.0, anyone could have a blog and interact with people worldwide through social media. The trade-off for the development of these networks is that corporations came to own most of the data. These corporations buy and sell highly sensitive information about our habits, jobs, income, locations, conversations, religious and political beliefs, health, and even appearance.

Web 3.0 and beyond integrates artificial intelligence, blockchain, virtual reality, and augmented reality into our daily lives for a more personalized experience. Instead of sitting in front of a computer and clicking away at a keyboard and mouse, you'll use eye-tracking, voice commands, and hand gestures to control your environment and your data seamlessly. Such widespread automation will eliminate 85 million jobs in the next 2-3 years. The workplace is changing forever. Imagine what an office job will be like; instead of a physical office, you'll wear a virtual reality headset. Inside you'll see your desk and interact with electronic paperwork and software. You'll attend meetings with holographic colleagues huddled around 3D models.

Even leisure and entertainment are changing. Instead of just watching sports on television, why not sit in your virtual VIP suite? Instantly switch views to any camera in the stadium, including what the athletes see! Skip the lines at the mall and step into your own virtual concierge luxury fitting room. Customize any outfit and see how it will look on you instantly. Purchase the digital outfit for your avatar in VR, and have the physical clothing delivered by drone in minutes. Gaming will be a Mixed Reality, where you complete tasks in the real world with a heavily augmented twist. Imagine doing an escape room in your house, with lava coming out of the floor, secret doors appearing in your wall, and every nuance of your movement triggering responses from lifelike characters. Or become your favorite superhero and save the universe!

Web 3.0 is bursting with opportunities for those with an active IMAGINATION. This expansive environment needs developers, blockchain experts, community managers, content creators, and more. You won't need anyone's permission to grow your net worth. Instead, own your virtual and physical presence, driven by your personal cryptocurrency. Take your profits and buy tangible or digital assets such as land to create generational wealth. The possibilities are only limited by your IMAGINATION!

FRANKIE FEGURGUR

About Frankie Fegurgur: Frankie's "burning desire" is helping people retire with dignity. Frankie distills the lessons he has learned over the last 15 years and empowers our youth to make better financial decisions than the generation before them. This is a deeply personal mission for him—he was born to high-school-aged parents, and money was always a struggle. Frankie learned that hard work, alone, wasn't the key to financial freedom and sought a more fulfilling path. Now, he serves as the COO of a nonprofit financial association based in the San Francisco Bay Area, teaching money mindfulness. He, his wife, and their two children can be found exploring, volunteering, and building throughout their community.

Author's website: *www.FrankMoneyTalk.com*
Book Series Website & Author's Bio: *www.The13StepsToRiches.com*

Fred Moskowitz

CURIOSITY AND IMAGINATION - POWERFUL HUMAN FACULTIES THAT WORK HAND IN HAND

IMAGINATION - What a powerful word. The classic definition of IMAGINATION is the faculty of forming new concepts, ideas, and images in the mind.

Suppose you have ever spent time with young children. In that case, it is for sure that you can't help but notice the ease in which they can let their IMAGINATION take center stage. Children will even invite everyone nearby to come around and actively participate in the experience.

It is quite interesting to ask a 5-year-old child what they want to be when they grow up. They will tell you without any hesitation about how they want to become an astronaut, firefighter, veterinarian, professional basketball athlete, superhero, or a movie actor. On the other hand, let's ask an eighteen-year-old preparing to enter college. "What major do you plan to take up in your studies?" While some may know exactly what they want to study, there will be a larger majority that simply does not know.

Unfortunately, it seems that for many of us, as we grow older, we often forget how to use our IMAGINATION. So, why do this ability get shut down as we grow up? It seems that has been a function of the negative influence of life and society at large on all of us. However, there are ways to reverse this trend.

One of the seeds of IMAGINATION is curiosity. And maintaining an active curiosity about everything in the world is a great way to flex that muscle constantly. Just as we might go to the gym to exercise our body and strengthen our muscles, we can be actively curious in order to stimulate our IMAGINATION. I have a mentor who taught me the benefit of going out and learning something new every year, whether a new sport, hobby, skill, or activity. It's an intentional way to be curious, and I have found this to be very powerful. As a side benefit, you may find that the activity can be quite fun and enjoyable while you are learning. And you may even meet some fantastic people in the process.

Curiosity is a very engaging and neutral emotion. Our human physiology really benefits from curiosity. It even helps the body grow new T-cells, improve our neurological function, and strengthen the immune system at a cellular level.

When you get into a state of curiosity, it tends to dispel negative emotions and negative self-talk. It also helps to open our creative faculties.

In his classic 1937 work *Think and Grow Rich*, author Napoleon Hill talks about two forms of IMAGINATION - Synthetic IMAGINATION and Creative IMAGINATION.

Synthetic IMAGINATION - The first form of IMAGINATION is Synthetic IMAGINATION, which arranges and combines well-known concepts, ideas, and plans into new combinations. This often draws from the person's experience, education, and observations. In addition, it incorporates prior work which has been taught or handed down from others.

Creative IMAGINATION - With Creative IMAGINATION, this is how nudges, whispers, hunches, notions, and inspirations are received. Some people even refer to this as receiving a "download." The creative ability becomes more alert and active through regular use. It is very much a mental muscle that grows when flexed on a consistent basis. Participating in creative activities can be one of the best ways to unleash and exercise that creative IMAGINATION inside you. I encourage you to consider taking up a hobby involving creative art of some type: painting and drawing, learning a foreign language, acting, theater performance, creative writing, or playing a musical instrument. Perhaps it was an activity you did when you were younger, and this could be a great time in your life to revisit that.

For much of my adult life, I have been a student of music, playing the styles of jazz guitar and bossa nova guitar. And, living in Philadelphia, I am afforded a very rich and vibrant live music scene right in my own backyard. As a result, I really enjoy going out to experience live music and the activity of playing jazz music in a group setting. This is certainly a place where creative IMAGINATION shows up in full force.

I have found that playing music is a powerful way to combine both concepts of Synthetic IMAGINATION and Creative IMAGINATION.

If we consider the established concepts and theories of music, these will all fall under the category of Synthetic IMAGINATION. So, let's pause to break things down to a more granular level, where we can look at some of the basic building blocks of music:

The Physics of Sound - The principles of physics, such as sound waves, wavelengths, frequencies, and harmonics, all come into play. Also, there are the notions of resonance, pitch, and timbre - these are the concepts that provide those sensory layers and richness to the sounds we are listening to.

Mathematics - With respect to mathematics, we use many numeric patterns, fractions, notes, and harmonics in music.

Time - The concept of time gives us rhythms and patterns built using sequences and periods of sounds and silence. Let's look at music through the lens of the other form of IMAGINATION - Creative IMAGINATION. The best place to see this at work is in different improvisational styles of music such as jazz, blues, rock jam bands, and Latin music orchestras. The common element you will notice is that the musicians will play a familiar song based around a very loose framework and structure. Then, they will improvise and take solos over this framework, and the music is made truly at the moment. There is very little pre-planning (if any), and once the music is played, it is a unique one-time experience. The band will never play the same song exactly the same way ever again.

For the audience, listening to these styles of music live can be a compelling experience. The band playing the music can connect with each other and with the audience, and vice versa. The energy oscillates back and forth between them, increasing the level of intensity of the experience. In observing the musicians on stage, we will notice that the band members interact musically all throughout, without speaking anything verbally. This effect is very evident if we ever have the opportunity to watch Cuban percussion musicians or Brazilian Samba groups. These styles, in particular, incorporate many rich layers of rhythms and counter-rhythms, all working together seamlessly.

You might hear the musicians having an entertaining conversation using call and response patterns if you listen carefully. The conversation is made up of musical banter going back and forth. Napoleon Hill describes this process of creative IMAGINATION by stating that "they can tune in and communicate with each other's subconscious minds."

In conclusion, I would like to emphasize that participating in creative activities and maintaining a healthy curiosity will have a very positive influence on your growth and personal development. This might be an excellent time for you to take action and revisit that instrument you used to play as a child or take some lessons in creative arts. I encourage you to set the intention to learn something new and see what kind of growth will come about in your life.

FRED MOSKOWITZ

About Fred Moskowitz: Fred is a best-selling author, investment fund manager, and speaker who is on a personal mission to teach people about the power of investing in alternative asset classes, such as real estate and mortgage notes, showing them the way to diversify their capital into investments that are uncorrelated from Wall Street and the stock markets.

Through his body of work, he is teaching investors the strategies to build passive income and cash flow streams designed to flow into their bank accounts. He's a frequent event speaker and contributor to investment podcasts.

Fred is the author of The Little Green Book Of Note Investing: A Practical Guide For Getting Started With Investing In Mortgage Notes and contributing author in 1Habit To Thrive in a Post-Covid World.

Author's Website: *www.FredMoskowitz.com*
Book Series Website & Author's Bio: *www.The13StepsToRiches.com*

Dr. Freeman Witherspoon

JUST MY IMAGINATION

IMAGINATION has been defined as "The image-making power of the mind; the act of mentally creating or reproducing an object not previously perceived; the ability to create such images." From this very definition, we can understand how powerful IMAGINATION can be. It is the medium to which things are brought into existence. There is no way to make something exist without them passing through the channel of IMAGINATION. IMAGINATION is a portal for creativity and innovation.

Looking at the things around you, the best books that have been written, the best houses that are built, or the best cars that are crafted, they exist because of IMAGINATION. Someone somewhere thought through and pulled that out of the mental realm. The mental realm embodies so many realities and possibilities, including the wealth and fortunes you seek to build. The way to engage that is through IMAGINATION. This principle that we are talking about that has contributed to many people's success is not a recent principle; it is an ancient reality for possibilities. It has been in place since the beginning of time. For ages, it has been believed that the way to realize success and progressiveness in life is through this instrumentality—that is, creative thinking.

IMAGINATION is an ancient principle that helps create success and usher people into stupendous wealth and health. The mind is such a powerful tool, and when we learn to use it well, we can access its latent power. In his book, *The Power of the Subconscious Mind*, Joseph Murphy asserts that the mind is created with powers that include even the body's ability to heal. When it is engaged well, then possibilities can be created as well. This makes us see the power of the mind. The tool that God gave man to navigate his way through life is through the mind. "How?" You might ask. Through creative thinking. We can attract, create, and fashion anything in life with this.

Success is a relational reality. If you look through every success in life, you will understand that success in one way or the other engaged this principle: creative and constructive thinking. Exploring this, they accessed ideas and theories that shaped their lives and the world at large. Reading through the pages of our magazines, blogs, websites, and books, we can see the theories and philosophies shared because the people sharing these stories or ideas engaged their minds constructively. Understand, friend, anyone who dares to engage in a positive IMAGINATION is unstoppable in this life. He becomes excessively successful and significant in life.

Let's look at how God encouraged His servant, Joshua, the servant of Moses, to engage in this very principle to enter into success and stupendous wealth:

"Only be thou strong and very courageous, that thou mayest observe to do according to all the Law, which Moses my servant commanded thee: turn not from it [to] the right hand or [to] the left, that thou mayest prosper thou whithersoever goest. This book of the Law shall not depart out of thy mouth; but thou shalt meditate therein day and night, that thou mayest observe to do according to all that is written therein: for then thou shalt make thy way prosperous, and then thou shalt have good success." (Joshua 1:7–8)

From this portion of scripture, God showed Joshua the way to increase prosperity. You don't need to be a Christian to embrace the realities that create success. The laws of success are universal. The moment we learn how to utilize them, we can become successful. In this portion of Scripture, God showed His servant how to maximize success. We will have to learn from them. Firstly, He spoke to him about the element of courage and also confidence. This makes people successful! I know no one under the sun who has risen to the top without these virtues. That is courage and confidence. To become successful, they are essential.

He further instructed that the book of the Law shouldn't depart from his mouth, and he should meditate on it day and night. What does the word "meditate" mean? It talks about creative and constructive thinking. The promise of one who engages in creative and constructive thinking is a success. Success will never elude a man who thinks and acts in the direction of those thoughts.

When we engage the mind, it releases the best insights ever for productivity. Remember, before the mind gets to that point, it must be "seduced." This seduction is what I call constructive IMAGINATION. In this place of mental engagement, anything can be created, including the money desires which occupy your sleepless nights. I understood the power of constructive thinking and IMAGINATION in my late fifties. It was then I saw that whatever a man can really think of, he can get it. I couldn't help but agree with the wise words of Solomon David, who asserts, "As a man thinks in his heart, so is he" (See Proverbs 23:7). Reading through this, I understood that the mind is an asset, and we can use it to create the life that we desire. Remember that desire is never enough to make one successful. We must couple that desire with constructive IMAGINATION to get us to that place of action.

Many people in the world today are merely wishful thinkers; therefore, they cannot manifest the things they wish for. The primary reason is that they are not constructively engaging their minds. The reality is that when the mind is engaged well, it will produce ideas that can guide one to success and wealth. Creative IMAGINATION is like a magnet; it draws your dreams and goals into realization. Therefore, I encourage you to learn to engage it for the life you envision.

When I set the goal of owning my own home, that house came into existence through constructive thinking. First, I wrote out the kind of house I wanted and the timeline. While meditating on this goal, details of creating the possibility kept flashing before me. Then, as I stepped out in obedience to the images and ideas, I attained the funding. I have used this principle to attract incredible results and fortunes from that point onward.

Friend, understand that constructive IMAGINATION is the pathway that creates possibilities. One who engages in it will become incredibly successful. As mentioned, there is a correlation between every success. You might be asking, "How?" Here is the thing: The principles of success and achieving riches are universal. However, the avenues for achieving them vary. So, learning to engage the principles makes success possible. One of the universal principles of success is constructive IMAGINATION.

Now here is the challenge. When you have a dream or desire of something you want to achieve, and you begin to imagine and constructively ponder it, learn the concept of writing as well. Get a notepad and journal the ideas that are coming to you. Some of those ideas are templates to achieving the very thing you are thinking about.

In the process of IMAGINATION, other ideas and thoughts are touched. Just as Napoleon Hill asserts in his book, he mentioned that the finite mind touches the realities of the infinite mind. These realities in the infinite realm begin to come to the conscious realm (this is what I call auto- suggestive realm). Your mind suggests ideas to you on possible ways to achieve what you are thinking about. The moment these suggestions are written down, you have initiated the process of manifestation.

In Habakkuk 2, God taught the prophet this very principle. He was told to write the vision down and then make it plain. The written dream or desire never dies out. There is always a way to manifest. We, therefore, ought to learn from this and engage it well. Thus, writing the vision or ideas down.

After writing the ideas down, keep going over them until it flames you up to act. When ideas are not processed or meditated upon, they don't trigger action. So, after writing and thinking through, keep revising. What you are doing is creating room for it to ignite a passion or flame for action. This flame is what is going to push you out of your comfort zone to make it happen.

Be specific and determined about the clear-cut goal. Ponder it. When that revelation comes, you will know. Your heart or spirit will bear witness that you have touched the exact idea that is going to create the change you want in life.

This is the way to success. Engage it, and success will befriend you. God showed us that success is possible if only we can meditate and ponder it. We can access success and stupendous wealth through constructive and creative IMAGINATION. I am challenging you today to think! If you don't believe so, you will sink. If you don't think, no one will mind you. Use your mind today to access the riches hidden inside of you. There are untapped riches and treasures within you. Be challenged through creative IMAGINATION and dare to access those riches.

FREEMAN WITHERSPOON

About Freeman Witherspoon: Freeman is a professional network marketer that manages several online businesses. He considers himself a late bloomer to network marketing. Prior to partnering with network marketing organizations, he served for over 20 years in the military. He has incorporated his many life experiences into managing successful business models.

Military service afforded him the opportunity to travel throughout the world. He has lived in Heidelberg, Germany, Seoul, South Korea, and many places throughout the United States. Freeman currently lives in Texas with his wife and three dogs; a Dachshund named Dutchess, a Yorkie named Boosie and a Pomchi (Pomeranian-Chihuahua mix) named Caesar.

Author's website: *www.FWitherspoonJr.com*
Book Series Website & Author's Bio: *www.The13StepsToRiches.com*

Gina Bacalski

HALLYU TO THE RESCUE

When I close my eyes, I can smell the damp, rich earth beneath the grass. I can feel the breeze as it caresses my face and teases my hair. I can taste and feel the grit of the limestone. I can "see" the emerald sea of meadows before me. Because of IMAGINATION, I can go back to the wall and my tree in England (which I talked about in Book 1) and live that moment time and time again.

IMAGINATION is really the linchpin to all the other chapters and books in this series. If you can't imagine something, how can you achieve it? Thoughts are things, but you have to think about them first.

Growing up, I almost had too much of an IMAGINATION. I would get lost for hours making up games and stories, pretending I was a princess in some long-forgotten castle (in England, of course), waiting to be rescued by a handsome prince. In other games, I was the warrior who did the rescuing. My fantasy world overtook even my chores to the point of my mother getting frustrated with my near-constant residence up in the clouds, a place my mother told me to get my head out of quite frequently.

My grand IMAGINATION has served me well in all of my career pursuits. I would make up stories and plays on the spot when I was a preschool teacher, I could see the hall fully decorated and the flower arrangement completed when I was a wedding planner and decorator. Likewise, as a real estate agent, I can help my clients see the potential in a home and help those I coach see the potential in themselves and their businesses.

Writing novels has been my go-to when my brain is about to explode with another story idea. Whatever the opposite of writer's block is, I have that when I write fiction. After I lay in bed and imagine the scene, I can write for hours on end and still have more to write. It has been a much- needed cathartic exercise and mental release for me.

My IMAGINATION has served me well in other areas of my life too. In addition to making up stories, plays, songs, poems, and places to put a sofa, I also use my IMAGINATION in manifesting changes I would like to see in my life.

As mentioned in a previous book, when I meditate at night, I use my IMAGINATION to make my mind and body actually believe the thing I want is already mine, and then I listen for the next steps to get me the thing I must have. Your brain will follow your IMAGINATION and your thoughts.

A word of caution, though, is that it works in undesirable situations as well. So, if I focus on bad things, those will just as surely come to life as much as desirable ones. While in general, I am very upbeat, have a happy disposition, and have a positive outlook on life, even I have bad days. They happen at least once a month for me and others like me (men have cycles, too!). I call them Spiral Days. You know what days I'm talking about! One thing triggers a bad thought (If it's a bad memory, those can be dealt with but more on that at a later chapter). That one negative thought will lead to two more. Then those will spiral down to five more and by the time your partner or loved one peels you off the floor, you're the worst cook and the worst wife, and you don't know why he could ever marry you to begin with. You're so fat no one could ever love you, and you have horrible hair, and you're terrible at make-up, and who let you pick out your own clothes, to begin with? And your cousin's next-door neighbor was right when she told you were ugly when you were six, and you weren't good enough to be the class president in seventh grade, so you surely aren't good enough to make any difference in anyone's life now, and—Sound familiar? Yeah, I see them for what they are on those days, and I know that I am a big fat liar and don't listen to my thoughts.

Instead, I know I need to distract myself from myself, so at the first hint of Negative Nancy tapping at my door, I promptly tell her to pack sand while I choose an activity that fills my entire brain. I do that activity until Nancy admits defeat, packs up, and goes back to sipping tea somewhere with Karen. Who invited her anyway?

My go-to activity on Spiral Days is Korean Dramas (KDramas). Think modern Jane Austen, only everyone is other-worldly beautiful, and there are subtitles. I like them specifically because they are subtitled, so I must use my entire brain to watch them. The acting is continually exceptional, and while the storylines and troupes are so reliable, they can be found on bingo cards (somehow, someone is consistently in the rain without an umbrella). I've always been a sucker for a good love story. Boy, do they nail the love story! So, there is literally no room for anything else to take space in my brain with all that going on. And the ample eye candy does a pretty great job of keeping Nancy in her place as well.

During these sessions, I am also very kind, and I permit myself to take it easy. I know I'll be much more productive if I take the rest of the day or evening off than I will be spending the three days to a whole week to get myself back together if I let myself entirely spiral.

Jay, my husband, knows my routine as well and will bring me chocolate and kisses throughout the binge session. In fact, when I'm watching a KDrama for pleasure, as they are my favorite, it happens often; I always let Jay know I'm okay and that I'm just watching for fun. But I still get chocolate and kisses anyway. Jay will always be my favorite love story.

Try it out. Let yourself dream like you did when you were five before the world told you that it wasn't possible. It is possible. You can be Batman and go to the moon and dance on stage! If you need to start small, do that as well. One of my mentors drove his brand new, fully loaded Ford F-150 thousands of times in his head before he drove it off the lot. I saw my beloved boy band BTS many, many times in my head before I went to LA and saw BTS live in concert four times! One of those times, I actually did get floor seats, and NamJoon (my favorite member) really did look at me three times, and yes, I really did stay in the same hotel as BTS.

Thoughts really are things. If your life isn't the way you want it, use your IMAGINATION to think better thoughts! Where will your IMAGINATION take you?

GINA BACALSKI

About Gina Bacalski: Gina is a Real Estate Agent, licensed since June 2018. Her background is in Early Childhood Education where she received her Child Development Associate from the state of Utah and has an AS from BYU-Idaho. For the past seventeen years, Gina has thoroughly enjoyed her experience in the service industry helping families in the gifted community.

In 2019, Gina helped Jon Kovach Jr. launch Champion Circle and is now CEO of the organization. She brings her genuine love for people, high attention to detail, and strives to exceed client's expectations to the Real Estate industry and to Champion Circle.

Gina married the man of her dreams, Jay Bacalski, in San Diego, in 2013. The Bacalskis love entertaining friends and family, going on hikes, and attending movies and plays. When Gina isn't helping her clients navigate the real estate world, she will most often be found dancing and listening to BTS, watching KDramas and writing fantasy, sci-fi and romance novels.

Author's Website: *www.MyChampionCircle.com/Gina-Bacalski*
Book Series Website & Author's Bio: *www.The13StepstoRiches.com*

Griselda Beck

IMAGINATION GONE WILD!

Imagination is the art and ability to dream without limitations and allow your mind to travel to a space where anything is possible. To be without limitations is to be without rules, conditions, or judgments. To believe, accept, give power to such limitations is what we refer to as "limiting beliefs." To bring this dream to reality, one must take committed action by giving power to their vision vs. their limitation.

The key to unlocking your imagination lies in permitting yourself to dream and permission to believe in the possibility that that dream is possible. These two permissions unlock creativity and inspiration.

Permission to Dream. Giving yourself permission to dream unlocks creativity. Think of it as allowing your imagination to run wild. We allow ourselves to dream and create something that provides us with an experience of what we want to feel or solves a problem we have—the possibilities are endless. As I write this, my mind keeps going back to the Wright brothers, and I imagine one of them sitting in a field somewhere watching a bird take flight and seeing himself as that bird, wondering how it might feel. Up until that point, no one had flown. Yet, they believed it was possible, and so it was.

Seven years ago, I sat in my office, staring out of the windows. I dreamed of a life where I could work from anywhere. I imagined myself sitting with my laptop at the beach on the rocks as the waves crashed in! People watched out of a coffee shop window with a beautiful view as a scenic backdrop behind them.

I could smell and taste the salty sea air, feel the ocean mist against my face, hear the sound of seagulls soaring and waves crashing as I watched tiny humans splashing at the water's edge and a pair of lovers kissing in a warm embrace. I deemed of having amazing conversations with the fascinating people I would meet on these adventures. Some would be just an experience in passing, while others may become life-long friends, business partners, and perhaps even lovers!

Many of these details described here have become cherished memories now!

I dreamed of this freedom because I wanted to experience the feeling of relaxation and all the beauty this world had to offer me. I wanted to eliminate the morning routine of waking up to the cringing sound of an alarm that sent pings throughout my body, always being in a rush, scarfing down a meal, brushing my teeth while applying makeup, a short workout, grab and go coffee and food. Instead, I wanted to stop just long enough to actually experience life, friendship, love, which, back then, I only experienced in moments such as vacations, massages, and the "big moments" with friends and family.

Detailed and vivid imaginations lead to conscious and physical awareness (think goosebumps, mind-body connection), which allows you to tap into your intuition. Unfortunately, most people stop at a thought or quick inspiration and leave it there because they don't believe it can happen. But what if it could?

Permission to Believe. When you believe that your vision is possible, it becomes a desire. This belief unlocks the subconscious mind allowing the desire to permeate the analytical mind (the barrier between conscious and unconscious mind) and seep into the subconscious. Our analytical mind is aware of all the reasons why we can't do something. It serves to protect us, but if we allow it to control us, then we are giving our power to limiting beliefs and therefore limiting our power to be extraordinary. Notice this and ask yourself, "Am I driving my mind, or is my mind driving me?"

When you believe that 100% is possible 100% of the time, even when you do not understand how anything is possible, your analytical mind only knows what it knows. It only knows our past based on experiences and information we have taken in and believed as truth. Therefore, anything that has not been done before is seemingly impossible until someone creates it — world records, breaking ceilings, human/civil rights, etc.

The belief in possibility is a channel between the conscious and subconscious mind, creating a manifestation portal. This results in conscious awareness of this desire. Suddenly, we hear things differently, see opportunities, communicate our desires, and thus open doors to resources we may not have otherwise come upon. This belief fuels our commitment. This conscious awareness is energy, source, the universe, or God. We trust when we genuinely believe it, which allows us to be open, surrendered, and in the flow. When we believe all thoughts, words, and actions align to make it happen.

Here are a few things that have helped me.

Create Space. A jam-packed calendar is neither sexy nor healthy. Constantly running from one thing to the next, or worst yet always running or "feeling behind," is not sustainable and a recipe for depression, loneliness, and apathy. You run on autopilot and become numb to a lot of the beauty and joy you were meant to experience in EVERY MOMENT. A few quick tips on creating time and space in your calendar:

Saying NO! I could write a whole book on this, but simply put, if it (or its outcome) doesn't light you up and make you want to bust out Michael Jackson level moves, then it's simply, "No."

Schedule enough time for sleep. Stick to it! Allow a minimum of 6 hours of sleep a night. I personally operate optimally on 9.

Schedule adequate and frequent hydro/bio breaks. Dehydration is the second thing after sleep that is MOST IMPORTANT!!! Low energy, digestion issues, mental focus, and headaches are all signs of dehydration.

Schedule meal breaks and actually take a break. Wolfing down food at your desk is not a break. Forgetting to eat and binging in one meal or skipping meals altogether wreaks havoc on your metabolism and energy.

Schedule time to MOVE your body every day. This could be a quick walk, yoga, dance, sport, gym, sex. It could be anything.

Schedule yourself first! That spa appointment, dance class, sports practice, etc. Schedule YOU first, then build around it. We often put ourselves last, and then there's never any time!

I used to pride myself on my ability to be so "dedicated" - I wore it as a mental badge of honor. The ugly truth? I was a Martyr and a resentful one! Martyrdom is not sexy and makes for a self- imposed "hard" and lonely journey.

Let it be easy and flow. Signs you need to create space: fatigue, lack of focus, stress, unhealthy relationships, overcommitted, always "busy," financial issues, and illness, just to name a few.

Meditation/Stillness. Meditation is one of the hardest things I've learned. This practice allows my analytical mind to rest, allowing that subconscious channel to open up flowing directly to the conscious mind, like bubbles bubbling up to the surface. We receive divine downloads, answers from within, and inspirational guidance in that space of stillness and openness.

Start by setting the timer for 1 minute daily and add a minute each week. If you can, ten or 20-minute increments can yield subtle results in just a few weeks. Give it time, and don't try to force or expect any result; simply practice stillness for 30 days.

When you get ideas or "downloads," jot them down immediately after the timer goes off. Set the timer for another 5 minutes after (or longer if you have the time) before you get to "the next thing." I jot down a few bullet points in my phone's notes app. If I have more time, I'll handwrite it into my journal. I also like to use the voice memos app on my phone, especially when I get that shower, dishwashing, or driving ideas (all active forms of meditation). That open subconscious channel can frequently be momentary, so it is best to capture these thoughts and these ideas in the moment, then come back to them later if you don't have time to flesh it out in that moment fully.

Energy Healing. While it is something I used to judge, fear (believed it was the "devil's work" as I had been taught), and in general thought was weird because it didn't not make logical sense, I have come to LOVE energy work. I have enjoyed the calmness of a Reiki session or healing energy of an assisted or live guided meditation and have experienced profound results of unblocking deep- rooted limiting beliefs through the Body Code (™) system by a practitioner. All this energy work has been transcending for me. What I love about the Body Code™, especially, is that I didn't need to recall the details of a story/incident, recount it or even have to know what "it" was. (Great for deep-rooted trauma.) Yet somehow, these limiting beliefs will be revealed and released during these sessions. Something beautiful happens once I'm conscious of the limiting belief, "the block," as it becomes very easy to see it for what it is, dispel it and be open to and choose the truth.

When we are aligned in that truth, our creativity can flow. Imagination has no limits here. 100% is possible 100% of the time. So let your mind let your imagination run wild!

GRISELDA BECK

About Griselda Beck: Griselda Beck, M.B.A. is a powerhouse motivational speaker and coach who combines her executive expertise with transformational leadership, mindset, life coaching, and heart-centered divine feminine energy principles. Griselda empowers women across the globe to step into their power, authenticity, hearts, and sensuality, to create incredible success in their business and freedom in their lives. She creates confident CEOs.

Griselda's clients have experienced success in quitting their 9-5 jobs, tripling their rates, getting their first clients, launching their first products, and growing their businesses in a way that allows them to live the lifestyles and freedoms they want. She has been featured as a top expert on *FOX, ABC, NBC, CBS, MarketWatch, Telemundo*, and named on the Top 10 Business Coaches list by *Disrupt Magazine.*

Griselda is an executive with over 15 years of corporate experience, founder of Latina Boss Coach and Beck Consulting Group, and serves as president for the nonprofit organization MANA de North County San Diego. She also volunteers her time teaching empowerment mindset at her local homeless shelter, Operation Hope-North County.

Author's Website: *www.LatinaBossCoach.com*
Book Series Website & Author's Bio: *www.The13StepstoRiches.com*

Jason Curtis

3 STEPS TO DAILY IMAGINATION MAXIMIZATION

"Man's only limitation, within reason, lies in his development and use of his IMAGINATION." – Napoleon Hill

Hill divides IMAGINATION into two parts:

Synthetic Imagination: Through this faculty, one may arrange old concepts, ideas, or plans into new combinations. This faculty creates nothing. It merely works with the material of experience, education, and observation with which it is fed. It is the faculty used most by the inventor, with the exception of the ones who draw upon the creative IMAGINATION, when he cannot solve his problem through synthetic IMAGINATION.

Creative Imagination: Through the faculty of creative IMAGINATION, the finite mind of man has direct communication with Infinite Intelligence. It is the faculty through which "hunches" and "inspirations" are received. It is by this faculty that all basic or new ideas are handed over to man.

I've never been, what you'd consider, very imaginative. I'm more of the Synthetic Imaginative to where I've used my experience, education, and observations more when making decisions. So, I have been trying to be more intuitive and apply Creative IMAGINATION in some aspects of my life, which has been somewhat impactful in many decisions I've made recently.

The Daily Application of Imagination

One of my best daily Habitudes to IMAGINATION has been investing 30 minutes every day in creative IMAGINATION time. Here is my routine:

Step 1: Get into a quiet place with a notebook where you won't be disturbed for a period of time.

Step 2: Close your eyes. Center your attention.

Step 3: Begin to imagine living your perfect life. See it, sense it and believe it. Then, see yourself performing the task or delivering the service that will help you obtain the things you desire on the physical plane.

Now, take the time to journal the ideas that came to you during your daily session.

Knowing what I know now, I wouldn't advise my younger self or anyone else differently. I wouldn't trade one second of my journey. I am sure I wouldn't have been open to embracing IMAGINATION then as I am now. It's all about readiness and timing. Are you ready to start imagining more than ever?

The Mentors of My Imagination

Think of some of your mentors you have learned from through the years. One person who has really helped me most with being more imaginative has been my friend and mentor, Dr. Robert Garcia. His path from where he was eating sandwiches out of moldy bread and struggling with ADHD to graduating with 2 Doctorate degrees and helping others through his

IMAGINATION and experience.

There is no way I would have ever imagined myself providing any value to what these other authors contribute in this historic book series. How I overcome adversity and obstacles is to approach my challenges head-on. I expect every challenge to come into anyone's path to success and greatness. I recommend collaborating with others if and when you need guidance.

My secret weapon in achieving levels of IMAGINATION is to allow myself to be open to any sort of IMAGINATION. My daughter especially helps me with that. I advise you to surround yourself with others who are more intuitive than yourself. Learn from them to become more imaginative, creative, and open. Without openness, you'll lack creative expectations.

Don't be afraid to work harder in your life and profession, but also smarter. Put in the time for self-development. Seek the coaching of others that have overcome what you want to achieve. You'll never go wrong.

JASON CURTIS

About Jason Curits: Jason has been a serial entrepreneur for 15 years and has enjoyed serving and helping his fellow entrepreneurs build their businesses and win in this game of life—on purpose! Jason created On Purpose Coaching because he knew, through his life experiences, that he could create an impact in others. He focuses on helping his clients create better relationships with their customers. This fosters trust and rapport while generating customer loyalty.

Jason is a Navy veteran of six years. He has sailed the seas and oceans in serving his God and country. Curtis and his wife, Brianna, have been married for eight years, and they have two children.

Author's Website: *www.JasonLaneCurtis.com*
Book Series Website & Author's Bio: *www.The13StepstoRiches.com*

Jeffrey Levine

IMAGINATION IS THE WORKSHOP OF YOUR MIND

As a young person, I never really thought about my IMAGINATION. It never occurred to me that man can create anything he can imagine. The power of my IMAGINATION appeared first at the beginning of my last year in little league baseball. I pitched the first game of my little league career. I lost 17 to 2. However, the night before my next pitching appearance, I saw myself pitching a no-hitter in my IMAGINATION. I saw it so clearly in my IMAGINATION that I knew when I took the mound the next day, I was going to pitch that no-hitter. Every inning went exactly as I had imagined. I still had a no-hitter in the last inning of the game. Now, I faced the best hitter in the league. He hit the ball really well, and my left fielder had to make an amazing catch, and I had my no-hitter. It was just as I had imagined.

Also, during my little league district championships, my IMAGINATION took over again. Even though we were losing the game in the last inning, I saw myself hitting the ball past the shortstop to win the game. In my IMAGINATION, the image was very clear and very vivid. When I swung the bat, the ball went exactly as I had imagined, and we won the game. The IMAGINATION in my mind became a reality in my life.

Again, the same thing happened next year when I started my Babe Ruth career at age 13. Again, my first game as a pitcher was against the best team and best pitcher.

Their pitcher threw so fast that he was impossible to hit.

Going to the last inning, the score was tied 0 to 0, and we both had a no-hitter. Before I went to bat, I saw a home run over the fence in my IMAGINATION. Because it was so vivid, it appeared real. As I stepped up to bat, the image of me hitting a home run appeared again. On the next pitch, IMAGINATION became real as the ball went over the fence. We beat the champs, and I had another no-hitter.

A few years ago, I was sitting in my bed at 7 AM on a Sunday. In my IMAGINATION, I kept seeing myself driving a white SLC Mercedes Benz convertible. The picture would not go away. In my IMAGINATION, I saw the words, "Go To The Dealership Now!" Since the dealership didn't open until 9 AM, I had plenty of time to get dressed and be there before 9 o'clock. However, I had like a pulling to get out of bed now and go directly to the dealership. I quickly got dressed, grabbed a bagel and a cup of coffee, and went to the dealership by 8:30 AM. Even though I was the first person at the dealership, many people were lining up behind me. Because I was first in line, I was the first one to test drive the white SLC Mercedes Benz convertible. Because it was the last day of the month, the dealership made me a very good offer. I also realized; I was not the only one who wanted this car. Because I acted quickly on my IMAGINATION, I was able to drive off the lot with a big smile and a brand-new car. Acting on my IMAGINATION was the key. If I had waited in bed, that car might have gone to somebody else.

Golf Tournament in Upstate New York—This was a big tournament. The morning of the tournament, I saw myself making a long putt to win. Since my partner and I came in last the year before, this didn't make sense to me. I was very relaxed playing on a beautiful day. For the first nine holes, I played the best golf possible. This continued for me through hole number 15. My partner, Chester, could do nothing right.

On hole number 16, my game started to fall apart. My tee shot went out of bounds. Chester hit the ball in the same direction as me, but it struck a tree and stayed in bounds. It only traveled 100 yards, and he still had 200 yards to go on a tree-lined green. I had never seen anyone go for the green from that point because it would've been an almost impossible shot because of all the trees. The risk was not worth it. I hit my next shot short of the green. I told Chester to just hit the ball a little further than me but not go for the green. Chester, unexpectedly, went for the green and hit the shot of his life. Somehow, the ball landed on the green. If I hadn't seen it, I wouldn't have believed it. I said, "Chester, what were you thinking?" He answered that he wasn't thinking and just hit the ball. He made the putt, and we had a birdie. The next hole was another tree-lined hole. Once again, I hit the ball into the woods. Chester hit a perfect shot. This came from a man who hadn't been able to do anything right for 15 holes. Chester hit the ball on the green and made the putt.

I missed the green on the last hole, a par three, and Chester hit another superb shot right next to the pin. He made the putt again. We handed in our scorecard with no expectation of winning. We sat down and had cocktails. Forty-five minutes later, we were called out for a playoff for first place. Because I don't drink, I was totally sober for the playoff.

We went to the first hole, and both of our opponents hit great drives. Chester hit it out of bounds. I hit a safe shot and was well behind our opponents. My next shot was a great shot that landed on the beginning of the green. My opponents didn't hit the green, and they both finished with a par. The only way to win was for me to make an extremely long and challenging putt. I didn't see that happening, so I planned on doing two putts to tie them and extend the playoff to the next hole. I putted it to the right of the hole just to be safe. Unexpectedly, off the radar, the ball went about a foot to the left near the hole, and it went in. The opponents couldn't understand how the ball went to the left.

That putt always goes to the right.

The golf tournament almost ended as I visualized. Even though it went an extra hole, the same ending I had envisioned became the result.

Your IMAGINATION is a powerful tool. If you can use this mental faculty to its fullest, magical things can happen for you. For example, as I talked about in this chapter, baseball games are won with my IMAGINATION, new cars appeared in my life, and a golf ending that only could be imagined in my mind.

Your IMAGINATION can help you have the same victories in your life. Remember, everything is created twice, first with the IMAGINATION in your mind, and second when it manifests in the material world.

JEFFREY LEVINE

About Jeffrey Levine: Jeffrey is a highly skilled tax planner and business strategist, as well as a published author and sought-after speaker. He's been featured in national magazines, on the cover of *Influential People Magazine,* and is a frequent featured expert on radio, talk shows, and documentaries. Jeffrey attended the prestigious Albany Academy for high school and then went on to University of Hartford at Connecticut, University of Mississippi Law School, Boston University School of Law, and earned an L.L.M. in taxation. His accolades include features in *Kiplinger* and *Family Circle Magazine,* as well as a dedicated commentator for Channel 6 and 13 news shows, a contributor for the *Albany Business Review,* and an announcer for WGY Radio.

Jeffrey has accumulated more than 30 years of experience as a tax attorney and certified financial planner and has given in excess of 500 speeches nationally. Levine is the executive producer and cast member in the documentary *Beyond the Secret: The Awakening.*

Levine's most current work, *Consistent Profitable Growth Map,* is a step-by-step workbook outlining easy-to-follow steps to convert consistent revenue growth to any business platform.

Author's Website: *www.JeffreyLevine.Solutions*
Book Series Website & Author's Bio: *www.The13StepstoRiches.com*

Lacey & Adam Platt

THE 2 TYPES OF IMAGINATION & CAN I DO IT?

The 2 Types Of Imagination

When we were kids, we lived by a few simple principles. One of those was "he who has the greatest IMAGINATION wins." By this, I mean whose ideas were chosen over and over? The person with the best IMAGINATION! Why? Because they were able to create the most amazing games, stories, and adventures! Now continue to think about that person later in life. Their ideas are constantly praised and given credit for. And after their ideas have been chosen by others repeatedly, they learn to form a habit of creating more. I like the school of thought that there are two types of IMAGINATION. Napoleon Hill once said that IMAGINATION can be either "synthetic or creative." At first, I was a little confused by this, and then I heard the term synthetic replaced with the word synthesized and finally understood what he meant. So, if we think about IMAGINATION as two different types, we can draw upon both! Then we find that our IMAGINATION is working a lot more often than one would think.

Hill goes on to explain that synthetic or synthesized is basically the components of other things like education, life experiences, or other resources pulled together to create something new. In comparison, creative is more about tapping into that "gut feeling," intuition, or inspiration. He gives several amazing examples of businesses that were created using synthetic or synthesized IMAGINATION. These were where other businesses fell short, which gave this person an idea to do something different to produce a better result. He also shows that businesses can stem purely from inspiration to create something new that hasn't previously existed but is needed. Both caused me to think about times in my life when I have used my IMAGINATION. I was able to think of times when I used things that already existed to create something and when I felt inspired to do something and created it out of that inspiration. Do you know what I noticed? The most interesting things that came to mind were when I used both together!

I want you to think back to a time when you created something. Maybe the idea sparked from someone else or something that already existed, and you added upon it and received some kind of inspiration that led you to create something entirely new. I don't know about you, but I rely pretty heavily upon that "gut feeling!" There are a lot of times when I do things that most people say they don't understand why I did it, and the only thing I can say is, "I don't know, I just had a feeling!" So, I would like to go back to when we were kids, and we were the ones being chosen to create new things to do and new adventures to go on.

When we are continuously being chosen to create new things and create a habit of doing that, we learn something I like to call leadership. Now stay with me for a minute. Leadership attributes or abilities can come from almost anywhere. But let's face it, when you're the most creative and fun person to be around, people naturally want to follow you. And aren't those usually the people who become leaders? I once heard a saying, "You can either choose to be a leader or a follower, and both roles are important; however, the most critical piece when choosing which one you want to become is what kind of financial compensation do you want to receive? Because leaders will always out-earn followers." What? When I heard that, I thought, why would anyone choose to be a follower? And then I realized it's because not everybody wants to be a leader. Now, don't get me wrong, there are good and bad leaders. And I wish I could say that I've always been a good leader, but honestly, it took a few times of being a bad leader to realize what a good leader was. I remember the first leadership position I was given. I was that dictatorship-style leader. The one that was like, "Do what I say and don't complain," and quick to blame somebody else when things didn't work out. Looking back now, I am shocked to think that that's what I thought leadership was. It took a few times to realize that leaders take responsibility for the outcome of their team because that outcome is a direct result of how they were led. A good leader jumps in, works longer, harder, and loves more than anyone else.

I read a meme that said, "A good leader will care more about the company than any employee because their idea is what created the business." When you put all of your love and effort into something, of course, you love it more than any of your employees are going to because they aren't the ones who created it or birthed it into existence! You can make the environment they're working in amazing or survivable. The choice is yours.

~ Lacey Platt

Can I Do It?

Everything that is created is created in the mind first from our IMAGINATION. Think about it and look at all the amazing things that have been created over the last century; they all came from someone's IMAGINATION. All advances in knowledge, technology, ideas, and so forth are the brainchild of someone's IMAGINATION or a group of people's imaginations. The telephone, cotton gin, iPhone, Google, Uber, putting a man on the moon, and so many other things that have been created or happened are because of someone's IMAGINATION. The problem is that most people have an idea, think about how cool something would be to create, and then don't do anything about it. I once heard the saying that the place with the most knowledge is the cemetery because so many ideas died with those who are there.

IMAGINATION is where all the proceeding steps start to take shape. It first begins with a desire for something, then having faith you can do it, and then programming your subconscious. After that, it can happen with autosuggestion, gaining the specialized knowledge you need to create something, and then having the IMAGINATION of how to make it happen. The IMAGINATION is where it all starts to be created; what if it can happen? But so many people don't think they can make it happen, so they give up. They don't let their IMAGINATION create the desired outcome they want. Like Napoleon Hill said in *Think and Grow Rich*, "Truly, thoughts are things, and their scope of operation is the world itself."

A few months ago, my wife and I went to a high-end networking event. The event brings experts in business, entrepreneurs, celebrities, and an amazing collection of people to meet and learn from. They bring these people up on stage and interview them about their life experiences. One of the most amazing people they had on stage was Karl Kani. Karl had an amazing story and view on his success. Karl Kani was born Carl Williams and is a fashion designer and CEO of a hip-hop fashion brand Karl Kani. When Karl was young, he would dream about creating his own fashion brand. He didn't know how to sew, but he had a great sense of combining different fashions together to create a unique design. He would come up with designs and then take them to a local tailor, cut them, and sew the clothes exactly how he wanted them. He would wear them to clubs and around town, and people would ask him where he got the clothes, and he would tell them that he created them. Well, one skeptic person said if you created it, why is your name not on the clothing anywhere? He knew that he had to come up with a brand name to be taken seriously, but Carl Williams didn't sound like a fashion name. The turning point came when Carl would ask himself, "Can I Do It? Can I create a fashion company and become world-famous?" He would ask himself, "Can I? Can I?" over and over again, and then it hit him; his brand name would be Kani which is a variation of "Can I." He had his name legally changed from Carl Williams to Karl Kani and created one of the hottest hip-hop fashions in the world.

Why do I tell this story? Because I thought it was a great example of someone who had a deep desire to do something. He had specialized knowledge of what he was doing; the only thing holding him back was his own IMAGINATION on if he could really do it. All other barriers started to fade when he took on the identity that he could by calling himself Karl Kani. He worked on his idea, and with his IMAGINATION and specialized skills, he created a famous fashion empire on the streets, hip hop circles, and the rapping world being worn by pretty much all famous rappers in the industry.

So, my question for you is, "Can You?" Can you create the life you want? You must first have that desire, faith you can do it, program your mind to think positively about what you want, learn some things maybe, but then let your IMAGINATION create it and then go to work, acting towards those things in your IMAGINATION.

Everything is created in your mind first, and then it can come to fruition in the world if you believe "You Can!"

~ Adam Platt

LACEY & ADAM PLATT

About Lacey Platt: Lacey is an energetic, fun loving, super mom of five! She is an Achievement Coach, Speaker and new Bestselling Author who enjoys helping everyone she can by getting to know what their needs are and then loving on them in every way that she can. Her ripple effect and impact has touched the lives of so many and continues to reach more lives every single day. Allow Lacey to help you achieve your goals with proven techniques she has created and perfected over years of coaching. Lacey and her husband have built an amazing coaching business called Arise to Connect serving people all around the world.

About Adam Platt: Adam is an Achievement Coach, Speaker, Trainer, Podcast Host and now a Bestselling Author. Adam loves to help people overcome the things stopping them from having the life they really want. Adam owns and operates Arise to Connect. Adam believes that connection with yourself, others, and your higher power are the keys to achievement and greater success in life. He is impacting thousands of people's lives with his message and coaching. He lives in Utah with his wife, five daughters, and their dog, Max.

Author's Website: *www.AriseToConnect.com*
Book Series Website & Author's Bio: *www.The13StepstoRiches.com*

Louisa Jovanovich

IMAGINE YOUR FUTURE

My parents did not come from money. They were immigrants who didn't speak English, had two children to take care of, and looked after my grandparents. They moved to the United States to give us a world they never had, even though they had no money. Nonetheless, they could still give my sister and me everything we needed to succeed.

My parents accomplished their dream. They sent my sister and me to private school, purchased a nice home to live in, and made sure we always had our needs cared for. My parents had a mission to succeed, and my sister and I to succeed as well.

Growing up, I was taking mental notes of my parents. I saw what they created with the power of mindset. So, I followed suit in my life, and my experience is similar: you decide what you want and then set off to achieve it.

Everything I wanted in life, I was able to achieve. I got everything my mind could create. Napoleon Hill famously said, "Whatever your mind can conceive and believe, it can achieve." The more I pondered that quote, though, the more I realized, "I'm not thinking big enough!" I was playing too small. I saw the results of my achievements, but my game was not big enough. My choices were from only what I could see possible. What if I imagined more possibilities? What would it look like to play a bigger game?

I always felt my parents' love and devotion, but there was this tension: my mom was committed to playing life safe, but my dad was a visionary. Their mission to give us everything they never had was the space they were in alignment. Their own visions for life, however, were not. It wasn't until they lost everything that I saw my mom become very creative.

My parents were in the middle of starting a business when their business partner died very unexpectedly. They needed this business partner's expertise for their investment to work, so they sold the business in a panic. The losses were significant, and this left my mother with a choice: she could play it safe, claim bankruptcy, and give up, or she could imagine a better way out of their financial hole. My mother chose to envision the possibilities. She got financially savvy and used zero percent credit cards to pay off one debt at a time slowly. My parents could have claimed bankruptcy and given up, but they didn't. Instead, they found ways to get out of debt, rebuild, and thrive. Still, what if they had turned to their IMAGINATION first instead of panicking?

When my parents panicked and sold off the business, they also sold off a piece of real estate they had purchased as part of the business plan. At the time, the property was worth $500,000, so it was understandable why they wanted that money back quickly, but what if they had considered other options. There were other options, and not considering them was a choice. If they had gotten renters and held onto the real estate, that property would be worth over $5 million today! By panicking and selling, they missed an opportunity.

I watched my parents through the ups and downs as I watched most adults around me. I noticed that when people made choices from freedom, it led to great success. On the other hand, when decisions came from fear, maybe a job got done, but there was no opportunity to ENJOY IT. There was no chance to imagine a job growing into something greater. Eventually, I realized it's not about the money in the end. It's about our experience along the way.

Despite this awareness, I struggled with fear-based thinking for much of my life. I did not realize how fear set deep roots in my thoughts and actions. I was afraid to ask for what I needed. I was afraid to charge what I was worth. I feared making others uncomfortable. By sacrificing myself and living in fear—Oh my God, I was becoming my parents!!

I didn't want to live in fear. So, I had to look closer at my core values. How can I make enough money, work from home as a single mother with two kids, and do it using creativity? I realized I would have to use my IMAGINATION and think outside the box.

I had the opportunity to do exactly that in January of 2021. I had a vision of hosting a global summit. This was ONE of the biggest undertakings of my life. My fearful thoughts began to take over. What was I thinking?! I couldn't do this! Even though I took a class that taught me how to do the job, I realized I only understood it in theory. I was freaked out, scared, and felt like fear would overtake me.

I had a choice to get stuck in my fear (no way!) or tap into my IMAGINATION (let's try this out). So, I started by visualizing the summit as if it had already happened. I celebrated the speakers that said yes to me. I celebrated the relationships I made with people all around this world. I celebrated the idea that the summit inspired breakthroughs in people's lives worldwide. I did it!

Of course, I only did it in my mind at this point. But the excitement I felt was real, and as that feeling set in, the ball started rolling. I took one step at a time. Whenever I got stuck in my fear, which happened a lot, I went back to my vision. I committed to that vision. And every time I went back to my vision, the next appropriate step (which I previously could not see) would appear.

Now I can say I actually did do it. I hosted the global summit. I did something that was SO outside the box for myself, and it felt thrilling. The opportunities from that job continue to expand and grow in ways that I could have never expected. My IMAGINATION did what logic could never do: it created magic. When we turn away from fear and to our IMAGINATION, we get to find the magic within us and enjoy the amazing opportunities it brings into our lives.

I won't lie. We cannot turn the fear off overnight. It's not that easy, but let's look at it for what it is. For me, turning away from fear meant that every time I became overwhelmed or thought about all the tasks I didn't know how to do, I had a choice: get stuck in the over-thinking, self-limiting beliefs and fear or tap into my IMAGINATION and vision. One thing I know for sure is that I will not wait until my last dying breath before I turn to my IMAGINATION. That's precisely what I witnessed with my grandmother.

My grandmother was a people pleaser, always worried about everyone else's needs. For seventy- four years, she took care of everyone around her. She was always putting herself second. When I was twelve years old, she was in the hospital, and my grandfather wanted to say his last goodbyes. But on this day, my grandmother did something different. She said no. At the end of her life, she finally found the courage to put aside her people-pleasing tendencies and choose herself. She finally put herself first. She knew she wanted to take her last breath in peace and decided to honor herself. It was her last day, her last breath, and she just wanted it for herself!

I often think of my grandmother and how it took her entire life to see that she had a choice. I think about celebrating the joy that wants to come through me, how I rejoice every time someone shares how they are taking action in their life because of what opened up for them through a conversation we had. I think about these things when I make my own decisions about whether to stay stuck in my fears or move forward with peace, freedom, love, and trust. Just as my grandmother did on her last breath, I shall do the rest of my life. My choice is clear.

Today, I am regularly in touch with my IMAGINATION. I ask myself big questions, even demand that I dream big, and then I settle in and visualize wherever my IMAGINATION takes me. My IMAGINATION paints beautiful pictures: I travel the world and speak on stage. I work with people who are committed to positively impacting this world. I purchase a beautiful home. I fall in love and have a magical relationship with someone who loves my children as his own. My children go to an extraordinary school and feel like they have structure and safety. I volunteer and give back to so many in need. I host dinners and book clubs, celebrating life with the people I love. When I am free from fear, the possibilities are endless in these safe spaces.

There are so many questions each of us can consider and so many possibilities to envision.

Where would you like your life to go? What kind of parent or partner would you like to be? What kind of a difference would you like to make in this world? What is your heart's desire that is trying to come through you? For me, these questions feel amazing to ponder. But, more importantly, I feel fearless when I allow myself to think about them!

Where does your IMAGINATION take you if you will allow it? How grand of a life can you truly allow yourself to see? How incredible, amazing, and impactful are you? So many of us hold back, not only in life but even in our dreams. But our dreams set the blueprint for what is possible. And you always have a choice. So, here is my challenge for you. Don't wait until your last breath. Don't let fear get the best of you. Forget what life has told you in the past and choose to imagine your future.

LOUISA JOVANOVICH

About Louisa Jovanovich: Louisa is the founder of Connect with Source. She is a mindfulness and emotional intelligence coach. She enjoys helping others identify blind spots and create new beliefs which empower her clients to access a life they have never dreamed possible. She has completed 20 years of personal and transformational growth including Land-mark Forum, Gratitude Training, and is a Clarity Catalyst Certified trainer. She works with entrepreneurs who seek clarity and want to up-level their lives.

Her life experiences and school of hard knocks are what make her a knowledgeable and compassionate leader and enable her to help guide others through the process of looking for answers within in order to find success and breakthrough their limiting beliefs. Her unique coaching techniques help her clients see the truth behind the stories that are keeping them stuck in the reality they created.

Louisa is a single mother of two teenagers living in LA. Her love and compassion towards others are her superpowers, helping others reclaim their confidence, find their voice, and know their worth.

Author's Website: *ConnectWithSource.com*
Book Series Website & Author's Bio: *www.The13StepstoRiches.com*

Lynda Sunshine West

IMAGINATION UNLIMITED

I want to be an astronaut when I grow up. I want to be a movie star when I grow up. I want to be the President of the United States when I grow up.

Did you ever say things like this when you were a child?

I wanted to be a child psychologist. It was just a dream. And I never became one.

What happened along the way? Were those dreams simply impossible to attain? Was your IMAGINATION too vast and wide that you knew you would never be able to turn it into your reality?

When I hear the word 'IMAGINATION,' the first person that comes to mind is Walt Disney. My favorite of his quotes is, "Laughter is timeless, IMAGINATION has no age, dreams are forever."

At some point in most of our lives, we forget that "IMAGINATION has no age." We, as humans, can keep imagining the "unreal," aka fake. It can be whatever we want it to be when it's in our IMAGINATION. IMAGINATION is literally "in the head."

It's when we share it outside of our head that it's possible to move it into action and to create something out of our IMAGINATION and turn that into a reality.

Imagine, if you will, if everyone in history who has ever had a crazy IMAGINATION never did anything with it because people will think, "That's impossible. You'll never be able to do that. No one will ever believe you. You're CRAZY!!" If that were the case, I wouldn't be writing this chapter on this computer using this computer keyboard sitting at this desk on this chair with the lights on while staring out the window looking at the beautiful blue sky with the golfers swinging their golf clubs while riding around in their Mister Magoo golf carts, etc.

The point is, had it not been for the curiosity (or IMAGINATION) of those inventors who have come before us and for all of those to come, the world would be vastly different today than it is.

One of my favorite inventors/imaginators of all time is Thomas Alva Edison, an American inventor and businessman. He is most widely known for his early versions of the incandescent light bulb. If it hadn't been for his IMAGINATION, we might still be using candles to light up a room. It was his IMAGINATION and never-give-up attitude that kept him moving forward. He knew without a doubt that what he saw in his mind's eye would come to fruition. He just needed to believe it to be true and needed to do the work to make it happen.

Sometimes when we have an idea, we work at it; it gets too hard, so we give up. If we are to be great, we must keep going. When I heard this Thomas Edison saying, "I have not failed. I've just found 10,000 ways that won't work," it hit me hard. I spent the first 51 years of my life quitting too early, not giving my IMAGINATION a chance, not believing in myself, not trying 10,000 ways to do anything. It was simple. I was a quitter.

While I don't regret my past, I realize that I allowed my IMAGINATION to be squashed and tucked away for decades. Having worked in the corporate world for 36 years, with 53 jobs, my IMAGINATION got buried deeper and deeper every year. As a legal secretary, creativity was not part of my job. As a matter of fact, my job was all about organization and making sure everything was in order and that everyone was where they were supposed to be when they were supposed to be there. It was a very linear thinking, task-oriented job.

But wait, that's not true. There IS IMAGINATION in that type of work. When faced with a situation that required becoming more efficient, my IMAGINATION was tapped into. My IMAGINATION was tapped into when faced with opposing personalities wanting different things at different times.

I spent so many years saying, "I'm not creative," and that was because I compared myself to famous artists, musicians, actors, performers, etc. I "compared" myself and, therefore, could not see my own creativity.

IMAGINATION comes in many forms. Sometimes you may imagine something that is literally impossible, like imagining yourself sitting on a cloud staring down at the planet. While that's a fun thing to imagine, it's not something you can do physically. Other times, your IMAGINATION may take on the form of reality and something that could actually happen, like imagining that my husband was going to marry me (which did happen after three years of dating, and we're still going strong 33 years later). I imagined it would happen, and it did.

When I quit my corporate job at the age of 51 and embarked on a journey called entrepreneurship, I had no idea what to imagine, so I didn't imagine anything. Then I started meeting amazing entrepreneurs who have made powerfully positive impacts on this planet, and, through their mentorship, I started RE-learning how to imagine. As a child, it came naturally, but I lost track of that piece of me. I forgot how to imagine because it was tucked away too deep.

There's a saying that people come into your life for a season, a reason, or a lifetime. I'm grateful for the people who have come into my life at various stages, particularly those who have helped me learn how to open my mind to the endless possibilities of what there is to be, do, have, and the impact I am here to make. If it weren't for their belief in me, I'm not sure where I'd be today.

I've been able to tap into their IMAGINATION by listening to what they have to say and hearing the wisdom and knowledge they have to share. It's through their teachings that this student has forged her way onto a more purposeful path and is making the impact she's here to make.

Imagine this. Imagine that. Imagine whatever you want. Simply imagine.

LYNDA SUNSHINE WEST

About Lynda Sunshine West: Lynda is known as The Fear Buster. She's a Speaker, 10 Time Best-Selling Author, Book Publisher, Executive Film Producer, Red Carpet Interviewer, and the Founder of Women Action Takers. At age 51 she faced one fear every day for an entire year. In doing so, she gained an exorbitant amount of confidence and uses what she learned by facing a fear every day to fulfill her mission of helping 5 million women entrepreneurs gain the confidence to share their voice with the world. Her collaboration books, mastermind, podcast, and many more opportunities give women from all over the world the opportunity to share their voice with the world. She believes in cooperation and collaboration and loves connecting with like-minded people.

Author's Website: *www.ActionTakersPublishing.com*
Book Series Website & Author's Bio: *www.The13StepstoRiches.com*

Maris Segal & Ken Ashby

IMAGINATION: THE POWER TOOL OF LIFE

"IMAGINATION is more important than knowledge. For knowledge is limited, whereas IMAGINATION embraces the entire world, stimulating progress, giving birth to evolution." - Albert Einstein

When we open the door to our IMAGINATION, we cross a threshold into the realm of pure potentiality. Imagine yourself hiking up a mountain, glistening snow on every peak, as far as the eye can see. Feeling warm energy move through your body, you remove your heavy protective coat. Your mind wanders playfully as you listen to the loud, peaceful silence and the sound of your feet crunching the pristine snow. Faintly, in the distance, you hear children's laughter drawing closer. The laughter now fills the air, joined with music and song. As the faces become clear, you witness yourself from early childhood and into your teens. Enveloped in the sense of joy, you recognize your childlike curiosity coming out to explore in an infinite space of possibilities. Finally, you arrive at the summit and stand in the presence of yourself at every age! You cheer loudly in celebration of your life! This imagined hike represents your journey, all you have faced, experienced, and overcome. From "here," where time and energy are infinite, without limits, nothing in your mind is holding you back, you are free to co-create with the universe, imagining your future "now."

What does IMAGINATION look like? We resonate with Napoleon Hill's two perspectives on IMAGINATION. He notes that "Synthetic IMAGINATION" connects existing concepts, inventions, and ideas to build upon. "Creative IMAGINATION" responds to an instinctual inner voice, a hunch from a blank canvas. They work in tandem! Using both synthetic and creative IMAGINATION as a collaborative duo is powerful! When working on innovation from a place of "synthetic IMAGINATION," an inventor may stumble on a completely different idea using "creative IMAGINATION." Here is a fun example: Richard Jones, a naval engineer, was experimenting on metal springs that have the capacity to stabilize and support instruments commonly used in ships. As he was working with tension springs, one of the springs fell off the bench and, coiling and recoiling, moved around the floor, seemingly alive. This inventor had no idea at the time that this would become one of the world's most famous toys, the Slinky (named by Jones' wife, Betty). Since its beginnings in the 1940s, this unlikely invention has walked down many steps and brought smiles to over three hundred million people worldwide.

DIVE Into Possibilities

Think of IMAGINATION as your personal and professional power tool that never wears out, and like a muscle, it gets stronger with use. When our IMAGINATION sparks us to engage in the actualization of an innovative possibility, then magic surrounds us. However, when not combined with empowered action, this power tool can shut down before it ever gains strength. Therefore, we invite you to DIVE into a sea of possibilities; Dare to Imagine, step into your Vision, and Empower yourself to act. It is flexing your IMAGINATION muscle daily that yields the best results. The only limit on our IMAGINATION is the restraining mind-messages, which stem from our past dramas and traumas.

Maris: Over the years, we have been blessed to work with our great corporate and not-for-profit clients to elevate the visibility and engagement of their causes and brands. From mindset-to-marketing, using our IMAGINATION power tool, we created partnerships and high-touch experiences with celebrities, global leaders, and changemakers to build and grow meaningful connections with their customers. These experiences ranged from special programming like hanging out with Whoopi Goldberg, private court time with tennis legend John McEnroe, hitting the slopes with world champion Lindsey Vonn, a private concert by Crosby, Stills, and Nash, and a studio interview and performance with rock and roll music icon John Fogerty. With each opportunity, we always began creating from a place of possibilities, imagining ourselves as the customer and asking, "What would move us to engage and feel valued?" Along the way, making an impact for our clients and their customers, we have learned that: When we put people first, what can be imagined is always possible, all the time! We are all creative beings. We all have access to our IMAGINATION, and each of us gets to use our IMAGINATION to spark creativity, innovation, resourcefulness, and solutions in all aspects of our lives. From navigating through our weekly family schedule to project management at work, challenges breed opportunities for flexing our IMAGINATION muscles. However, if we ignore that innate creative spark, we are not serving ourselves or others. Change happens when we see every choice as creative and practice imagining the possibilities. As partners, in business and life, we live by the notion that; "It is not a question of IF we will create, the question is, WHAT will we create."

Ken: If I visualize my life as a building, IMAGINATION is the cornerstone of that structure. As a songwriter, I have experienced the flow of creative energy in a life-fulfilling way. I am so grateful to be participating in the enchanted forest of IMAGINATION. As a result, I have danced with hundreds of songs that have flowed through me and then performed worldwide. When I think about the pride I felt with my first song, my hundredth song, commissioned songs, and especially those I am writing now, I am acutely aware that IMAGINATION is rooted in "being" versus "doing." Although there are mechanics used while songwriting, the primary energy is being a conduit of open possibilities. I step into my vision from this daring-to-imagine space and then take empowered action to bring a new story to life with music and lyrics.

I can remember where I was, who was in the room, what I was feeling, and the undefinable magic I experienced for almost all the songs I've written. It is in those moments that I am "being' open to both "synthetic" and "creative" IMAGINATION.

As you read my word "songwriter," you can easily substitute your own word. For you, it could be painter, coach, banker, author, executive, entrepreneur, healer, community leader, or parent. IMAGINATION is foundational to personal and professional life choices and, at the core, is problem-solving.

Imagining One Song

Intending to cultivate creativity and spark productivity in individuals, we launched "One Song." Our purpose with this program is to share the experience of writing a song with anyone who wants to play in the zone of curiosity and the potential of freeing their IMAGINATION. The intention of using songwriting in this way was sparked by a question that we have posed to hundreds of people worldwide: "Have you ever written a song?" The general reply was, "No, I'm not creative!" So, we began exploring creativity from all angles and invited individuals and teams who had never written a song to **DIVE** in and join us without any limitations or concerns about their results. There is no right or wrong in this zone of childlike curiosity; there is only imaginative expression. As mindset coaches we have experienced individuals, families, and business teams standing in a place of play and IMAGINATION to unleash creativity and unlock possibilities.

We have a conviction that every soul on this planet has a song inside, echoed in the saying that "music is the universal language." Nikola

Tesla proposed that the "secrets of the universe" are found in "energy, frequency, and vibration." My song, your song, and all our songs express our unique energy, internal frequency, and natural vibration. We listen and feel connected to another person's song, words, or voice because it resonates with our own core's energy, frequency, and vibration.

We invite you to consider this thought; we are all songwriters. A song is a vibration combined with words! Our voice is a melody, and our words are poetry. In our personal and professional lives, we are all writing songs every day with everything we say. In our tone and choice of words, the listener hears the music!

IMAGINATION knows no age, gender, or class limitations. Our innate ability as humans is to use our IMAGINATION to create solutions and innovations for a thriving life and planet. Martin Luther King used his IMAGINATION to dream, visualize, and create a movement for a socially just and equitable world. He said, "Out of a mountain of despair, a stone of hope." We can act on our IMAGINATION, envisioning a future world where human suffering is healed, every human voice is heard, human engagement and compassion is constant, and every child and adult feels safe and has a bright tomorrow.

IMAGINATION, our personal and professional power tool functions better and better each time we put it to use. IMAGINATION, left in the darkness of our toolbox, can grow dusty and rusty, becoming sluggish, and glommed up with goop. Yet, the more we tap into and unleash our IMAGINATION, the greater it functions and supports our desires and vision. Like water, IMAGINATION flows with energetic connections creating possibilities.

When we accomplish this in a way that lifts, propels, and orbits our onboard IMAGINATION to exceedingly higher realms, we convert probable impossibilities into reality, using the IMAGINATION: The Power Tool of Life!

Reflections:

How does using your IMAGINATION energize you?

What do you imagine for yourself in 1, 3, and 5 years? What will it take for you to realize the possibilities that exist?

How will you tap into and exchange your IMAGINATION and creative energy for something that matters?

MARIS SEGAL & KEN ASHBY

About Maris Segal and Ken Ashby: From Mindset to Marketing, Ken Ashby & Maris Segal, a husband and wife dynamic duo, have spent the last thirty-plus years bringing an innovative, collaborative voice to issues, causes, and brands. As entrepreneurs, activists, business strategists, executive producers, coaches, authors, speakers, and trainers, Ken & Maris work with the public and private sectors from boardrooms and classrooms to the world stage. They are known for creating high touch experiences that unite diverse populations across a broad spectrum of business, policy, and social issues.

Their leadership expertise in Business Relationship Marketing, Organizational Change & Cultural Inclusion, Personal Growth, Project Management, Public Affairs, and Philanthropy Strategies has been called upon by companies and their agencies. Their experience includes: consumer and financial brands, Olympic organizers, Super Bowls, America's 400th Anniversary, Harvard Kennedy School, Archdiocese of LA and NY Papal visit planners, the White House and celebrities across the arts, entertainment, sports, and culinary genres.

With Ken's expertise as an award-winning singer-songwriter, they launched ONE SONG, a songwriting workshop series designed to unleash creativity in individuals and teams.

Their **DRIVE** method: **D**esire, **R**elationships, **I**ntention, **V**ision and **E**mpowerment sits at the core of their companies Prosody Creative Services, ONE SONG, and Segal Leadership Global to set a path for every client to Build High Performing Businesses & Elevate Personal & Professional Leadership for Maximum Impact & a 360-degree Thriving Life!

Author's Website: *www.ProsodyCreativeServices.com*
Book Series Website & Author's Bio: *www.The13StepstoRiches.com*

Mel Mason

IMAGINING THE POSSIBILITIES
HOW TO STUMBLE UPON YOUR EUREKA MOMENT

We all know the lyrics.

"In that case, I don't want no part.

That would only break my heart.

Oh, but if you feel like loving me, if you've got the notion,

I second that emotion."

Smokey Robinson's "I Second That Emotion" is a song that withstands generations. Somehow, it just keeps getting better. But believe it or not, the song wasn't born out of a long, grueling songwriting session. Instead, the inspiration for this hit was pure luck.

According to Smokey Robinson, he and his songwriting partner, Al Cleveland, were shopping at a department store. Smokey wanted to buy a gift for his wife, Claudette, and decided on a string of pearls, saying, "I sure hope she likes them."

Al responded, "I second that emotion." He misspoke, of course, but they both knew they'd stumbled upon something special.[1]

The song "Mother and Child Reunion" by Paul Simon has a similar story. Simon was eating at a Chinese restaurant, browsing the menu, and came across a chicken and egg dish called "Mother and Child Reunion." He thought, "That's it."[2]

More recently, Miley Cyrus wrote "Malibu" while letting her mind wander in an Uber driving through Malibu.[3]

What is my point in telling you about these random backstories on hit songs? I want to show you what a spark of IMAGINATION looks like and remind you of its vital importance in our lives.

Remember when, as a child, we'd create entire worlds in our heads? Our bed could become a pirate ship, or the couch could become a stage. We could see it all so clearly, and for those moments, we really believed it. Our Imaginations became our realities. Somewhere along the line, though, we've taught ourselves to shut our vivid IMAGINATION down.

As we grow older, we buy into the "more mature" idea of getting serious, buckling down, and working hard. Who's got time for silly games? I get it. I'm not saying to pick up a tube of wrapping paper and pretend it's a sword (although if that sounds fun to you, go for it). IMAGINATION is so much more than pretend fantasy battles, but we are using our

---

1 Blistein, J. (2021, June 3). *Smokey Robinson reveals origin story behind 'I second that emotion'*. Rolling Stone. Retrieved January 7, 2022, from https://www.rollingstone.com/music/music-news/smokey-robinson-i-second-that-emotion-origin-story-1177296/
2 Morales, C. (2018, July 11). *10 fascinating stories behind Classic Rock Songs that will blow your mind: Herstyleasia*. Her Style Asia. Retrieved January 7, 2022, from https://www.herstyleasia.com/fascinating-stories-behind-famous-songs
3 Songfacts. (n.d.). *Malibu by Miley Cyrus - Songfacts*. Song Meanings at Songfacts. Retrieved January 7, 2022, from https://www.songfacts.com/facts/miley-cyrus/malibu

IMAGINATION every day in some form or another. You might imagine sleeping in for an extra thirty minutes just thirty seconds after waking up. You might imagine how you could have handled a client differently. Maybe you imagine scenarios where you tell your boss what you really think. The IMAGINATION is there, but it needs some room to breathe. Only when your IMAGINATION is free to expand will you be privy to the sudden insights that many musicians seem so attuned to.

I received the inspiration for my business in the unlikeliest of moments: watching an episode of Hoarders.

In 2013, I was released early from a year-long contract as a personal assistant. Since the job fell through, my employer gave me a $50,000 check (to cover the rest of my contracted year), and just like that, I was free. I had six months off with money in my bank account, and I needed to figure out what to do with it all. I knew that I loved creating order out of chaos, and I had a background in energy healing, but I had no idea what that passion and knowledge could mean for my life. I didn't feel like finding an answer right away, though. I needed to unwind. I wanted to turn my brain off. So, one day during the six months I took off, I turned on the television. In 2013, the show Hoarders was in full swing, but I'd never seen an episode. The premise of the show, confronting people's clutter, sounded appealing, so I gave it a chance.

After a few minutes of watching, I was utterly horrified! To me, it seemed so apparent that these "hoarders" were using their clutter as some sort of distraction from their trauma, and the show hosts were ripping their possessions away so quickly that people had no time to address the root cause of their pain! It's as if these poor folks had built up their Great Wall of China, and in swoops the TV producers tore down the protective barrier and then bounced. This left the show's subjects with no defenses from their pain. How could the people behind this show not see the damage they were causing by having hurting hoarders make huge decisions in such a short amount of time?

This moment of frustration became my moment of clarity. I knew what I wanted; I knew where I was being led. I decided right then to start a business that would succeed where Hoarders had failed. First, I would help people understand the root cause of their clutter and only then deal with their physical mess. Then I could help them keep the clutter from coming back. An evening of mindless television became the moment my company was born. It was clear in my head, like a childhood bed becoming a pirate ship.

Our moments of inspiration come to us when we aren't looking for them. Smokey was shopping. Miley was in an Uber. I was splayed out on the couch! Our IMAGINATION is most potent when we are most relaxed.

For our IMAGINATION to flourish, we must give it room to breathe. We cannot be *nose to the grindstone* all the time. There must be space in our lives for rest and reflection. The answer doesn't always come when we are actively searching for it. Sometimes our brain needs a break so our IMAGINATION can have a chance to run the show. Even Archimedes, the famed Greek mathematician, had his "Eureka" moment in his bathtub. Tell me he wasn't relaxed!

When we give our IMAGINATION time and space, ideas don't just come out of thin air with no assembly required—quite the opposite. We must be prepared and ready to act. Smokey Robinson recognized his friend's accidental phrasing could be a hit song because he had years of songwriting experience under his belt. He'd thrown out more ideas than he'd saved and was actively honing his talent. So, when his IMAGINATION handed him the gift of "I Second That Emotion," he was primed and ready to receive it.

If you haven't put in the work, you won't recognize your eureka moment when it appears. Worse yet, your eureka moment may never arrive if you haven't put in the work. In my case, the reason I was ready to receive my eureka moment was that the seed which would someday grow into my company was planted decades earlier, and I had been tending to it.

During the most trying years of my life, I was confident I would use my pain to help others one day. I knew the universe could take the trauma of my sexual abuse and drug addiction and use it for good. Of course, I didn't yet know what that would look like, but I held onto that thought for years until it ultimately formed into my idea for my business. In the meantime, I trained in yoga and reiki, learning about healing energies and being fully present.

I followed these breadcrumbs of the spirit throughout my early life, trusting they would lead me where I needed to go. I put in the work, continued to grow, and the lessons percolated within me. Finally, when the moment was right, my IMAGINATION delivered, but only because I'd been feeding it inspiration for years.

Preparing your IMAGINATION for a eureka moment is like cooking a stew. It takes a lot of effort on the front end. You've got to peel, chop, thaw, and dice, but then, once you've thrown all the ingredients into a pot, you can sit back and wait for it to simmer. You've done the work, and now you get to rest. It won't be long before you can enjoy the fruits of your labor.

Our IMAGINATION is a handy tool, and we never stop using it. Even after my Eureka Moment, I continued to need my IMAGINATION. My company didn't appear overnight. In the beginning, I was mainly being hired to declutter, which was fine, but I'd get discouraged because I kept returning to the same clients and clearing the same spaces. My message wasn't getting through.

As long as we were cleaning and organizing, my clients were less interested in addressing the root cause of their clutter. I began to understand that my sincere desire was to coach people through the process of decluttering their lives and not just help them clean. This shift in my business model wasn't fully realized until the Covid-19 Pandemic when I was forced to reimagine my game plan. I needed to adapt to the circumstances, and that required my IMAGINATION.

Life evolves quickly, and we must be willing to reimagine what could be to keep up constantly. Even when things are going smoothly, ask yourself, "But what if?" Wait and see what your IMAGINATION hands you. You never know. When I reimagined my business model to virtual coaching while social distancing during the pandemic, the results were night and day. My clients were actually experiencing the long-term benefits I had always hoped for them. The clutter was leaving and not coming back. This meant they were healing!

Don't miss opportunities to reimagine your great ideas. For your IMAGINATION to deliver consistently, you must consistently give it space and allow the process to happen. Allow the Now. You can't force it—it's your IMAGINATION! It will do what it wants, but you can gently lead it by constantly growing, evolving, and resting. Then, when a burst of inspiration finally happens, suit up and take action.

In the book *Think and Grow Rich*, Napoleon Hill says, "Man can create anything he imagines." I love that quote because it is simple and true. Our imaginations form our realities. Even now, we imagine that we are living, existing, struggling, seeing, grasping. But we are just a mere thought in the mind of The All. The world exists in your own IMAGINATION.

Like that scene from The Matrix, when Neo struggles to catch his breath, and Morpheus says, "Do you really think that's air you're breathing?" We think we are breathing air because we imagine we are breathing air. If we can imagine breath, then what can't we imagine? You are limitless, but only if you can imagine the possibilities.

MEL MASON

About Mel Mason: International Best-Selling Author Mel Mason is The Clutter Expert, and as a sexual abuse survivor, she grew up depressed, suicidal, and surrounded by clutter. What she realized after coming back from the brink of despair and getting through her own chaos was that the outside is just a mirror of the inside, and if you only address the outside without changing the inside, the clutter keeps coming back.

That set her on a mission to empower people around the world to get free from clutter inside and out, so they can experience happiness and abundance in every area of their lives.

She is the author of *Freedom from Clutter: The Guaranteed, Foolproof, Step-by-Step Process to Remove the Stuff That's Weighing You Down*

Author's website: *www.FreeGiftFromMel.com*
Book Series Website & Author's Bio: *www.The13StepsToRiches.com*

Dr. Miatta Hampton

THE POWER TO CREATE

Your IMAGINATION is your mind's ability to bring things into existence. Excellent concepts that agree with your future. Have you created objections or barriers that prevent you from creating? What have you been telling yourself that keeps you from the life you truly want to live? "Someone had done it before." Have you become so distracted by everyday life that your ability to re-imagine your life has been stifled? Everything that you need to succeed is on the inside of you. You just need to tap in. Tap into your greatness. You must see it before you see it, or you never will see. Using your IMAGINATION, you can reach into your future and bring it into your now. I dreamed of becoming a nurse before I actually became a nurse. I saw myself walking into patients' rooms with my stethoscope around my neck, calling the physician to get orders for my patient, and answering the phone on the nursing units. My IMAGINATION fueled my desire. I knew that if I created the plan and stuck to it sooner rather than later, I would get those two letters behind my name R.N. As I accomplished my goals, my desire for more grew. There was a calling inside me that required more of me.

I imagined myself as being a successful business owner, but not just any kind of business owner. I imagined I owned multiple six-figure businesses. As I imagined what could be, I could hear the negative voice in my head asking me, "Who do you think you are? Who is going to buy you products?" The loudest voice in your head wins, and I had come too far to allow self-limiting beliefs to get in the way. I had the creativity. I had the power of my mind to create anything that I wanted to, and I believed that I could do all things through Christ that strengthened me. I am capable of producing whatever I put my mind to.

It is incredible what you can accomplish if you just put your mind to it. I remember feeling like I was pinned into my 9 to 5. I showed up every day, gave my gifts and talents, and felt like I was not getting anything in return. "There has to be a better way; surely there is something more," that is what I told myself. I felt trapped between the income I was earning and truly living my best life, and it was getting the best of me. Most days, I felt like the energy, the very life of me, was being sucked out by non-supportive, toxic co-workers. I was annoyed by voices and faces, but I continued to show up every day with a smile on my face. They say, "insanity is doing the same thing and expecting a different result." I was expecting the days and months to get better, and the truth is they were not.

I needed something different. As I sat cemented behind my desk, my mind began to wander, and I imagined what life could be like out from behind this desk. This desk that was filled with piles of paper, this desk displayed overwhelm, this desk that represented a padlock. My mind had a padlock on it, and I needed to be free. Free to create and free to re-imagine my life. At that moment, I realized I had the power of my mind to create. Working a 9 to 5 was no longer working for me, and I needed a strategy, but I was dealing with an idle mind.

As the saying goes, "An idle mind is the devils' workshop." An idle mind is wandering, not task- oriented, unproductive, and unfocused. Strategies for dealing with an Idle Mind:

1. Plan to be productive, no, I mean actually fill your calendar with productive activity, focused activity, if you are thinking about starting a business, new to business, writing a book, plan to write a

book? Fill your calendar with items that move the needle. It is not about perfection but progress.

2. Cut down distractions and things that will cause your mind to idle and engage in mindless activities such as scrolling on social media, going through emails when you should be doing other things, watching television when you should be studying your craft, and entertaining unnecessary things conversations, and overthinking.

3. Stop procrastinating. You are not lazy; you are a procrastinator.

I realize if felt like this and if I was experiencing this, how many other busy working women building legacy felt the same way. I discovered a problem that I could solve. I imagined myself giving direction and guidance to like-minded women, busy working women who are working a 9 to 5 while building a business simultaneously, who lacked clarity, felt overwhelmed, undervalued, and was combating an idle mind. So, I created PIVOT to Success Academy.

For women working a 9 to 5 and building legacy, days can be chaotic. Splitting my time between work, business, family, and self was a lot. I was trying to do everything, and as a result, things were getting missed. I lacked clarity, felt overwhelmed, and undervalued. I had made everything and everyone a priority, and I made myself an option, and I began to re-imagine life. My life was on a constant pivot, and I was not a priority. I stopped investing in myself and stopped celebrating myself. I just needed that one great idea. "You only need one idea to make a million dollars," is what I keep telling myself. Failure is not an option, and it is not the opposite of success. If I activate my IMAGINATION and keep putting forth the energy to create the products, goods, and services, then it is just a matter of time before that one idea, that one product, is created that will change to trajectory of my life. What you must know is that it is not about how many times you have tried and did not find your actions favorable, but you tried, and you discovered a way not to do a thing, and you are closer than you were before. Activate your IMAGINATION and let your creativity flow. What is your perfect day? What is your ideal life? Can you create your next level and design a life that you want to live simply by the IMAGINATION?

Three Affirmations to keep you aligned with your IMAGINATION and unleash your greatness.

1. I have the power to create. Anything that I can imagine, I can have it. There is not anything that I can imagine that I cannot create. There is greatness on the inside of me. My greatness is waiting to be released. I was born equipped. I do not need validation, only IMAGINATION.

2. Nothing can stop me but me. There is no force that can stop me from achieving what I imagine is mine. The things that I am dreaming of are already mine; I simply need to position myself and go after them properly. If I can imagine it, I can attain it. Realize that it is mine, in my future, and is waiting on me.

3. When my mind attaches to my limitless wisdom, the possibilities and creativity are endless. When I believe what I can imagine I can attain, I seek the strategy to bring it to fruition. My ability to create is unending. When I have purpose and a plan, I create wealth.

Spend some time and reflect on these four questions:

What is your life re-imagined?

What is your purpose?

What problem do you solve?

What is the plan to use your IMAGINATION to create wealth and build a legacy?

To book me as a speaker, email info@drmiattaspeaks.com

Follow me on Instagram @drmiattahampton

Follow me on Clubhouse @drmiattahampton

Follow me on Facebook @drmiattahampton

DR. MIATTA HAMPTON

About Dr. Miatta Hampton: Dr. Miatta Hampton is a nurse leader, #1 best-selling author, speaker, coach, and minister. Miatta impacts others with her powerful, relatable messages of pursing purpose, and she empowers her audiences to live life on purpose and according to their dreams. She coaches and inspires women to turn chaos into cozy, pivot to success, and how to profit in adversity. Miatta provides tools and resources for personal, professional, and financial growth.

Author's website: *www.DrMiattaSpeaks.com*
Book Series Website & Author's Bio: *www.The13StepsToRiches.com*

Michael Butler

IMAGINATION

As a child growing up on the farm in Oklahoma, I always had an active imagination, overactive, my parents will tell you.

Imagination is what helped me overcome a five-year struggle to speak without stuttering. It was on my family farm that I imagined I was the movie producer making movies for Hollywood, TV episodes and cutting to commercials, and selling products to my viewers during the breaks.

According to Merriam Webster's dictionary, the meaning of IMAGINATION is the act or power of forming a mental image of something not present to the senses or never before wholly perceived in reality.

History is filled with inspiring stories of people like Victor Frankl, who survived unspeakable atrocities during the holocaust to share his story of victory with future generations, to scientists, inventors, and pioneers, and even athletes who endured hardship to become great, advance mankind and solve the worlds collective problems.

What you see in your mind will happen in time.

When I was an eleven-year-old child who stuttered, someone gave me a book by an eleven-year-old kid. It had a picture of a yacht on the cover sailing on the ocean. This book, along with the fact it was written by someone my age, forever changed the course of my life.

I began to dream. I began to imagine my life beyond the family farm. Planes would fly over, and I'd begin to say to myself, "Someday, I'm going to fly on those planes and speak all over the world to thousands of people."

It's true that we move in the direction of our most predominant thought. I can remember the painting on the wall in the wrestling room of my high school wrestling team's training room.

"What you see in your mind will happen in time." Realizing this was a quote taken directly from Scripture, "As a man thinketh in his heart, so is he," I began to incorporate the principles in this Bible verse into my heart and mind. It became a part of who I was and not just an affirmation I recited from memory.

Leveraging Imagination and using the God-given power of visualization is found in the Bible. God told Abraham that his descendants would be as the stars of heaven and the sands of the sea in spite of the fact that he and his wife were old and having a baby looked impossible.

The creation of this series by Erik Swanson was first a thought in his mind. Then it became a dream in his heart that manifested in this 13 book series that you now hold in your hand, Volume 5.

Glenn Lundy, the celebrity Co-Author featured in this IMAGINATION Volume 5, went from being a drug-addicted teenager and homeless to running the top morning show The Breakfast of Champions across all social media platforms and is now a married father with eight kids. I've heard him tell his story from the stage more than once live and in person and at 5 am in The Breakfast with Champions room, and he talks about HOW he changed the image on the inside of himself before his circumstances changed and how that was the catalyst for all of the change that manifested in his life shortly thereafter. He's gone on to mentor and coach thousands of entrepreneurs to rise above mediocrity by mastering their morning routine to change their future.

The Greatest Nation – IMAGINATION

One of my school teachers said the greatest nation is IMAGINATION. And her story went something like this: "What if there was a nation called Imagination and all the kids could dream of what the world could be? And what if there was a nation called Imagination, and people could see that they are truly free? If all of our nature were positive imaginations, there'd be no war, and we'd all stay free."

Our Imagination controls our future, so it's important for us to upgrade our Imagination, so it gives us the images to take us where we want to go.

Have you ever noticed that negative people seem to have all the bad luck, and things always seem to work out for positive people? Life's outcomes are not based on what month you were born or what "sign" you were born under. No, success is a planned decision, not a matter of fate. I agree with the farmer who said, "the harder I work, the luckier I get."

This short acronym helped me frame my life picture and alter my Imagination from a negative one to a mostly positive one:

IMAGE

I–Image

M–Me

A–acceptance of who you were born to be

G–God

E–Enjoy

By changing the way I see myself it changes the way others see me. By choosing to have a positive mental attitude, I can have a good day regardless of the circumstances. When I choose to change my image to one of positivity, it affects me and others around me in a positive way. It increases my productivity and improves my self-esteem and the self-esteem of those around me.

Me

It's okay to think about taking care of me. In fact, if I don't take care of myself, no one else will. It's not until I take care of myself that I can help anyone else. Not only is it selfish of me to NOT take care of me. It is irresponsible. If I don't take care of myself, then I codependently make someone else responsible for me, which will create stress, frustration, and lack of productivity for me and my family and friends.

Acceptance

Accepting who I am, who I was created, accepting my assignment brings me joy, happiness, and freedom. I accept the fact that I cannot change anyone. I accept the fact that I can only change myself. I accept that my assignment is unique to me and that I'm different from the eight billion other people on this planet.

God

He's bigger than me and has a good plan. I acknowledge that I am not God; I did not create myself. I was created by a higher, more intelligent being, and God's plan for me is good, and His assignment for me is unique and profound.

Enjoy

I choose to enjoy my uniqueness.

I choose to enjoy myself.

I choose to enjoy my family.

I choose to enjoy my friends.

I choose to enjoy my hobbies.

I choose to enjoy trying new things.

When it comes to the things you will do as the result of this book and this entire series, I can only imagine!

As a global book publisher and speaker Butler is a recognized authority in the book publishing space. Helping authors and speakers evolve and create platforms of influence in an ever-changing marketplace.

Founder at BeyondPublishing.net, his authors have spoken in fifty countries and on six continents. With more than 650 titles published by authors in 30 countries, he's most proud of his four grown sons and two grandsons.

MICHAEL D. BUTLER

About Michael D. Butler: As a global book publisher and speaker Butler is a recognized authority in the book publishing space. Helping authors and speakers evolve and create platforms of influence in an ever-changing marketplace.

The CEO of The Mark Victor Hansen Library with over 80 New York Times Bestselling titles, global distribution and sales with over half a billion books sold.

Founder at BeyondPublishing.net his authors have spoken in fitty countries and on six continents. He's most proud of his four grown sons and two grandsons.

Author's Website: *MichaelDButler.com*
Book Series Website & Author's Bio: *www.The13StepsToRiches.com*

Michelle Cameron Coulter & Al Coulter

IMAGINATION...
THE SEED TO ALL CREATION!

A Tribute to an incredible woman of inspiration, vision, and possibilities; my mom - Jacqueline Cameron (who we tragically lost this past year to Covid).

Growing up in the big, blended family of 10 kids, my mom was the most significant influence of possibilities; creative, resourceful and always found a way.

Two things she always said were, "There is always a way to make things work" and "Something good comes out of everything."

Rewinding the story a little bit to share some examples of the power of her vision and IMAGINATION of what was possible: She found this little piece of land on the outskirts of the city that had been an actual junkyard. I'm talking full-on chairs, mattresses, dump yard. No one ventured past the main ring road in the city and thought she was crazy to buy this little piece of land and move to this little acreage. I was in grade 3. Shortly after that, my birth dad left, leaving her with four young babies, all under nine years old and five dollars in her pocket.

That didn't slow her down. I can only imagine that was the toughest time for her, with four little kids. I remember camping in the living room in a tent in front of the fireplace, having bread, milk, sugar in a bowl, and Tang orange juice for dinner. She made it fun and an adventure for us. I didn't know until years later that we were camping out because there was no power. She was determined to keep our home and not have to turn to welfare

I had major migraine headaches, was in and out of the hospital, and missed many school days that year. The doctors could not find any answers, so she took me to this wonderful chiropractor. It was the first relief I had. When she stopped going to the appointments, he did a doctor's house call to check in on her and her little kids and found them camping in the living room with no power. He wanted to help. She came up with a solution; she would sell him her beloved horse King for $500 to meet rent that month and then repurchase the horse when she saved up. She did this three or four times before getting her feet under her.

She got her real estate license and quickly became one of the top realtors in the city in just three months! She was the first actual "Extreme Makeover" Realtor. She would find a property that needed some TLC and get in there with paint, wallpaper, clean, decorate, stage, and bake cookies or fresh pies and buns for the open house.

She was on purpose and had a big vision and four babies to feed.

She had a passion and loved restoring old antique cars. Priceless - nothing stopped her. Us kids always looked amazing; she would get beautiful second-hand clothing and imagine and create the cutest clothes for us all, like snowsuits from an older man's ski coat.

We started seeing more of Dr. Cameron, who became more of an uncle to us until I remember when he asked my mom to marry him, one of the best days ever. I remember asking him, "Does this mean we get to call you dad?" So they became 2 Jacks: Jack and Jackie. He adopted us all, and our family of four kids became nine with his five, and they had one together, making it an even ten kids, five girls and five boys - the Brady Bunch on steroids.

The homestead was expanded and added on to about as many times as there were kids. It was an incredible place to grow up. My dad's chiropractic clinic ended up being built and based out of the house, and his patients *loved* coming out to the country to this special place.

My mom went on to work for the airlines. Could you imagine trying to go on a family trip with ten kids? We became the first original "Amazing Race."

My parents would pick a destination, everyone got to pack a carry-on bag only, and then we would split up in teams going standby to see who could get there first. If there was any complaining or whining, the game was done. You could be standing by for a flight for hours, half-day, or overnight. It was so much fun. My mom would have an envelope of money allocated for where we would stay. With ten kids, you can imagine that hotel rooms could be hard to come by and very expensive. So we would stay one night in a hotel, and she would go and scout out accommodations, usually finding a house to rent and source everything we needed. They were the most amazing adventures.

Once I started my swimming career (which I'll share more about in other chapters), I couldn't go on those family adventures anymore, as I would miss too much training. One of the last big ones I remember was after I retired from swimming. It was one of the first big trips for some of the married siblings and had little ones. Our family was growing and making it even more challenging to travel with that many. My mom had an entrepreneurial venture on the side that she was making these creative, beautiful jackets, up-cycling out of denim jeans for the arms, using the pockets strategically for the front and back. Her designs were called "La Pouch" ("the pocket" in French). They were beautiful one of a kind with terry towel designs inlaid and were in a number of stores all over the place.

Her denim supplier phoned her and said, "I have two thousand pairs of "seconds," which means slightly flawed jeans. Would you like them? "She didn't hesitate. "YES!"

She ended up sourcing and renting an abandoned bank, and all of the kids either sorted jeans or sold jeans or babysat the little ones. An entire family team effort. In two weeks, she made a blowout sale and sold out 2000 pairs of jeans! Enough to take 36 of us on a family adventure!

We went down to Cabo San Lucas back when they had just expanded the runway, and it was the first 747 to land 25+ years ago. It has changed so much since then.

She negotiated for 36-airline seats this time since we took up a big chunk of the plane. In usual style, we got there at Christmas with no reservations for accommodation. No problem, IMAGINATION, and adventure would begin. We stayed at a hotel the first night as my mom did her magic. She sourced two presidential suites at a hotel that she found out were vacant. She returned to them the second time and asked, "Is the President coming?" They were like, "What?" So again, she asked, "Is the President coming?" "Well, no," was the response" "Well then we will take both Presidential suites." She handed him an envelope of cash, which she had budgeted for the trip. They accepted the cash and just looked stunned as to what just happened!

It was amazing; it was like a two-level castle in the middle of the compound.

We had a big duffel bag that we brought full of a Christmas tree and lights and decorated the center of this compound, "The Cameron Christmas Castle," I will always remember and cherish.

IMAGINATION - what's possible

~Michelle Cameron Coulter

You have probably watched the cartoon "Sponge Bob Square Pants" if you have kids. There is a scene where Sponge Bob and Patrick Star are playing in an empty cardboard box, having the time of their lives. His friend Squidward gets them out and tries to jump in and have fun, but nothing happens. Finally, Squidward can't figure it out and asks Sponge Bob, "How do you have so much fun?" Sponge Bob draws a rainbow with his fingers and answers, "IMAGINATION." Look it up on YouTube, Episode Idiot Box if you get a chance. We would ask our kids to think outside the box and use their IMAGINATION to solve a challenge, and they would draw the rainbow with their fingers and say "IMAGINATION." It always made us laugh.

This was actually an incredible lesson as the girls learned to solve challenges and think through things.

My Father, who passed away 20 years ago, was a Rheumatoid Arthritis Specialist Doctor. He was a brilliant man and had a good sense of humor. He loved playing basketball and the trumpet growing up. I really looked up to him and also played the French horn, basketball, hockey, then volleyball in high school. In my first year of university, I decided to follow in his footsteps. So I took Natural Sciences to lead into medicine. During my first year at university, I really excelled at volleyball and was selected to the Provincial and National University All-Star teams. Then I made the Junior Provincial Team and Junior National Team. Just before my second year of university started, I was asked to join the Senior Canadian Volleyball Team and move to Calgary.

I remember talking to my dad and being quite nervous as I told him, "I was thinking of taking a year off University and moving to Calgary to train full time with the Canadian Team." My dad told me he went to university for ten years to specialize in medicine, and he always wondered how far he could have gone in basketball as he was the captain and leading point scorer in high school.

"If I were you, while you are young and have a good body and so much talent, why not push yourself and see what you can do. School will always be waiting here for you.

That made the transition so much easier, knowing my dad supported me in this crazy venture. After that talk, my IMAGINATION started to fly. What my future could look like. Training with like-minded athletes, pushing ourselves way beyond what I thought our bodies could handle. Then I found out that Canada had never qualified a team (men or women) in the sport of volleyball into the Olympics. So we started imagining what it would look like and feel like. We started concentrating on the best teams in the world and seeing what they were doing differently. As we cracked into the top 10 teams, we started getting invited by top teams to play in tournaments and tour in countries like Russia, Poland, France, Japan, Italy, East Germany, Holland, and the USA. We learned from each team and became better and better. By the beginning of 1984, we had beaten every team in the world. My dream came true in 1983 as our hard work paid off, and we qualified for the 1984 Los Angeles Olympics. We were so proud to be the first volleyball team in Canada ever to achieve this.

~Allan Coulter

MICHELLE CAMERON COULTER & AL COULTER

About Michelle Cameron Coulter: Michelle is an Olympic gold medalist, entrepreneur, mother of four, community leader raising millions of dollars for charities, global inspirational leader, and founder and CEO of Inspiring Possibilities.

About Al Coulter: Al is a two-time Olympian in volleyball, captain of Team Canada, world record holder in matches representing one's country in any sport, with over 735 matches, entrepreneur, father of four, and personal best coach, specializing in relationships, team, and resilience.

Michelle and Al are the embodiment of today's leaders. Strong and empowering, they embraced life's challenges with strength and courage. They bring insight, compassion, depth, and inspiration to the table with multiple world championships, three Olympics, an Olympic gold medal, marriage, and four children.

They are sought-after inspirational leaders. Through their speaking, workshops, and retreats, their gift and passion is to inspire possibilities and support people to embrace their greatness in a real, authentic, healthy, and vibrant way—creating thriving community, connection, and one's own gold medal results.

Author's website: *www.MichelleCameronCoulter.com*
Book Series Website & Author's Bio: *www.The13StepsToRiches.com*

Michelle Mras

IMAGINE THE OUTCOME

"There is no life I know to compare to pure imagination.
Living there, you'll be free if you truly wish to be."
- Willy Wonka

Our minds are powerful, multifaceted biological computers. They can create or destroy with a single thought. You see this demonstrated hundreds of times on a daily basis. One of the first thoughts for many is, "I need caffeine to wake up." You go about your morning routine with the anticipated reward of your caffeine fix to keep you going for the next part of your day. The reality is you have already been functioning without the caffeine until you grasp a cup in your hand. Do you need caffeine, or do you believe you need it? Perception, reality, and IMAGINATION play integral parts in our daily lives.

In 1987, I was a young woman working as an Administrative Assistant at a credit union in Omaha, Nebraska. One of my morning tasks was to make sure there was coffee ready before everyone else arrived. I mistakenly made two batches of decaffeinated coffee. I observed as each employee dragged themselves into the office and zombie-like beelined to the break room for a cup of coffee. Their eyes were barely opened until they took their first sip. Instantly, their eyes would widen, their posture straightened, and a smile would come across their faces. One by one, I observed a mind-over-matter transformation instantly occur. These people believed caffeine was in their cups, recharging them for their day. Out of the 12 employees who drank the coffee, only one complained that they were not feeling a caffeine boost. I observed, noted, and proceeded to make another double batch of decaffeinated coffee later that day.

Why run such an experiment? First, it started as an accident. Secondly, I was an engineering student who enjoyed testing a reasonable hypothesis. After several runs of this experiment over several weeks, I discovered only one person was sensitive to the lack of caffeine. That information caused me to run other experiments around facts and IMAGINATION throughout my lifetime. What did we see versus what we expected to see, rather than what was actually there? In my college classes, I discovered if I imagined that I knew the material then walked into class, my professors would not call on me. On the other hand, if I walked in appearing clueless, I was sure to be called to the board to explain all I did not know to the class. I learned quickly to embrace the "I know this" look into the core of my existence.

Please note, perception of what is expected or has happened before has no place in pure IMAGINATION. It will cloud the possibilities. Think of your childhood. Whether you were rich or poor, happy or sad, your IMAGINATION was a source of comfort in times of need. When lonely, we created friends; bored, created adventures; stuck inside, built worlds. Regardless of your circumstances, IMAGINATION was the key to distraction and inspiration. As children, our IMAGINATION fueled us. When asked as a child, "What do you want to be when you grow up?" how did you answer? Whatever you said, you declared with enthusiasm! I know my answer was always something to the effect of, "I'm going to be a doctor, pilot, and sing with Gene Kelly!" What did your dream job look like? Did you land anywhere close? Are you using any of the skills you admired? I'm always fascinated by people who break the perceived norms of occupations. People like:

- Brian May, guitarist for QUEEN, Song Writer, and a Ph.D. in Astrophysics.

- Hedy Lamarr, Actress, and Inventor, pioneered the technology that became WiFi, GPS, and Bluetooth.

- Arnold Schwarzenegger, Body Builder, Actor, Film Producer, businessman, Politician.

- Michael Jordan, Athlete of multiple sports and businessman.

Just because you chose one career path in your youth doesn't mean you must stay there. We grow up—our point of view shifts. Our priorities change. Dream big and outside your perceived lane. What can you use in your current job that can be applied to what you really want in life? What can you pull from your experiences that can be applied to your dream? What do your heart and mind imagine?

I remember watching the television show Star Trek back in the 1970s, thinking about how cool it would be to have a phone on my hip, talk to my room to dim the lights, and push a button to receive meals, even if it was in pill form. The kids in my neighborhood would build forts of cardboard and scrap wood that we would name different starships. We recreated worlds from neighborhood to neighborhood, and we used phrases like "Beam me up, Scottie" as someone inside the fort would drop a rope to pull us up or make us climb into our "ship." We pretended our Walkie-Talkies were flip communication devices. We wanted it all to be real. So much so that what was pure science fiction imaginary tools became a reality within our lifetime. That is the power of IMAGINATION!

I challenge you to stop seeking outside affirmations of what can and cannot be done. Close your eyes for a moment. Use your IMAGINATION to see yourself accomplish a goal. How are you receiving this accomplishment? How do you feel? What is happening around you? What are you wearing? What are you driving? What do you see? What do you hear? Smell? Taste?

Now, embody those images. In your mind's eye, walk into it. You are there. Bask in the feelings. Remember what this moment feels like. Now, open your eyes and keep the overall feeling. Your task is to live every day in that feeling. Wake, eat, exercise, walk, work, talk and interact in your world holding that feeling. Live emotionally in that state. Your ideal state of existence is waiting for you to catch up to it. Keep walking. I like to say, "Live and act as if what you want has happened. You are simply catching up to it." You've probably heard or seen Dream Boards and the term "Manifestation." Each of these tools and terms helps clarify what you want in the future until it becomes a reality.

Why did I share different scenarios about perception and IMAGINATION? Because it is a large part of what I do as a professional speaker and speaker coach. You must be able to imagine the outcome. Release all preconceived notions of "what-if" and create in your mind what you want your audience to leave with. My example of walking into my college classes with an air of confidence is not "faking it until I make it." It was knowing I would understand by the time I left that class. This lesson can be used to walk into any room with confidence. See the end in mind. The examples of people who didn't limit themselves to their initial career lane prove that it can be done. Lastly, the Star Trek example proves that just because it hasn't happened before doesn't mean it can't become a reality.

IMAGINATION is the key to our future. Without playing into fantasy scenarios, there isn't progress. If you can't imagine what "it" you want, then what drives you to try? Think of this scenario: When you say some task or invention is impossible, only a few will fight to prove you wrong. On the other hand, if it is declared that a task or invention is possible, far more will strive to solve the "how" to make it a reality. Break through the mediocre. Use your IMAGINATION, dream, and make the supposedly impossible possible.

Our minds are powerful, multifaceted biological computers. They create or destroy with a thought. You might as well use that powerful thought for good. As Spider Man's Uncle Ben wisely said, "With great power comes great responsibility."

ABOUT MICHELLE MRAS

About Michelle Mras: Michelle is an International TEDx Speaker, Communication Trainer, Success Coach, co-Host of the Denim & Pearls podcast, the Author of *Eat, Drink and Be Mary: A Glimpse Into a Life Well Lived and It's Not Luck: Overcoming You,* and Host of the *MentalShift show on The New Channel* (TNC), Philippines.

Michelle is a survivor of multiple life challenges to include a Traumatic Brain Injury and her current battle with Breast Cancer. She guides her clients to recognize the innate gifts within them, to stop apologizing for what they are not and step into who they truly are. She accomplishes this through one-on-one and group coaching, Training events, Keynote talks, her books, Podcasts and MentalShift television show.

Awarded the Inspirational Women of Excellence Award from the Women Economic Forum, New Delhi, India; the John Maxwell Team Culture Award for Positive Attitude; has been featured on hundreds of Podcasts, radio programs, several magazines, and lends her voice to audiobooks and has a habit of breaking out into song.

Michelle's driving thought is that every day is a gift. Tomorrow is never promised. Every moment is an opportunity to be the best version of you… Unapologetically!

Author's Website: *www.MichelleMras.com*
Book Series Website & Author's Bio: *www.The13StepstoRiches.com*

Mickey Stewart

THE SWINGING DOORS OF IMAGINATION

IMAGINATION is the software program of our future, where ideas are built into creation. Napoleon Hill called IMAGINATION the 'workshop of the mind,' meaning everything created was first thought up in someone's mind.

I think of IMAGINATION as a parallel universe where the answer to everything lives, just waiting to be called into existence. In this chapter, I'll discuss two types of IMAGINATION and show how IMAGINATION is both a RECEIVER and TRANSMITTER of ideas, allowing us the potential to turn our future-imagined life into reality.

In *Think and Grow Rich*, Napoleon Hill states there are two types of IMAGINATION – Synthetic and Creative. Synthetic IMAGINATION draws on existing ideas that we can then mold into our own vision. The ideas born here are comparable to pieces of clay already set up on a pottery wheel; the ingredients already exist (the clay), but then we get to shape them into our unique forms. Creative IMAGINATION, however, draws from the energy that has yet to take physical form. Ideas born here may come in the shape of hunches, flashes, feelings, and intuitive 'knowing.' Instead of working with a pre-existing piece of clay, never-yet-discovered ideas await you in the creative IMAGINATION.

I've always had an extremely vivid IMAGINATION and couldn't help but notice some people seem to have an exclusive 'VIP PASS' to a secret backroom of this special 'workshop of the mind.' My husband, Mark, is one of those people. He's an incredible musician and composer who has published a book containing 45 original compositions. His tunes are played by some of the top traditional musicians and bands in the world. Mark doesn't think of the creative process as tapping into a higher power, but you don't HAVE to think about it, or even understand it, to use it; some people just do it unconsciously.

For those of you who *would*, however, like to understand how to use creative IMAGINATION consciously, I've provided some suggestions below. The actual key to accessing both types of IMAGINATION is to get yourself into a 'high-vibe energy' state, where you feel in alignment (tuned-in) with something bigger than yourself (a higher power), and you strongly sense something wants to come forth through you. It's important to also listen to that call. Peter Parker calls this his 'Spidey-Sense.'

All of Mark's brilliant tunes came to life when he was in this 'high-vibe energy' state, with many of his tunes being composed immediately after spending a full day teaching bagpipes in the Highlands of Cape Breton. After being musically stimulated and inspired the entire day, much of the magic occurred during our two-hour journey home (from Inverness to Sydney Mines). It would often start with a 'flash' of inspiration while driving, which would inevitably result in me reaching for our portable cassette recorder to quickly capture the never-heard- before tunes that magically flowed from his practice chanter. Fully formed, perfectly complete pieces came to him like a high-speed download. It was incredible to witness!

Watching Mark pull something from his IMAGINATION (bringing the 'formless' into 'form') so quickly and effortlessly before my very eyes is mind-blowing. If you saw it for yourself, you would 100% agree with me.

It comes to him so incredibly easily that he doesn't really think much of it. To me, however, this is Einstein-level creative IMAGINATION; it's how something that comes to you in a flash while driving down a windy-dirt road can later end up in TV shows, films, and even become a ringtone in Indonesia.

In lay terms, when we're using our Synthetic IMAGINATION, we are more 'in our HEAD' accessing ideas to help us figure something out. These ideas are also born from passionate enthusiasm and high energy and are strategic (and similar) to the development of plans.

Every successful entrepreneur makes excellent use of their Synthetic IMAGINATION!

Creative IMAGINATION, on the other hand, is accessed when we are truly 'in our HEART,' as opposed to 'in our HEAD.' In the state of creative IMAGINATION, you receive impulses that are often accompanied by thoughts like, "Ooh, I didn't even know I knew that!" To me, it's a tingly feeling and almost like an out-of-body experience.

Our IMAGINATION is an incredible resource that is ready and willing to assist us at every moment. As previously mentioned, our IMAGINATION is not only a RECEIVER of ideas (similar to Mark's musical download experience), but it's also a TRANSMITTER of ideas.

When I think of TRANSMITTING ideas, I think of a website where you see (only) the result – the beautiful colors, the professional photos, and the well-thought-out text. But behind the scenes is a technical language called coding, a language that developers use to get a website to look, perform and behave a certain way.

Aside from meditation, gratitude journaling (writing my 'code') is one of the easiest ways for me to get into a 'high-vibe energy' state. Being grateful has been the number one thing that has changed my life above everything else. Keeping a journal is also a great collector of evidence to look back upon.

I have several journal entries where I wrote about how grateful I was to live in Scotland, see a castle from my window, go to a ball at a castle every year, be married to a Highlander in the Duke of Atholl's private army, and live inside my favorite Scotland-based, time-traveling fiction book series. A few years after writing those entries, I found myself on set filming the TV series for those exact books. I was literally LIVING inside my favorite novel. I wrote about feeling IN it – and then I WAS IN IT!

This is just one example of how I turned my future imagined life into reality by using my IMAGINATION as a TRANSMITTER. Stuff like this happens to me ALL THE TIME because I believe anything is possible.

The communication between us and IMAGINATION (which I also often refer to it as God, Source, The Universe, Infinite Intelligence) goes two ways, like the swinging doors between a restaurant dining room and its kitchen. I have been consciously playing with those swinging doors - practicing both 'RECEIVING from' and 'TRANSMITTING to' IMAGINATION for the last fifteen years. The below practices have allowed me the opportunity to strengthen my Synthetic and Creative IMAGINATION muscles.

Here are some ways to fling those swinging doors wide-open. I invite you to give them a try! For RECEIVING:

Ask for inspiration. Close your eyes, still your mind, and ask the question you want to be answered. Such as, "What is the solution/idea I'm looking for?" Don't try to come up with the answer yourself. Instead, allow some breathing space for that door to open wider and wider. I use this method daily to find things. In our home, we say, "Have you asked the Universe for it?" and within minutes, and often seconds, we find what we're looking for. Try it. It works!

Write down inspired thoughts immediately after they come to you or immediately following your meditation time. Don't censor or edit. When you try to censor the ideas coming in, it's like you're pushing back on the door that is trying to open.

Make gratitude journaling part of your morning routine. You know you're on the right path when, during journaling, your chest feels like it's going to burst with love and joy. Every day you start with gratitude makes the rest of your day feel like bliss.

For TRANSMITTING:

Think of the outcome you desire and then daydream, write, and speak about it with immense gratitude – REPEATEDLY! Pure gratitude is the super juice that fuels your magic wand.

Think 'from' the dream rather than 'of' it. (I learned this from Neville Goddard)

Act as if the outcome has already happened, to the point of self-belief. Repetition of the two above steps will get you where you need to go with this.

"Feeling is the secret.
If you persist until you see exactly what you want to see, fix your
position with the glue of feeling and remain there
- it will be reflected on the screen of space.
There is no fiction!
Every thought you think will come to pass."
- Neville Goddard –

MICKEY STEWART

About Mickey Stewart: Born in Cape Breton, Canada, Mickey Stewart is a musician, coach, and author who has been a player and instructor of the snare drum and bodhrán for forty years.

Responsible for heading up the drum program at Ardvreck School in Perthshire, Scotland since 2002, Mickey is in high demand to teach throughout the U.K. and North America.

Creator and founder of BodhránExpert.com, her YouTube videos have received more than two million views from students and fans from every country throughout the world.

Over the past eight years, she's been involved in the TV and film industry as a supporting artist. Even more recently, she's begun following her newest passion, which is teaching others how to share their talents with the world.

Stewart lives in Crieff, Scotland with her husband of twenty-four years, Scottish musician and composer Mark Stewart, along with their 16-year-old son, Cameron, who is also a piper.

Author's Website: *www.MickeyStewart.com*
Book Series Website & Author's Bio: *www.The13StepstoRiches.com*

Natalie Susi

IMAGINATION. MEDITATION. MANIFESTATION.

The thing I am about to say is the thing you're not supposed to say. It is a sentiment that is not always acceptable in the personal development industry and certainly not in the entrepreneurial world. Still, I am a woman who often says the things you're not supposed to say, so here it goes.

You don't have to work hard to get what you desire. You don't have to hustle, grind, or grit your teeth to prove that you care enough, that you're good enough, or that you've paid your dues enough in order to cash in on your desires. What you do need to do is get clear on your desire, imagine what it looks and sounds and feels to have it in your life, meditate on that vision daily, and then take consistent, inspired actions towards that desire every single day. It is simple, but it is not always easy.

I will model how this process works with a simple story.

As I mentioned in previous books, I am a UCSD professor for a communication course called *The Pursuit of Happiness* and the former CEO and Founder of a beverage company called Bare Organic Mixers. After I sold my company, I had a very clear desire to get back to teaching, but this time around, I wanted to teach how to live a happier life, not how to write about literature. My first business was a valuable learning experience, but it was the kind of work where I was hustling and grinding every day. It felt like I was constantly pushing a boulder up a hill. When I sold the company, I made a promise to myself that I would make at least $100,000 a year on my own schedule doing only the work that made me feel happy and purposeful. Most people thought I was a little nutty when I shared this desire. Teachers who earn a 6-figure salary on their own schedule teaching what they want to teach is a dream, not a reality. I disagreed with this mentality, and I respectfully stopped listening to the people who doled it out to me. Instead, I wrote down my specific desire, and then I meditated on what it would look and sound and feel like to live this life every single day. I allowed my IMAGINATION to take over, and I stepped into this world where I got to live and work in a reality that my dreams were made of.

If you'd like to take the first step towards bringing your IMAGINATION to life, check out the below. This exercise is designed to walk you through the process of writing simple statements that ask you to state your desires clearly. It also asks you to use your IMAGINATION to detail what your ideal situation looks like in any given area of your life. It may feel elementary, formulaic, or repetitive as you complete it; however, this is the most efficient and effective way to support your brain to think and believe in new possibilities. The sentences are designed to get you to consider your desires and then clearly write them on paper in a way that asks you to tap into your senses, emotions, and beliefs to paint a picture of the desired outcome that you can genuinely believe and get excited about.

Manifesting Magic Exercise:

Check out the below for the 6-sentence exercise for manifesting magic.

Set aside about 30-60 mins to do the below. Fill in the blanks and write your descriptive visualization about what you'd like to manifest in each area (or just one specific area) of your life on a piece of paper. Then, write your final version on a white notecard, and read these every morning and every night (white notecard is optional, but I prefer this color).

Once you've completed the exercise, put your hands over your heart and breath into your heart 3- 5 times. Close your eyes and imagine feeling what it would be like if this were your current reality. Try to smile while you're doing this process. If you'd like to add better energy to this practice, light a small tea light and place your notecard under it. Focus your attention on the candle flame and drop into a meditation where you allow your IMAGINATION to take over. Stay focused on what it would be like to have your desires in this very present moment.

1. I intend to create a reality in which I FEEL (3 emotions that you want to feel) _____ in XYZ area of my life (example: in the professional area of my life).

2. When I wake up in the morning, I THINK (write down the first thought that you'd think about in this area of your life if it looked the way you want to manifest it) _____ (Example: "I am so excited to open my emails and get started with the day).

3. When I go to bed at night, I THINK (same thing here—can be repetitive or a new thought) _____ (Example: I feel so accomplished and satisfied today).

4. When I talk about this area of my life, I often SAY things like (something that sounds like you and is something you'd be really proud to say out loud or something you'd be so excited to say) _____ (Example: when I was manifesting my relationship, I wrote here "I manifested the guy on my freaking vision board.") *Make it sound like YOU!

5. When I FEEL into this area of my life, I feel it in my XYZ part of my body _____ (Example: my heart feels

warm and open, I get goosebumps on my arm, my brain feels clear and calm.

6. In perfect divine timing for the greatest and highest good of all involved. And so, it is. (Close with this sentence).

Have fun with this exercise, and trust that it is very powerful. Get into a daily practice of reading your sentences and meditating on them, and you will start to see some magical shifts very quickly in your life. If you'd like to learn even more about the power of setting intentions and using your IMAGINATION to manifest, read *The Map* by Boni Lonnsburry. The first sentence of this exercise comes from her book, and she will explain in more detail why it is essential to use this specific language when writing out your desires. Happy Manifesting!

NATALIE SUSI

About Natalie Susi: Natalie has more than 14 years of experience as a teacher, speaker, entrepreneur and mentor. Currently she's a 5-year UCSD professor focusing on communications and the Pursuit of Happiness. As an entrepreneur, she founded and grew Bare Organic Mixers beverage company for 8 years resulting in an acquisition in 2014.

After selling the company, Natalie combined her educational background as a teacher and her experience as an entrepreneur to provide personal development coaching and consulting to individuals, businesses, and creative entrepreneurs. She developed a program called Conscious Conversations and utilizes a step-by-step process called The Alignment Method to support leaders in cultivating conscious teams and businesses through a process of self-reflection, self-discovery, and self-ascension that ultimately increases profits, productivity, and the growth of the individuals personally and professionally.

Author's website: *www.NatalieSusi.com*
Book Series Website & Author's Bio: *www.The13StepsToRiches.com*

Nita Patel

POSITIVE POSSIBILITIES

The very first time I watched The Secret, my eyes were opened to a world of positive possibilities. At first, I laughed. If you've seen the documentary, it has a sense of exaggeration to convey the messages. A few weeks later, I watched it again. This time it piqued my curiosity in a new way. The main message I got out of The Secret was the Law of Attraction. But there was still something more profound that was being said, which I couldn't quite process. So, I watched it again. Except this time, I paused it, took notes from almost every speaker, and went back to reflect on what they meant.

I discovered the book *Think and Grow Rich* from this process. The IMAGINATION chapter is one of the most powerful chapters that spoke to me in this book. My moon sign is Pisces, and we're known to be dreamers. We live in a world of fantasy. So as pragmatic as we may be, the world is our oyster. What a beautiful validation from a personal development-business book! I was just told that I should continue to fantasize to be successful in life.

There was only one problem with this. My fantasies until now were of pain and trauma. I spent my time reliving my past pain. Having been around dysfunctional relationships made me think it was normal, and that's what life was supposed to be like. So, what ran through my mind all day? Dysfunctional conversations and unhappy endings were exactly how I had observed in my real life. The music that made me feel was that of pain and sorrow. I loved alternative music. I had recently attended a Coldplay concert around this time. I was absolutely in love with their songs, as anyone is when they see their favorite band perform. Feeling the sadness and pain from their songs made me feel alive. This was my version of IMAGINATION. I loved Coldplay, I thought about them deeply, and I manifested seeing them. But I also manifested the pain and sorrow I so deeply felt from the lyrics.

We have over 70,000 thoughts a day, and most of these thoughts are on autopilot to be defensive negative and protect our ego. But after studying the IMAGINATION chapter, what a revelation! I could use the same process to find happiness! Can this be real? This was the question that piqued my interest. Because of this, I had to go back and watch the movie a third time while taking notes. Once I took notes, it was crystal clear to me. I heard Bob Proctor give the example of gravity. He said something to the effect of, just because you don't believe in gravity doesn't mean it exists. It's a law of nature. That was the moment I realized I had been practicing IMAGINATION all along, but only to my detriment.

I thought to myself if I can rewire these thoughts to be positive, imagine the life I could create!

One thought at a time, I went from negative to endless positive possibilities of dreams and fantasies. I learned how to feel through joy instead of pain. I learned how to love with an open heart. My Piscean mind knew no bounds.

At first, I was embarrassed to share my dreams with those even in my inner circle. So, I started writing them down. I wrote them in the form of goals, affirmations, journal entries. I would even write out a full detailed day in my life three years out. The more I practiced writing my dreams, the more I became comfortable with them. This went on for a few years. I felt judged and ashamed of being a dreamer. I didn't want people to tell me that I was full of it. I didn't want to be discouraged and shown back to my past. It was My Secret of Positive Possibilities.

Time went on, and one day I realized that I was actually living my dreams. I realized that anything I had thought of with intention and taken inspired action towards, I was living. And by no means was it perfect. But the fact that I had proof of my new life was enough for me to start talking about it. So, I started sharing with my family, friends, staff, clients, and the more I shared, the bigger my life became. It was the most rewarding thing I had done until that moment. FINALLY, I took something that changed my life and told everyone I knew about it.

Of the many things that I have experienced from this concept, the one that sticks with me the most are of all the loving, trusting, like-minded, beautiful people in my life today. Coming from a competitive corporate culture, there was no room for collaboration, let alone love. I deeply craved a sense of connectedness filled with pure and positive intent. I shared this with my coach at the time. She helped me articulate it in the form of a goal, and she helped me rewire my IMAGINATION process and painted a beautiful picture that resonated with my IMAGINATION.

I took that foundation, expanded upon it, set intentions, and took inspired action when it felt aligned. The results of this have been unimaginable. It's been my most precious and priceless gift. I never thought I'd have the love and support from people all over the globe as I do today. I can't believe the people I call my friends today. Sometimes I ask myself what I did to deserve this. But a moment like this reminds me that there's a process to everything, and I followed that process.

With that, I want to express my sincere gratitude for everyone in my life right now and those who will be a part of my future. Thank you, and I love you.

Namaste.

NITA PATEL

About Nita Patel: Nita is a best-selling author, speaker, and artist who believes in modern etiquette as a path to becoming our best selves.

Through her professional years, Ms. Patel has 25 years of demonstrated technology leadership experience in various industries specifically with a concentrated focus in health care for 14 of those 20+ years. She's shown her art across the world to include the Louvre in Paris. She's a best-selling author and performance coach, pursuing her master's in Industrial organizational (I-O) psychology at Harvard. Her investment in psychology theory and practice is what led her to a deep interest in helping others. She has become deeply and passionately devoted to nurturing others and in building their confidence and brand through speaking and consultative practices.

Author's Website: *www.Nita-Patel.com*
Book Series Website & Author's Bio: *www.The13StepstoRiches.com*

Olga Geidane

WHAT ARE YOU GOING TO DRAW ON YOUR CANVAS TONIGHT?

Tomorrow… I am going to become an international speaker!

Tomorrow… I will compose myself right before getting onto the stage; I will tell myself that THIS is the moment to inspire and empower others!

Tomorrow I will put on my best dress: that red one, or actually, no, I will put on the black dress with long zip and my Louis Vitton shoes. No, not those as the heels are too high. But damn, I will feel so good in them on the stage. I wonder what people will think of me: better or worse if I put those shoes on?

Oh CRAP, I got DISTRACTED here!

Ok, ok, ok, let's go back to this again:

SO…

TOMORROW I will do my first international speech! I will be calm; my breathing will be deep and relaxed! I will be feeling EXCITED, instead of nervous (or at least I will be telling myself that)! Once I hear the emcee announcing my name, I will take a deep breath in, and with a big smile and confidence, I will come out onto the stage and enjoy this moment of becoming an international speaker!

For days and weeks, those were my thoughts, way before "tomorrow" actually arrived!

Those thoughts were with me every single night, as we were in the darkness of English nights, in our bedroom with white horizontal blinds on the windows, in our house.

I so damn hated those "dust collectors" on the windows, but they were the last thing I saw before leaving to my own world of my IMAGINATION when I was closing my eyes.

The reason WHY I was escaping to my world of IMAGINATION was my BIG dream of that time to become an international speaker. And the reason for my dream was the vision I had: many people transforming their lives as a result of coming to my events, retreats, and seminars, just like I transformed mine when I went to Tony Robbins events. One of his events after another was helping me to unlock and reveal more limitations within me that would lead to me growing so rapidly and becoming the new version of me.

One evening I felt very brave and shared this vision with my partner, and he screamed his lungs out:

"WHO, Olga, you?!?! who are you kidding? WHO DO YOU THINK YOU ARE? To become a speaker, you must have something important to say, and you've NOTHING to say; in fact, you are totally worthless! You came from a small village in Latvia, your English is horrible, you're a single mom for years, struggling financially, and you don't even own a house!"

OUCH.

Have you EVER had a feeling of wanting to just melt in the split of nanoseconds and disappear through the floorboards?

That is precisely how I felt that moment, at the table as we had our dinner. Suddenly I wasn't even hungry.

Suddenly I felt sick.

Suddenly something switched inside me, and mentally I was already out of that relationship right that moment. We were supposed to get married, and I ALREADY KNEW right that moment - it would NOT happen!

All I said was that I wanted to be a speaker.

I wanted to shift my impact from 1-2-1 coaching sessions to one-to-many.

All I wanted was to inspire and motivate others. I had this desire to help hundreds and thousands and maybe, MAYBE, one day even a million people to live the life they deserve and desire!

That evening I knew one thing - my dream was smashed to pieces as well as my confidence by this man.

I knew one more thing: this man did not belong in my future.

- I also knew that right that moment, I HAD A CHOICE:
- To listen to him, forget my dream, to get married and have a normal life.
- To leave him and pursue my dream, trusting myself.
- I actually came up with the third one:
- To leave him, pursue an even bigger dream: to become not just a speaker, but an international speaker!

It would be the perfect story for the movie: I moved out the next day and started pursuing my dream.

But this is NOT a movie, so let's go back to reality.

My big dream was the reason for the next god-knows-how-many-nights I was living in my own world, becoming an international speaker every single night!

You see, when we let our IMAGINATION flow and be creative, we literally CREATE our world!

Think about it; your mind is like a blank canvas, and every day, every single hour, even a minute, you have the CHOICE to pick one crayon or another, dark and depressing or bright and vibrant color and…draw your art, create your future.

What are YOU choosing?

What did you choose a minute before, when you were reading my story of my partner verbally abusing me? Did you choose to think how awful he was, or did you choose to think he was right? Or perhaps, you were puzzled why are you even reading something so personal from my life.

See, every single thought of yours is there because you ALLOWED that to be there.

- It can be negative or positive.
- Self-disruptive or self-motivational.
- Making you feel worse or better.

And that is the impact of just one SINGLE thought.

You and I know that you never end up with just one thought. Where is one, there is another, similar, and then another one, and you end up having an argument in your own head!

So now, just for a moment, imagine a white canvas and a pack of crayons in front of you.

And imagine for a moment that ANYTHING YOU WILL DRAW on that canvas with those crayons, using different colors, will come true. What would you draw?

That white, plain canvas was your subconscious when you were born.

And then every single person who came into your life: parents, siblings, schoolmates and teachers, neighbors, movies, bedtime stories, cartoons, adverts on TV and radio programs, podcasts and YouTube videos, magazines and books, and so much more - left some sort of a mark, a smudge, a line, a strike on your canvas using THEIR own colors while having THEIR own intentions.

I want to invite you to sit back, close your eyes, and imagine what your canvas looks like after all THEIR work on it. Scary, right?

And this is the scariest part: the longer you are on this planet of Earth, the messier your canvas is because you came across so many MORE people who messed it up!

That canvas represents your life, my friend. Brrrrrr....

That's the feeling my clients and audiences I speak to have every time I take them on this journey.

So far, I haven't met even one person in my life saying, "Oh, I am totally happy with my canvas; it is PERFECT!" But, perhaps, you met someone like that?

"So, what do we do with that messy canvas, Olga, and how is it even connected with this book's title, "IMAGINATION"?"

There is a very strong connection, my dear.

Your IMAGINATION is exactly what you need to start owning your own canvas.

Remember this; you have permission to start a brand-new life at ANY stage and ANY moment. Read that again!

- It doesn't matter how old or young you are.
- It doesn't matter where in the world you reside.
- It doesn't matter what your past was like.

You CAN, and you WILL create a brand-new life from a fresh start once you decide and are committed to that!

The minute you CONSCIOUSLY, DELIBERATELY DECIDE to have your canvas fresh and crispy white, your life will change.

Remember, your subconscious controls you when you don't make choices of your own will - it makes all decisions FOR you. So, the minute you step in and take over - it backs up.

How do we step in?

So here, let's go back to the crayons!

"Crayons" are your thoughts, which are the ingredients for your dreams becoming a reality.

The better drawing you create in your IMAGINATION - the sooner and closer you will get towards your dream. The brighter colors (positive, supportive thoughts) you choose, the easier it will be for your brain to see that dream. Once your brain can see what you want, your subconscious will start doing everything to deliver your order.

The more you draw on your own canvas, the sooner you replace the messy one, and your subconscious will become your best friend because now it will start delivering to your life what YOU want, not what others programmed you for!

Let's go back to my story here.

On the 4th of September, I was lying in my hotel bed and thinking:

Tomorrow… I will become an international speaker!

And that was my new reality: only 13 months later, since the day I said out loud I want to be a speaker, followed by my dream being smashed by my ex-partner and me drawing my own new canvas, my dream BECAME REALITY right there, on the Frankfurt's stage.

What are you going to draw on your canvas tonight?

OLGA GEIDANE

About Olga Geidane: Olga is an International Speaker, an Event MC/Host, Facilitator, Mindset Coach, a Best-Selling Author, and a Regional President of the Professional Speaking Association in the UK. She is a host of Olga's Show and A World-Traveler.

Olga helps ambitious people to unlock their extraordinary performance and their true, authentic side. She is passionate about helping people to live their best lives. Olga knows how tough it is to be broke and unfulfilled in life: at the age of 24, just after her divorce, Olga came to the UK from Latvia with no spoken English, with just £100 in her pocket and a 2.5-year-old son. Olga is a very inspirational survivor: she went through abuse, betrayal, cheating, financial loss and emotional breakdown. Matt Black (Business Model Innovation & Disruption Consultant - Snr. Advisor to CEO, CSO, CCO, COO - Author & International Public Speaker) said: "Olga really takes it up a notch beyond anything I have seen before. She is one of the bravest people I have ever seen on stage. If you are looking to book a speaker or attend a talk that will be inspiring, challenging and leave you wanting to take action... She is perfect."

Author's Website: *www.OlgaGeidane.com*
Book Series Website & Author's Bio: *www.The13StepstoRiches.com*

Paul Andrés

THE 6 POWERS OF GENIUS

There is no question that IMAGINATION is a powerful tool. It's what allows us to create new things, come up with innovative ideas, and dream about the future. It's also what allows us to remember the past. It is our friend when it comes to planning, and it even helps with empathy when we try to understand how others think. IMAGINATION, in a sense, is what truly unlocks our genius.

IMAGINATION, in its purest form, does everything in its power to help people be happier, more productive members of society. It has no agenda or ulterior motives; it simply wants you to succeed in life by showing you limitless possibilities and an abundance of ideas.

Yet, for such a wonderful mental faculty, IMAGINATION is one of the most misunderstood and underrated tools we have. We don't think to thank it or treat it with the respect it deserves; instead, you might find yourself struggling against your own IMAGINATION as it feeds you images and ideas that make you uncomfortable. Sometimes our IMAGINATION can seem like our biggest enemy and the reason for the negativity we see in our lives.

But just as easy as our IMAGINATION can see the dark, it can also create the light. It is in our control, and understanding our genius by unlocking the power of our IMAGINATION is the key to creating the life we deserve.

Over the years, I have struggled to truly understand the power of my IMAGINATION and the true depths. But I have found six insightful understandings of the IMAGINATION that have helped me unlock its power and truly expose my genius.

1. It's Not Just for Kids

Children often get a bad rap when it comes to IMAGINATION. However, the truth is that the ability to imagine and daydream isn't something we outgrow; it's just something we're told to stop doing as adults.

Unfortunately, dismissing our IMAGINATIONs like this can have serious consequences. When children daydream, they begin forming ideas about themselves and their capabilities that affect how they feel about their future selves. In other words, when you tell a child not to imagine, you may be reducing her chances of being a successful adult.

2. IMAGINATION Is a Tool of Exploration

IMAGINATION isn't just helpful in solving problems. For readers who love science fiction, it can also offer a glimpse at potential solutions. By envisioning distant worlds or alternative futures, authors give us tangible ways of understanding abstract ideas and characteristics. For example, if we want to understand the true nature of love, then we can look at how it appears in our favorite stories. We can also do this for other emotions like fear or anger—and even more abstract concepts such as trust, betrayal, revenge, hope, redemption, etc.

In a sense, IMAGINATION is a tool of exploration. It can help us better understand our own lives and the problems we might be having with them. But it also offers a window into the potential solutions available to us, which is precisely what IMAGINATION was designed for!

3.   You Can't "Imagine" Something into Existence

Do you have an idea for a movie that would be amazing if only Hollywood would make it? Maybe you think it's a shame that your favorite band doesn't have more recognition. Perhaps it bothers you that the person who should fix the potholes on your street still hasn't shown up. Maybe there is some problem in society that could be easily resolved if only people would "wake up." These are all examples of popular complaints which sound perfectly reasonable until you realize one thing: they cannot happen through pure IMAGINATION alone.

You may wonder why this is, and the answer is simple: IMAGINATION is about the possibility, not actuality. Sure, you can imagine a world where people are willing to accept public displays of affection or where the mayor shows up every day on time. But this doesn't make it possible for these things actually to happen within our observable universe. Of course, they might happen if extraordinary events occurred—be they Armageddon-level catastrophes or sudden unexpected miracles—but this isn't how humans have ever experienced the reality of working.

4.   You Can Imagine Something into Being

This does not mean that you cannot change your experience by imagining something new! In fact, one of the coolest aspects of IMAGINATION is that it's an active mental exercise rather than a passive one. So instead of simply thinking, "There should be more love in the world," you can imagine what it would be like to see people holding hands and exchanging warm glances. Instead of hoping that someone will come and fix the potholes on your street, you can try to remember a time when they did and then re-imagine that experience in 3-D.

You may not get exactly what you want simply because you want it, but IMAGINATION has many benefits besides this. If nothing else, using your IMAGINATION helps revitalize your mind and body -- which is why so many meditation exercises ask people to visualize themselves walking through a forest or looking out over the ocean. Once again: these scenarios are only possible if extraordinary events occur; we've never seen them happen under normal circumstances. But that doesn't mean that imagining things in this way isn't helpful. We've all heard the expression "seeing is believing." And if you're not sure what to believe, seeing can help you sort it out.

5.   Your IMAGINATION Can Be Controlled or Contained

Here's where things start to get interesting. While your IMAGINATION isn't real, you can still control it if you put in the time and effort. For example, if I'm upset because I want more love in my life, I can imagine what that might look like, but only for so long. If I keep focusing on the problem rather than the solution, my mood will stay stuck in a "scarcity mindset." My subconscious won't be able to move past this issue unless I deliberately switch over to imagining how happy it would make me feel to see people holding hands or exchanging loving glances with each other.

This idea of switching between realities has been used in psychotherapy for decades. For example, it's the basis behind Cognitive Behavioral Therapy, which challenges people to examine their negative thoughts and then re-imagine them as less harmful or untrue. So, if someone says that your IMAGINATION is real, they're actually incorrect. And if they say that it can be controlled or contained by an outside source, then there are even deeper problems with what they're saying - because obviously, you have control over your mind!

6.   You can train your mind to imagine better things

I'm glad I didn't grow up believing that whatever popped into my head was true because I would have grown up thinking that imaginary elephants were real. During my childhood, I had some very active dreams where imaginative things would occur; nowadays, those same dreams seem completely boring to me because through sheer repetition, I've trained my brain to imagine better things.

Even as an adult, it's easy to train your mind to imagine more positive thoughts and concepts because you simply have to focus on them and repeat that process often enough, and those thoughts become ingrained. If you want a good example of that, check out what happened when Reddit user Tulpamancy decided he wanted his Tulpa Galatea to be goth.

The same thing can happen with more abstract thought processes as well. In 2011, scientists asked a group of men and women between the ages of 25-45 how they felt about their bodies. They found that 66% of the men judged themselves against the "ideal" male body, which is defined by being muscular yet lean. Of the women in the study, 69% judged themselves against some "ideal" female body that is apparently fit yet curvy.

At the same time, these men and women were shown pictures of both male and female bodies, many of which had flaws or imperfections on them. The scientists found that when they showed these images to their subjects, their brains responded very differently depending on how people felt about themselves: Subjects who thought more positively about themselves (men and women alike) saw flaws in the photos where others didn't; conversely, those who felt negatively about themselves tended to ignore any issues with the picture they were looking at because it was too similar to what they were expecting

Clearly, we can't rely on the real world to judge us on meaningful terms because our individual mentalities will always skew it. That's why it's essential to block out these negative images of ourselves and replace them with better ones until the positive images become ingrained into your mind.

It's clear that IMAGINATION is one of the most powerful tools we possess as human beings. It can make our impossible dreams possible and help us unlock new perspectives on life that we never imagined before. We may sometimes let it take us down a dark path, but if we use our IMAGINATION to change ourselves for the better, it also has the power to create an extraordinary future for all of us. So, what will you imagine? What do your goals look like in five years or ten years from now? How would you feel living this reality today? Whatever dream you have inside of yourself-go after it! Unleash your inner genius by using these six helpful insights into how to unlock the true power of your IMAGINATION and unleash your genius to transform your life with your own unlimited possibilities!

PAUL ANDRÉS

About Paul Andrés: Paul is an award-winning conscious entrepreneur, visual storyteller, and intuitive coach. From digital and interior design, to business clarity and personal growth coaching, to social justice advocacy and volunteering, Andrés is proof that aligning your passions with your purpose is the true magic to success. He currently devotes his time to helping awakened entrepreneurs and heart-centered creatives design the life they deserve through personal and professional coaching and consulting, as well as shedding light on uncomfortable topics that bring awareness to the social justice issues of today as the host of his video podcast, In Your Mind. Andrés is also a two-time #1 best-selling author. You can catch him as a featured guest speaker at events across the country.

"Home is so many things, but ultimately, it's where life happens. It's where we sleep and grow a family, it's where we play and grow professionally, and it's where we learn and grow within. Each home plays a key role in helping us design a whole life—the life we all deserve." — Paul Andrés

Author's Website: *www.PaulAndres.com*
Purchase Book Online: *www.The13StepstoRiches.com*

Paul Capozio

WHAT'S FOR LUNCH?

One of my income streams involves a company I partner with based on the West Coast. I fly out a few times a year to visit the owner and his team, plan the future, and rehash the past. While sitting on the plane during my last trip out before writing these words allowed me time to reminisce about the book and get my thoughts together for what you are about to read.

I had breakfast in New York (Newark Liberty International Airport, to be exact) and had lunch in San Francisco. Fans will know exactly what I'm referring to and realize that the possibility of a fast transnational flight was just someone's IMAGINATION when the original book was written. As with all my submissions to this book series, I will be completely honest about my thoughts. The concept of that day being an impossibility back when *Think and Grow Rich* was written was lost on me. Until that is when I had the epiphany that it has become all too commonplace, expected, and the wow factor has worn off. People fail to keep those realities in their frontal lobe, which is a mistake. So, when I think about what is to be, not only for me but for the world and our collective future, I have to say I have some reservations.

Ida Auken, a member of parliament in Denmark, said, "Welcome to 2030. I own nothing, have no privacy, and life has never been better."

Now I want you to think about the world of NFTs, the metaverse, virtual real estate. With all the excitement around cryptocurrencies and our pursuit of all things, are we moving in the right direction? Are everyone's imaginative ideas worth building upon? Are the powers that be allowing us just enough rope to hang ourselves? With the shrinking of free markets and the move towards a more socialist society, we may be giving up our power of IMAGINATION. No, I'm not spewing conspiracy theories; I'm considering the potential for imaginative thinking to be diminished. Not fewer dreams being realized but no dreams for some of us at all. It may be far off, but yet here we are discussing the impact of a book written 85 years ago. Time flies when you're not paying attention, and things thought impossible are now not even a thought to most not paying attention. Yes, anything is possible, even dystopia, if those in whose IMAGINATION it exists are successful. Things are moving super-fast, and they will be getting faster, but that makes it easier, and incubation times for IMAGINATION to become a reality are much shorter. The good news is your idea will get going quickly. The bad news is if it's a bad idea, you'll know just as fast.

IMAGINATION is a powerful tool, and many of these virtual concepts are exciting. I have a question? Would you give up your physical real estate and be happy owning only virtual real estate? Could it be that A.I. is not what will be our demise when our machines are smarter than we are? We will not give it a second thought to freely give up what is real for what is virtual? Some of us already have and are super excited about it, are they right? I have news for you. We are all going to find out whether we like it or not.

So, while my writing up to this point may seem foreboding, the good news is we have proven that both coexist. One of my heroes, Nikola Tesla, the father of modern electricity, had a vision that electricity should be free and available to all. Alas, he died penniless, and we all pay a monthly electric bill. But his IMAGINATION led to some of the greatest inventions and conveniences we enjoy every day. All because of his impressive IMAGINATION. Other people's imaginations gave way to creating great wealth by building the infrastructure on which we all receive our electricity, gas, and even water. Most of us gladly pay our bills for convenience, and those with the foresight are billionaires. Others built physical and then online stores so we could purchase devices based on imaginative designs created by others.

All are necessary, but we must not kill the goose that laid the golden egg, the mind that imagined. So, my reason for pointing this out is that we must foster our IMAGINATION and dream bigger. We must encourage our children the value, passion, and joy of IMAGINATION.

"I don't care that they stole my idea... I care that they don't have any of their own." ~Nikola Tesla

Caveman Sex

To be truly successful is to understand the laws as outlined; you must understand the power of your thoughts and hold your ideas as your power center. I made the mistake of trying to understand the seemingly mystical nature of this instead of just knowing it is real. By not allowing it to do its job without my interference, I worked against myself. The input of the minds and thoughts of others will be broadcast to you to help you along. If you believe in or have a great gut instinct, collective intelligence is the root. The key was accepting that this is not mysticism, witchcraft, or voodoo. Is it so hard to believe that we have not yet fully evolved? We have all read about primitive man believing lightning and other natural occurrences as acts of the gods. Punishment for behavior not suitable to the greater power. Laughable huh? Well, have our egos become such that we think we've fully arrived? That this is as good as it gets, and we know it all? As far as the universe is concerned, we are still cavemen. If what we think are aliens turns out to be our future selves or some other notable discovery not be the same as understanding that static electricity from two clouds is not the gods upset with us for caveman sex?

Now, do you understand the force of IMAGINATION and the power of the idea? Think about the great ideas you have seen and figure out what yours are. How will you profit from them? While most cannot take their concept from the cradle to the grave for whatever reason, lack of funding and so on, get it out and profit from it. If you develop your IMAGINATION, it is a never-ending waterfall. If you wait for a home run pitch, you will never get on 1st base. Don't be greedy; sell the idea, sell the design, build the prototype, and partner with or sell to the people who can get it to the next level. Heed this advice, understand the value of what you have at the stage it is at, not your emotional attachment to it. When someone comes to me with just the idea and has valuations based on the finished and realized result, or calls it their baby, in most cases, that idea will die unrealized. It is worth the value of the sum of the parts, and most times, the biggest parts are funded by someone else. Think in abundance and do more each time; Elon outsources, and so should you.

IMAGINATION can be learned and developed, and people think it's silly, mostly the broke ones. Your brain needs and loves stimulation. I make sure to take a brain supplement every day. It was impossible to find one that really worked, so that idea was hatched, and the group out on the west coast formulated it. My brain is worth it. It's funny how people will drink a protein shake when they work out but not a brain drink for thinking. I went to a catholic grammar school where discipline was as important as Jesus. I would get hit with a yardstick across my knuckles for daydreaming. I was a massive daydreamer. That was the worst thing you could do to a kid! Now I must work extra hard to stop thinking like an "adult mind" and daydream as much as I can.

Call To Action

Start daydreaming about anything and everything, 10 to 15 minutes a day. Don't worry about a great idea, just start imagining, they will come. Then, start pitching your imaginative thoughts about products, services, or new business concepts to anyone who will listen. Train your brain, exercise it, don't tell them you're practicing, just pitch. Think about synthetic IMAGINATION, better versions of existing ideas. Nurture the creative IMAGINATION; allow yourself to listen to the voices in your head. See the flying car with actual flapping wings! Go wild! Your concept might only turn into a drive-in buffalo wild wings, but now you're on your way.

PAUL CAPOZIO

About Paul Capozio: Paul Capozio was born in Hoboken, New Jersey and grew up on the streets of Hudson County. At 35, he was recruited to be the President of Sales and Marketing for a 350-million-dollar human resources firm. In 7 years, he drove the top line revenue of that firm to over 1.5 billion.

Capozio owns and operates Capco Capital, Inc., an investment and consulting firm. The majority of Capco's holdings are of manufacturers and distributors of health and wellness products and human resources firms. Capco provides sales consulting and training, helping companies increase sales through traditional and direct sales disciplines. Making the invisible visible and simplifying the complex is his stock and trade.

A dynamic public speaker, he provides motivation and "meat and potatoes" skills to those in the health and wellness field who do not consider themselves "salespeople," allowing their voices to be heard above the "noise."

He is a husband of 32 years to his wife, Linda. He is also a father and grandfather.

Author's Website: *PaulCapozio.com*
Purchase Book Online: www.*The13StepstoRiches.com*

Phillip McClure

IMAGINATION TURBO SPEED

Slamming down on the accelerator pedal and holding onto the steering wheel for dear life, I ripped around the racetrack. Every moment, I gained on every other racecar still in front of me. Feeling the engine roar and the sight of the crowds cheering me on to victory propelled me even faster. Weaving in and out and around the competition slowly overtaking every single opponent. Finally, there it is, the coveted checkered flag in front of me. If I can pass this last car, I will be the winner. I did it, but just barely, as we were side by side the entire last lap. I am the best racecar driver who has ever lived; I had just won the world championship once again until my mom called out the window again, reminding me about coming inside.

There I sat in an old Go-Kart with faded blue paint and a rusted frame that was rotting away on the side of my uncle's house. It still had remnants of a seat and a steering wheel, which were all I needed to be a racecar driver. After racing, my mom said I had to take off my racing gear and come inside for dinner. So, as I walked over to the house, all proud of myself and excited to tell my mom that I had retaken first place that day, I began to take off all the sweet racing gear I had acquired. This included my racing goggles, which were just some oversized swimming goggles that probably belonged to one of my sisters. My cape gave me turbo speed, which was always a sheet safety- pinned around my neck. And, of course, my rubber irrigation boots, which were my racing boots. I knew I looked so cool. Thinking about it makes me want to dig up the old picture again.

Why do we stop imagining these great adventures we used to live out in our lives every single day? It did not matter where we were: hours in the sandbox, the side of a hill, a stream, even grounded to your bedroom. We always had the power and entertainment our minds provided us. It was simply a wonderful time of our lives for many of us. Where would we be if we just simply did not allow our IMAGINATION to be dulled but instead embraced it and fed it, keeping it alive? I'll tell you where you could be, and you know deep down what could have happened. You would be having more fun with life and start getting the things you want or wanted. Now let's talk about how this works.

> *"What you imagine imagines you."*
> - Neville Goddard

There is so much power in IMAGINATION, it can be used for or against you, and the effect it has is up to you. What you imagine over and over becomes imprinted in your mind. You start acting and living in ways to react to what you imagine will happen. But beware, as there is a poison to life that you can expose yourself to if you are not paying attention. You must carefully guard what is in your IMAGINATION. Some people spend their time imagining terrible things such as disease, pain, death, and financial ruin. Why in the world would someone imagine this? Because 90% of all mainstream media focuses only on the negative, we are continuously bombarded with fear-based thinking and risk-taking dangers. Guard against this way of thinking as if your life depends on it. Once someone begins to imagine repetitive negative outcomes coming for themselves, they will begin to bring them to fruition as they are putting themselves in that life and following that frequency.

However, IMAGINATION can also be used positively and bring you to, or closer to, the abundance in life you seek. Use IMAGINATION for good. Use it for the good of you, your family, and even strangers. Spend your time imagining all the wonders that will happen for them and the great experiences they will have in their lives. The more you imagine, the faster you will believe it is happening. Once you believe, you naturally will act as though it is happening, and there you find yourself possessing the habits that made the things happen.

"As soon as man assumes the feeling of his wish fulfilled, his fourth-dimensional self or spiritual self finds ways for the attainment of this end, discovers methods for its realization. This also knows that whatever can be experienced in the IMAGINATION can be experienced in our reality or outer world."
-Neville Goddard

As Napoleon Hill stated, "The workshop of your mind is IMAGINATION." So put the workshop into action; get the lights on. Get the cogs moving and start taking those steps towards your goals. The NorthStar Journal, my company, helps you break this down and accomplish this faster and keep you on track.

Here is the part that you have probably heard repeatedly. That's good, though, as it is what really needs to be understood and soaked into your mind. When IMAGINATION is used in detail, you are helping your brain create clarity of what you are really going for. Everything is in the details. Love the details to the point that you are excited when you begin to imagine your goal, and you know the next thought coming to mind because you have previously designed it in your mind. Once you get to that point, you are really on to something as your subconscious aligns with your goals. Imagine the fragrance of the new car smell or the fresh, clean air of your house surrounded by trees. Imagine what it feels like, what it smells like. Put yourself where you want to be, and you will follow.

This should be done in small steps until you get it exactly right. Then, as you imagine where you are going or what you are accomplishing, it will slowly morph and evolve until it is just right. For example, suppose you are having trouble clearing your mind and calming yourself down so you can refocus yourself and imagine a different outcome. In that case, I recommend the "Take six, Calm the Circuits" Neuro exercise by John Assaraf. First, close your eyes in a safe environment and take six slow deep breaths. Then, on the exhale, breathe out slowly as if you're breathing out through a straw. This exercise can be done with the eyes open as well if needed.

Let me walk you through my current IMAGINATION exercise as an example. When I begin my morning meditation and imagine living in my future, I get as detailed as I can be. Right now, I am replaying driving up my 200-meter driveway through the trees that lead up to my tucked-away brick home. The car I am in, the trees, the grass, the lake, even my kids playing outside. Then the slow opening of the garage doors. I know what cars are inside and what I'm driving, but I still miss so many details once that door opens. I have been using my NorthStar Journal to document this, as I'm excited to read them in the future as each of these comes true and use them for lessons for others.

IMAGINATION reinforced by memories will begin to dip into the threshold of predictability. It is predictable if you do something that generates a similar result; this is even accomplished on tasks you have never completed or attempted. Imagine the desired outcome, backward plan what needs to happen, and look back at the steps required to figure it out and get started. Now, this next part might entertainingly go against much that you have heard but hear me out as it's in a different context. BE PREDICTABLE. In the sense that from your peers or those dependent on you say and speak the words of:

"I knew he/she could do it, that is _____."

Write your name

Or,

"Of course, _____ would be the one to figure it out."
Write your name

You have all seen this before, especially in the sports arena. "I knew he would make that shot or catch that ball." This is you. Imagine it and take the actions towards being it or achieving it. Here at NorthStar Coins, we build these beautiful coins for people just like you to keep you on track and accelerated, to remind you to pursue your goals constantly. It is incredible what a simple reminder can do to have you imagine reaching your goals and then putting you back on course to achieve them. For me, I am now driving on the racetrack, and it's surreal that it has been in the making for decades. Now I just need to win the world championship. I need to find that old picture now so I can place it next to a modern one.

In closing:

I challenge all of you to dig up an old photograph of yourself. Rekindle your IMAGINATION of where you were at that time of your life and what you believed was possible for you. Then, write that down on the back of the photograph and use it as your bookmark, starting with this book.

Stay *in* the flow, not with the flow.

PHILLIP D. MCCLURE

About Phillip D. McClure: Phillip is married to the love of his life, Maaike McClure, and is a very proud father of two exciting kids. He was raised in the Great state of Montana before moving to Utah. Phil lives life to the fullest. His accomplishments consist completing a full Ironman, deploying four times with the Army, earning multiple decorations along the way. Including two Utah crosses! Which makes him the only soldier in history to receive that medal twice. Currently, Phil is the Owner of NorthStar Coins, Events by NorthStar, the co-owner of P.B. Fast cars and recruits pilots for the Army Aviation program. It was during his last deployment that he accidentally created his first mastermind and it has forever changed his life as well as the others involved. He mentors and coaches in self-improvement and physical fitness.

Phil is an exotic-car enthusiast who spends as much time behind the wheel as possible, whether it is carving through canyons, ripping around the racetrack, or coaching others to see their potential. Competitive driving is the best therapy in the world.

Live life to the fullest and have fun while doing it. You don't get a rewind in life so take mistakes as the lessons they are and improve, don't make the same mistakes twice.

Live in flow, not with the flow.

Authors website: *NorthStarCoins.com*
Book Series Website & Author's Bio: *www.The13StepsToRiches.com*

Robyn Scott

THE POWER TO CREATE SOMETHING FROM A THOUGHT IN YOUR HEAD!

I have to say first and foremost; I LOVE MY IMAGINATION!

I am the hugest and biggest Walt Disney nerd you will ever know! He knew how to harness his IMAGINATION to create one of the most successful and richest dynasties ever! When I think of IMAGINATION, I go to children right off. I have taken care of so many little humans in my life, and I know them intimately. What fuels them, what drives them. What they perceive and understand is so simple and easy. So why do we make things so gosh darn difficult? All of this talk wants me to take you back to our first book and principle, "Desire." *WHAT DO YOU WANT?* Do you know yet? Have you been trying to figure it out? You *HAVE* to see what you want, to get it!

When I was in fourth grade, I was smitten with Peter Pan. Not the musical or stage productions. I was in love with Peter Pan from Walt Disney's version. I had a real crush on him. I did. I would draw pictures of him and pretend my bed was the pirate ship covered in pixie dust and flying off into the sunset with him now that he got rid of that Wendy Bird! I know this is where my passion for glitter comes from! I remember vividly the day I realized how animation worked and that, like my drawings of Peter, which are all they were, were drawings. In my mind, he was so tangible and real. I cried! A lot! Luckily, "my little pink squishy heart" (thanks Neal Hooper) recovered, and I am married to a pretty spectacular swashbuckler, who is quite real! Although I was a little bit crushed, most of all I was curious! How did he do it? I started reading everything I could about the man behind the mouse!

In December 2020, I braved the pandemic world and took a group of aspiring entrepreneurs looking to help level up to Disney World. As entrepreneurs, I thought there was no better place on the earth to evoke more innovation and IMAGINATION than what Walt Disney had created and shared with the world. So, I had our group look for ways to solve problems they found as they visited the parks. We had two teams, and they created some phenomenal super-cool additions. They took the "principles" they applied in their simulations, and we had A-MA-ZING masterminds about how to apply them to the businesses they own!

Walt Disney knew movies. He knew animation! He started right where he was and dreamed, DESIRED more! Bigger! I don't know if Walt could even fathom where his dream has grown to. Did he imagine it could be the biggest international brand it is today? Could he see in his IMAGINATION that he would dominate all other movie franchises? Do you think he knew he would have 12 "Happiest Places on Earth?" I doubt it.

Who would have ever foreseen Star Wars being sold to Disney? I sure didn't! And they are two of my all-time favs! When I was six, watching Sleeping Beauty and seeing Star Wars very shortly after, I did not imagine Princess Leia being a Disney princess, here we are today in 2022, and SHE IS! Princess Leia is a Disney Princess! This is why when we walked into Smugglers Bay in Hollywood Studios Park, I was instantly transported to the world I grew up watching and loving! To see the Millennium Falcon blew my mind! Talk about IMAGINATION and innovativeness!

Spoiler Alert! Real Storm Troopers and AT-AT walkers! I was whisked away and loved every second!

Now, Princess Diana. She was a real-life princess! Regal and beautiful! I did my research projects about her in 5 grade. She was a person living in the real world, and she was a PRINCESS! So, if she could be, why not me? Olympian diver? Why not me? Miss America? Why not me? Why NOT me?! Well, let me tell you. I was not that talented. My subconscious mind doesn't realize royalty is kind of a family thing. I was not competitive. Not super athletic. According to my teachers and leaders, my greatest attribute growing up was being a good friend.

What?

I had a friend who was phenomenal on the piano! One of my dearest friends is the most amazing artist and another who competed in dance! My talent was being a good friend. What the heck do I do with that? It took me years to really understand how to love my talent. I LOVE PEOPLE! I LOVE CONNECTING! I LOVE EMPOWERING PEOPLE THROUGH MINDSET! So that is

where I started. As I entered the entrepreneurial world, it was evident that I am a Connection Catalyst! (I coined the phrase in my first book, *Rediscovering the Lost Art of Face to Face Connecting, Collaborating, and Creating*. Working with other Connection Catalysts is so much fun and rewarding. To have yourself surrounded by like-minded people is a great way to get your IMAGINATION going again. The more you use it, the stronger it becomes! I am not sure I could play with barbies sunrise to sundown anymore, I know I get lost in people's stories, and I adore brainstorming and really working through problems! I have talked all night to PLENTY of people!

IMAGINATION is uber important! *Acting* on your ideas and IMAGINATION is even MORE important! Then it turns to innovation! This is where the magic happens. This is where we change the world. As Napoleon Hill teaches in *Think and Grow Rich* that we have the power to harness this magic and use it to fuel our dreams and aspirations! Do you have access to little kids? Volunteer to hang out with them. Ask them questions! Get as curious as they are about the world around them, and then stay present and listen! Can you go to a park and simply "BE" there? Ok, be careful not to give off a creepy vibe or anything, just *being*. Watch as they swing and slide. I think "lava" is a universal game, and it's fun to watch the plethora of ideas and games children come up with!

My sincere challenge to you for the next 30 days is to discover what inspires YOU! I go to children. You may find yours at the zoo or opera house. Music is another tool you can use. Of course, I go to Disney tunes for inspiration. Find what music actually moves YOU! Have fun with this and really find something that you love! Nature is a place I know many people go to as well. Whatever it is for you, FIND IT and IMAGINE MORE!!!!!!

Now, I have to continue imagining and creating my own empire, AND YOU do too!

ROBYN SCOTT

About Robyn Scott: Robyn is the Chief Relationship Officer for Champion Circle. She manages the prospecting program for Divinely Driven Results. Scott is a Habit Finder Coach and has worked closely with the president, Paul Blanchard, at the Og Mandino Group. She is also a certified Master Your Emotions Coach, through Inscape World. Scott is commonly known in professional communities as the Queen of Connection and Princess of Play. She has been working hard for the past 9 years to hone her skills as a mentor and coach.

Scott strives to teach people to annihilate judgements, embrace their own stories, and empower themselves to rediscover who they truly are. Scott is an international speaker and also teaches how to present yourself on stage.

Her first book, *Bringing People Together: Rediscovering the Lost Art of Face-to-Face Connecting, Collaborating, and Creating* was released in August of 2019 and was a bestseller in seven categories.

Author's website: *www.MyChampionCircle.com/Robyn-Scott*
Book Series Website & Author's Bio: *www.The13StepsToRiches.com*

Shannon Whittington

THE SUBCONSCIOUS ROAD TO DREAMS

When we transition from child to adult, something happens to many of us, something that I believe is quite tragic. The tragedy is that we lose our IMAGINATION. We're conditioned by our parents, teachers, jobs, and the media that being an adult with an active IMAGINATION is silly at best and downright irresponsible at worst. And because we want to be safe and secure and not push the limits of our comfort zones, we take this idea as gospel. So we limit ourselves and our goals, and we remain conservative as humanly possible (e.g., "I just want to make a decent living"; "I just want a car that doesn't break down every thirty miles"; "I just want to be comfortable"). After all, if we dream small or don't dream at all, we will never be disappointed, right?

But deep down inside of us, there's an inner childhood version of ourselves that is desperately yearning to emerge, to have a little fun, and to let our inner spark of IMAGINATION run free. This inner child doesn't think about disappointment. This inner child isn't concerned about comfort zones or practicality or all of the other fears we have been taught. To the inner child, the entire world is at their fingertips! They see it, and they imagine it, and they know joyously, beyond a shadow of a doubt, that their dreams are indeed possible.

What if I told you that you could reconnect with this inner child, and by doing so, you could harness the power of IMAGINATION to help make your wildest - and I do mean wildest - dreams come true? After all, some of us spend a lot of time dwelling on our fears and anxieties with no positive outcome anyway. What if we tweaked our brains and our hearts to focus on the goals and feelings we wanted to have instead? The possibilities are endless, and here's how to do it.

Let your IMAGINATION go wild

Many of us have been taught the "S.M.A.R.T." model in our workplaces and schools when it comes to goal setting. We're taught to set goals that are Specific, Measurable, Attainable, Relevant, and Time-Bound. This is a great formula for practical daily work tasks, and it works really well. But when it comes to your personal life, if you have big dreams (and I'm hoping you do), be smart and toss that S.M.A.R.T. model right out the window.

Case in point: When I moved to New York City, I lived in a 3-story walkup in Manhattan. Whenever someone would stop by, they'd have to walk upstairs to the first apartment, another flight to the second apartment, and another to the third. My apartment was on the first floor, but I had a dream of owning the entire building. A big dream for a young country bumpkin from Tennessee, right? At the time, this seemed like a complete absurdity and outright foolishness. In fact, when I mentioned it to some of my friends, they quickly confirmed my foolish idea. I made decent money, but not nearly enough to own a three-story building! Even though I realistically knew this, my subconscious mind didn't, so I figured out a way to trick it.

Whenever someone would ring my doorbell, I wouldn't just answer the door. No. No. I'd run all the way up the stairs and back down - every single time the doorbell rang. I imagined that I owned the building and had to run down two flights of stairs to get to the front door, and I did this for 12 years! I never told anyone this little secret. It was between me and my subconscious.

Fast forward to today, and believe it or not, I live in a beautiful 3-story house. I have to run down two flights of steps to answer my door! This was a dream that my brain thought the practical (S.M.A.R.T.) side was very foolish, but my subconscious mind didn't. So now, when my doorbell rings and I skip down the steps, I stop and think, "Wow, Shannon. Remember that apartment you lived in and how far you've come? You're living in the exact house you imagined for so many years!"

I encourage you to permit yourself to do the same and think about what you desire with zero regards to how practical or impractical it is. Instead, I want you to imagine everything you want out of life and to embrace that little version of yourself who didn't know the difference between fantasy and reality; that child is going to become one of your best friends on your road to success!

Write down your goals

I have a colleague with whom I share a friendly sense of educational competition. He got his Masters, and I got mine. He got a second Masters; I got my Doctorate. Then, one day, he asked me, "Shannon, why are you getting all of this education? You're clearly smart and successful as you are." I told him that I'm pursuing education because I want to be the expert, the go-to person, in the field of LGBTQ+ health; that whenever someone needs a nurse consultant regarding inclusive healthcare or workplaces for the LGBTQ+ community, I want to be the first person who comes to mind.

Sounds lofty, right? But I don't stop there. I told this man that I'm also getting this education because I want my yearly income to become my monthly income. Dear reader, I promise you that when I told him this, he looked as if his eyeballs were going to pop out of his head and land on the floor! He indicated that these goals were absolutely loony and outrageous in an unspoken but very clear way! Maybe you think that too, and perhaps I'm a little foolish for writing this, but heh, after all, we are talking about IMAGINATION, right?

I learned a very useful lesson that day: I can't tell everybody about my goals without thinking I'm reckless or overly imaginative. And yet, I still need to somehow get my goals out into the open. I can't just contain my IMAGINATION in my mind. So, this is what I do: I write down my goals every single morning. I write down all of my wildest goals (e.g., "My yearly income is now my monthly income"), I run my fingers across the page, and I read my goals back to myself. Then, I write that this goal is easy and already done. I've even gone a step further and created a laminated vision board with images of all the things I want to give my subconscious a healthy dose of sensory stimulation. I keep it within my eyesight while I'm working, and it is the screen saver on my phone. Every time I look at it, I literally see my future every time I pick my phone up. Not only that, but I imagine the feeling of having achieved everything I've written down. Talk about fun! I love imagining this!

When I do all of this, I don't just think about personal financial security. I think about the countless lives I can impact, all the people struggling in ways I can't even comprehend. I imagine being able to help make a genuine, long-lasting difference. And when I write it down, when I intentionally translate my outlandish fantasies into something tangible that I can read and see and touch, I imprint it onto my soul and keep lovingly tricking my subconscious into making it happen. And I simply wait for it to happen because I know that eventually, it will.

Stay consistently imaginative

When it comes to achieving goals, any successful person will tell you that consistency is key. And while this is true, that same mindset can and should be applied to harnessing the power of your IMAGINATION. Being imaginative one day a week and practical the other six days simply isn't going to cut it. The truth is that you have to dedicate time every single day to let your IMAGINATION run free.

Recently, I spent twelve full hours lying on my couch imagining. First, I dreamed about all the incredible, amazing things I could manifest, all of my goals, most of which the average person would find wholly ridiculous. Then, I imagined what it would feel like to achieve them. Finally, I saw myself living the life I wanted, having the income I wanted, using my skills and knowledge, and lived experiences to change the world for the better. To say that I was blissful and elated and felt like a little girl again is a drastic understatement; the level of joy I got from purely imagining my dreams was indescribable.

You might think, "That's all well and good, Shannon, but I don't have twelve hours just to sit down and imagine my dreams." I totally understand. I had Covid at the time, so it was sort of convenient. But maybe you have 2 hours or even 1 hour! Check your screen time usage on your phone. I bet you have the time! Some of us spend a lot of our free time watching TV or scrolling when we're bored; imagine taking just one hour or even thirty minutes a day away to dream, to think about all the things you desire and how you'd feel after achieving them. Aside from giving you a momentary sense of pure bliss, try and comprehend just what such a daily act will do for your subconscious. You will start thinking and behaving in ways that lead you to those goals. I promise.

With all of this said, I leave you with a quote by Albert Einstein: "IMAGINATION is everything. It is the preview of life's coming attractions." When you are consistently, relentlessly imaginative, you create a subconscious roadmap to your wildest dreams. So please don't ignore that whimsical, beautiful inner child; hold their hand and run with them into the future with the power of your mind and soul and watch your life transform.

SHANNON WHITTINGTON

About Shannon Whittington: Shannon (she/her) is a speaker, author, consultant, and clinical nurse educator. Her area of expertise is LGBTQ+ inclusion in the workplace. Whittington has a passion for transgender health where she educates clinicians in how to care for transgender individuals after undergoing gender-affirming surgeries.

Whittington was honored to receive the Quality and Innovation Award from the Home Care Association of New York for her work with the transgender population. She was recently awarded the Notable LGBTQ+ Leaders & Executives award by Crain's New York Business, as well as the International Association of Professionals Nurse of the Year award. Whittington is a city and state lobbyist for transgender equality.

To date, Whittington has presented virtually and in person at various organizations and conferences across the nation, delivering extremely well-received presentations. Her forthcoming books include *LGBTQ+: ABC's For Grownups* and *Kindergarten for Leaders: 9 Essential Tips For Grownup Success.*

Author's Website: *www.linkedin.com/in/shannonwhittington and on YouTube at ShannonWhittingtonConsulting-for 101 LGBTQ videos*
Book Series Website & Author's Bio: *www.The13StepsToRiches.com*

Soraiya Vasanji

PERMISSION TO IMAGINE

"Once upon a time, in a land far, far away...."

Do you feel nostalgic too? When I close my eyes and hear these words, I feel a little spark of curiosity inside. What fantastical tale will unfold before us? And will I guess the plot twists and ending? It makes me feel like a child again, as this is how many imaginative and creative stories begin. When I think about IMAGINATION, I immediately think about Walt Disney and Disneyworld. I am a Disney lover at heart! I even built my own 4-foot Disney castle out of foam shapes and dressed up as Walt Disney for my seventh grade "Who Inspires You Most?" presentation. The fantastical characters, the storylines with heroes/heroines, and magical fairytale endings are more than just entertainment and childhood whimsy. I remember researching Walt Disney in middle school and being fascinated by how we could even come up with these characters and worlds, as well as his perspective on IMAGINATION. He believed that IMAGINATION is necessary for living our best life and is the best-equipped tool to navigate life's challenges. The worlds he created allowed us to escape our lives, but what if it is not about escaping life but creating our most magical life yet?

We had planned to vacation and celebrate my daughter's birthday in Disneyworld this winter, but the ongoing pandemic interrupted that plan. I was genuinely looking forward to breathing in the creative fantasy and getting inspired for a grander vision than I currently held. When I am at Disney, it feels like anything is possible. And honestly, in life, anything is possible if we believe, and we can picture it first. And by anything, I mean everything! 100% is possible 100% of the time. And the first step is to dream it, suspending disbelief and your current reality limitations to imagine what doesn't exist. Take the "could, should, and would" out of your thoughts! What do you envision for your life? Okay, now let go of any constraints that rise up. What is awaiting you in your magical life? We don't need to be at Disney physically to conjure up and go deeper in manifesting our latest desires.

IMAGINATION is not just about fantasy, creativity, and dreams; there are many types of IMAGINATION. Those that help us navigate situations and problem solve by thinking outside of the box, flexing that IMAGINA-TION muscle, using a different method of thinking, or a new approach to solving something with a tool that doesn't even exist. And yes, it tru-ly is a muscle, and like all muscles, when we don't flex and exert them, they start to atrophy. But, as we use and stretch our IMAGINATION, the good thing is that it becomes easier and easier to think in these ways and dream. We also have emotive and empathic IMAGINATION to feel and see what others go through. We have all either said or heard this, "I can/ can't imagine what you are going through!" We may not always realize or associate these imaginative ways, but we flex these daily thinking chan-nels.

Imagining or visioning our greatest possibilities indeed orients us to-wards our North Star. We can use it as a compass, and it's okay if what we may need doesn't even exist yet. Because the truth is, there may be something beyond what we can conjure up that may be even better than we could have thought at first anyways. This is the benefit of iterating on our vision and desires of life. In fact, Dr. Murray Hunter posits that there are eight types of IMAGINATION and while we may use these in both the conscious and subconscious, they support stringing our knowledge together. He suggests that "IMAGINATION is the ability to form mental images, phonological passages … of something that is not perceived through our senses. IMAGINATION is a manifestation of our memory and enables us to scrutinize our past and construct hypothetical future scenarios that do not yet but could exist." I have included his 8 Types of IMAGINATION in the table below. Which of these types do you excel at? Which of these do you desire to delve deeper into?

As we mature and get into our life patterns, our habits and routines take over, and we don't consciously push our limits. We don't push ourselves into "stretchy" situations, where we "stretch" beyond what is comfortable, usual, and routine. So when my clients share that they feel stuck in life, I ask them questions about other areas of their lives. And most times, it reveals that they feel stuck or are not making decisions or traction in other areas of their life. How we do something in one area often shows up in other areas of our lives. So I coach and advise them, and it usually includes some version of you gotta start taking small steps to "shake things up!"

I want to ask you now: What feels routine for you? What are you waiting to do? What story are you telling yourself? When was the last time you caught yourself thinking, "When X happens, then I will do Y?" Why are we waiting? You deserve to live your best life and get Y now!

Seriously, don't wait. Go do and get what you want now! You know what you want. Go do it! This reminded me of last summer when I cleaned out my old boxes, books, and toys from my parent's basement (you know, where you shoved all your adolescent, childhood, and college memories). I found a bead set that I loved to look at, and I would always tell myself that I had to wait to open it. So what was I waiting for? I waited so long that 25 years have passed, and now I have no interest in making some friendship bracelets. So I ended up donating it, and I sent out energy that some 10-year-old girl will receive and open it up and use it right away.

What are you going to start using or get up and do differently? You can also shake things up by getting a different haircut, walking a different route than you usually do, go up a street you have never been down in your neighborhood, swap items from two cabinets in the kitchen, or heck, put your underwear in a new drawer. I am telling you, shifting things up messes with our orderly head and makes us spin a little, which in my experience, leads to some kind of breakthrough, growth, or calling upon the IMAGINATION to see things in a new light!

Sometimes I find we are looking for permission to imagine, create, dream, or manifest. As kids, we have this innate sense of wonder, and it seems routine to use our imaginations to view everything around us. And yet, as we get older, we lose that permission to go to our creative edge. We need to be reminded and given permission just to leap, to let go and feel inspired to dream the impossible. So, voila! Here is your permission slip to jump deeper and higher than you ever dreamed possible.

IMAGINATION has served me most deeply and profoundly in my journey to begin a family. If you have been following this series, you will already know that I have endured my truth of neonatal loss and heartache like many women. I bring this up because in grieving and emerging from the darkness, dreaming and imagining being pregnant and one day holding my baby is what gave the first shreds of hope when it seemed like it would never happen. I have been in the family creation mode for a decade now! Yes, a whole decade going through the trials, troughs, and trepidations of all things fertility to manifest the family that my husband and I envision. It is with complete certainty that I manifested my daughter Naila. I imagined what she would look like and be like and spoke to her daily before she was even a possibility growing inside me. While she doesn't necessarily possess all the characteristics I conjured, she is even more impressive than I could ever have imagined. This is the epitome of IMAGINATION: opening oneself to the power of positive thinking beyond what reality tells us, what history dictates, and it confirms the growth mindset outlook. When we believe that things can change, that there is something more that is possible or can come beyond our current skills or perspective, this is IMAGINATION at work.

Table 1: Dr. Murray Hunter's Eight Types of IMAGINATION

1	Effective IMAGINATION	combines information together to synergize new concepts and ideas.
2	Intellectual (or Constructive) IMAGINATION	is utilized when considering and developing hypotheses from different pieces of information or pondering over various issues of meaning, say in the areas of philosophy, management, politics, etc.
3	Imaginative Fantasy IMAGINATION	creates and develops stories, pictures, poems, stage-plays, the building of the esoteric, etc.
4	Empathy IMAGINATION	helps a person know emotionally what others are experiencing from their frame and reference.
5	Strategic IMAGINATION	is concerned with the vision of what could be, the ability to recognize and evaluate opportunities by turning them into mental scenarios.'
6	Emotional IMAGINATION	is concerned with manifesting emotional dispositions and extending them into emotional scenarios.
7	Dreams	are an unconscious form of IMAGINATION made up of images, ideas, emotions, and sensations that occur during certain stages of sleep.
8	Memory Reconstruction	is the process of retrieving our memory of people, objects, and events.

SORAIYA VASANJI

About Soraiya Vasanji: Soraiya is a Certified Professional Coach (CPC), Energy Leadership Index Master Practitioner (ELI-MP), and has a Master's in Business Administration (MBA) from Kellogg University. She inspires women to be present, not perfect, ditch what doesn't serve them, and create their best messy life now. She loves sharing her wisdom on mindset, the power of language, self-love, self-worth, and leadership principles. She is the founder of the Mommy Mindset Summit series, where she interviews experts on topics that interest moms, so they can create a life of authenticity, abundance, and joy—and show their kids how to have it all, too.

Soraiya is married to her soulmate, has a four-year-old daughter, and lives in Toronto, Canada. She is a foodie and a jetsetter, and she loves collecting unique crafting and stationery products!

Author's Website: *www.SoraiyaVasanji.com*
Book Series Website & Author's Bio: *www.The13StepstoRiches.com*

Stacey Ross Cohen

LET YOUR IMAGINATION RUN WILD

"It has been said that man can create anything which he can imagine."
– Napoleon Hill

The preceding book in *The 13 Steps to Riches* series explored the importance of specialized knowledge, something that Napoleon Hill urged people to "never stop acquiring." Indeed, specialized knowledge gives individuals a competitive edge in the workplace because in-depth expertise can help solve even the most complicated problems.

Specialized knowledge becomes even more potent when mixed with another ingredient: IMAGINATION. IMAGINATION has sparked life-changing discoveries such as the light bulb, automobile, and television throughout the ages. More recently, it's led to 3D printers, augmented reality, smartphones, AI, and the metaverse. In short, IMAGINATION enables the future.

Hill described IMAGINATION as "the workshop of the mind" and defined two distinct types:

Creative IMAGINATION. Creative IMAGINATION works automatically, generating new ideas through "hunches" and "inspirations." These ideas are considered disruptive and the first of their kind. A classic example of creative IMAGINATION is Thomas Edison's invention of the lightbulb. A more contemporary example is Elon Musk, with his electric cars and Martian colonization ambitions. Yet another disruptor? Uber is the app-based transportation platform launched in 2009 and now operates in over 900 metropolitan areas worldwide. This innovative take on urban travel disrupted taxis and private transportation significantly.

Synthetic IMAGINATION. Whereas creative IMAGINATION is about creating something new from nothing, synthetic IMAGINATION creates something new from something old. Synthetic IMAGINATION takes existing ideas, inventions, or products and transforms them into something more. Most ideas and inventions fall into this category, as very few truly original inventions are created today. While Uber is a work of creative IMAGINATION, Lyft is an example of synthetic IMAGINATION: It built on top of Uber's concept, offering new and different features.

IMAGINATION is often linked to the arts. It's something that creators aspire to immerse themselves in, whether musicians or painters. But IMAGINATION is just as important in business, especially in marketing and communications, where you have to imagine creative ways for clients to stand out from the clutter.

I have a client story that really exemplifies the need for IMAGINATION in marketing and communications. I worked with the CEO of a sizable senior-living campus that offers a continuum of care, from independent living to assisted living to skilled nursing. The CEO approached me to write a news release announcing a new cyber senior program in partnership with a local university. Essentially, the college students came to the facility to help 70-plus-year-old residents navigate the internet, connect with their grandchildren, and use email. In my mind, I knew that if we sent out this announcement, it would get very little play in the media since there were many similar programs already out there in the world. So, I told her to give me a day or two—and I put my IMAGINATION to work.

The breakthrough idea? We created a graduation ceremony following the 13-week program. The seniors went on stage (by walker, by wheelchair, or by their own two legs) to receive course completion certificates from the college students. And the cost? A sheet cake and some fruit punch. The CEO instantly loved it, especially the affordability, since the organization was a non-profit. She also agreed to my suggestion of inviting staff and the seniors' families. The event ended up garnering broadcast coverage and front-page ink. But it also went deeper. It touched seniors, staff, families, college students, and college faculty. Making this idea come to life was one of the most joyous moments in my career. To see the proud smiles on the seniors' faces as they accepted the certificates will forever be ingrained in my mind and heart.

But take note: Without action, IMAGINATION is just ideas. To make it a reality is a relentless effort. You need to go all-in with a solid game plan and follow through with precision.

Fuel Your IMAGINATION

While IMAGINATION is natural for children, adults need to regularly invest in, cultivate, and practice it. Our IMAGINATION "muscle" calls for consistent exercise, or else it will atrophy. Just like memory, IMAGINATION is a skill that can be improved by challenging and nurturing it. Our brains are our most valuable asset and need to be stimulated regularly to produce original ideas and concepts. Here are some sure-fire tips to strengthen your IMAGINATION and drive it to new heights:

Practice meditation. The very first step to spark creativity is to clear your mind—and meditation can help you do exactly that. Indeed, research has shown that meditation is linked to increased creative thinking. A clear and alert mind is better able to learn new things and develop new ideas. So look for ways to incorporate meditation techniques into your daily life, whether just a few minutes of mindfulness or a more dedicated regimen of an hour each day.

Experience the new. Challenge yourself to get out of your comfort zone, embark on an adventure, and experience new things. Such opportunities provide new perspectives and supple ground for originality and creativity. Need some inspiration? Plan a trip to a new country. Take a performing art, writing, or painting class. Teach yourself how to do your own taxes. Try cooking a new recipe or learning a new language. Or take up white water rafting. New experiences of any kind, big or small, can spur you to think in new ways.

Become a lifelong learner. Learning is a guaranteed way to nourish your IMAGINATION. Indeed, successful people are obsessed with learning. So train yourself to be curious and ask questions: Why? Where? How? What? Who? If ever you encounter something that you don't understand, ask. And seek out new knowledge and skills through books, podcasts, YouTube, and online courses.

Make time for play. I have a confession: I love Legos. Any chance I get, I will buy a Lego set as a gift for friends or family with kids — and then politely remove myself from the "adult" room to play with them for a bit. What can I say? There's a part of me that will always be a playful builder. I recall my love growing up for Mr. Potato Head and exchanging different body parts to make new creations. Whenever I assembled a new version, Mr. Potato Head became a different character. If you're not up for playing with Legos and Mr. Potato Head in the office, no worries: Plenty of other options are available. Maybe it's a game of Scrabble or a few minutes of Minecraft on the computer. The point is to embrace imaginative play as an escape and a way to see things differently, which is the essence of IMAGINATION.

Foster a positive mindset. Passion and enthusiasm are critical to a rich IMAGINATION (and other successful attributes, too, like reaching big goals). It's challenging to feel imaginative when you are tired, bored, stressed, or angry. When I have a writing assignment and find it difficult to focus, I first do a 10-minute meditation and then set a positive writing stage: light a candle, play soft background music, and get into my most comfy clothing.

Build a creative community. I am a big proponent of brainstorming to keep creative juices flowing. Exchanging ideas with co-workers, mentors, family, and friends brings fresh perspectives. And it's even more productive when you blend in the right and left-brained people. In my business, communications require true partnership with others. The kind of partnership where ideas are born, exchanged freely, executed, and, yes, sometimes tossed out. For example, when we create a new logo for a client, this is precisely the process that we use. We typically develop ten logo concepts and boil them down to four or five final ideations to present to the client. It is creative collaboration at its best and truly produces the best result.

Use visualization. Napoleon Hill said it best: "If you do not see great riches in your IMAGINATION, you will never see them in your bank balance." So, learn how to use visualization, the practice of creating vivid and desirable images in your mind. Indeed, "seeing is believing" and "visualize to materialize" are more than just motivational phrases —they are proven and effective psychological methods backed by science. Just ask the Olympians and professional athletes who use visualization to focus on achieving victory. Create a detailed vision board with pictures, words, and quotes to get started.

In wrapping up this chapter, I hope you have some new inspirations and tools to get out there, imagine and create. But have realistic expectations: Indeed, expect failure more often than success. Remember, each failure is a stepping stone toward success. Best-selling author and organizational psychologist Adam Grant, who studies original thinkers, believes that the ability to embrace failure is essential. In his TED Talk "The Surprising Habits of Original Thinkers," he explains that "the greatest originals are the ones who fail the most because they're the ones who try the most." But, he adds, "You need a lot of bad ideas to get a few good ones."

Here's to letting your IMAGINATION run wild.

STACEY ROSS COHEN

About Stacey Ross Cohen: In the world of branding, few experts possess the savvy and instinct of Stacey. An award-winning brand professional who earned her stripes on Madison Avenue and major television networks before launching her own agency, Stacey specializes in cultivating and amplifying brands.

Stacey is CEO of Co-Communications, a marketing agency headquartered in New York. She coaches businesses and individuals across a range of industries, from real estate to healthcare and education, and expertly positions their narratives in fiercely competitive markets.

A TEDx speaker, Stacey is a sought-after keynote at industry conferences and author in the realm of branding, PR, and marketing. She is a contributor at *Huffington Post* and *Thrive Global,* and has been featured in *Forbes, Entrepreneur, Crain's* and a suite of other media outlets. She holds a B.S. from Syracuse University, MBA from Fordham University and a certificate in Media, Technology and Entertainment from NYU Stern School of Business.

Author's website: *www.StaceyRossCohen.com*
Book Series Website & author's Bio: *www.The13StepsToRiches.com*

Teresa Cundiff

IMAGINATION NOW & THEN

Why is it that we have such fertile imaginations as children, but as we grow older, our IMAGINATION begins to wane? Of course, I am speaking in broad strokes because this is certainly not the case with everyone. I think it's partly a function of responsibility that we take on as we grow up that begins to crowd out our IMAGINATION. We have harder classes in school and must study more, and there is only so much gray matter to expend. Middle school turns into high school that runs into college, and then we are off on our career working for "The Man." At this point, IMAGINATION is all but a fleeting childhood pastime that only comes back to mind when we see it through the eyes of our own children. Then it's like, "Hello, old friend!"

So, are we to leave IMAGINATION only to the entrepreneurs of the world? Is it to be left in the past while we toil away at a 9 to 5? I say NO! It doesn't have to be this way! Let's think back to the world's great inventors and what IMAGINATION they must have had to come up with the light bulb, the telephone, the steam engine, the airplane, the personal computer, and the cell phone. What incredible imaginations they must have had. These inventions revolutionized the entire world! And how about Ron Klein, who put the magnetic strip in the back of our credit cards? Brilliant right? And let's face it, don't we all want to be brilliant? But it seemed like thinking and using their IMAGINATIONS was their full-time job! Who's got time for that these days?

In Napoleon Hill's chapter on IMAGINATION in *Think and Grow Rich*, he states, "It has been said that man can create anything which he can imagine." That is a very powerful and bold statement. I challenge you here – Do you believe it? The chapter goes on to explain "the moment you reduce the statement of your desire, and a plan for its realization, to writing, you have actually taken the first of a series of steps, which will enable you to convert thought into its physical counterpart." Every idea that has been brought to fruition was born in the IMAGINATION! It's just as simple as that. How much time does it take to use your IMAGINATION to come up with an idea? I don't know either! I'm asking the question so we can think about it together.

What are some things you do to nurture your IMAGINATION? I will confess that I wish I had more opportunity to be out in nature to free my mind of the day-to-day so I could imagine more. I am of the thought that I must release some things from my brain to make room for free-flowing ideas to take place. You may disagree. But I will confess that I am a dreamer. Perhaps that is akin to using my IMAGINATION. I imagine being on white, sandy beaches with my toes in the sand. I imagine that my whole family is there at that same location, and we are enjoying a wonderful vacation. I imagine writing my first solo novel and it being wildly successful, but these imaginings are not what Hill is referring to. He's referring to using your IMAGINATION to generate ideas that will transmute into money after writing them down and formulating plans.

So, as I usually do in my chapters, let me ask you some pointed questions. Are you currently using your IMAGINATION on any money-making ventures? As of this writing, I can say that I have applied my IMAGINATION to some commercials for my TV show and my proofreading business. I have also sent my ideas to update my website to my website guy to make the changes. I have also been formulating my ideas for what I am writing to you right now. So, the THINK part of *Think and Grow Rich* definitely applies to engaging your mind on ideas for all aspects of your business.

You can brainstorm with your staff, family, peers, and associates about what you're thinking. It's certainly wise to write EVERYTHING down! There are no dumb ideas. Keep it all because one thing could be a seed for something else. You just never know. I'm preaching to myself here because sometimes I write things down, and sometimes I don't. Hill puts it quite succinctly when he says, "Ideas are the beginning points of all fortunes. Ideas are the products of the IMAGINATION."

It would be nice to go back to the innocent days of our childhood if only to feel the freedom to imagine and be carefree. However, I know that everyone does not have a carefree and innocent childhood, so I do not mean to sound cavalier. I personally had my innocence stripped away from me in childhood, so there weren't many carefree days. Still, I remember playing with my paper dolls and pretending and using my IMAGINATION and having a wonderful time with them.

There is freedom in our IMAGINATION that can't be found anywhere else and fun as well. We can pose the question to the group, "What would you do if you had a million dollars?" That really gets people's imaginations going, and it costs nothing! Hill encourages us to read his book through and then come back to the chapter on IMAGINATION because it is just that powerful. Writing this chapter has made me want to spend time cultivating my own IMAGINATION! It truly only takes carving out some time actually to do it!

Here's what the steps for me will look like as I move forward, spending time nurturing my IMAGINATION in a way that would make ole Napoleon Hill proud of me. With a notepad and erasable Frixion pen (made by Pilot) in hand, I'm going to spend 30 minutes or so just thinking and writing everything down. If I'm blessed enough to have a colleague free at the same time, then we will brainstorm ideas together. This would be my preference. I currently have a mentor, so she and I always are working on great things for me! Everything will get written down! At this juncture, I will just stop and THINK! Again, the THINK part of *Think and Grow*

Rich because I believe that rolling over ideas in the brain will begin to understand whether the idea has application to my business. It could be that an idea warrants further brainstorming, and that's awesome!

Let me offer a word of wisdom here regarding intellectual property. I am writing all this assuming that you already have in place protections with your staff about nondisclosure or proprietary material at your workplace, etc. and that any work product/idea developed therein belongs to the company. Just make sure you have all that covered.

I'll share a quick story that I wrote in third grade with you. I entitled it, "Stop, Caution & Go." Of course, I only remember the basic premise of it, so this will be much better than a third-grader would have written!

In the middle of the intersection hangs the big yellow traffic light. The cars and trucks pass underneath it without any thought given to the busyness going on right over their heads as they pass through! Because little do they know that three little men work feverishly to keep the traffic flowing. Their names are Stop, Caution & Go. These triplet brothers are five inches tall and are each the color that matches their station. Stop is a bright red with a serious disposition, and he takes his job of stopping traffic very seriously. Caution is as sunny as his personality, but he is anxious when turning the light yellow to warn the passing traffic that the red light is about to trip. Go is happy-go-lucky and as carefree as can be as he allows the traffic to zoom by cheering on each car as it goes through.

The traffic light in which they live is also their playground. It has a super fun slide when moving from top to bottom. Each triplet has a swing on his level for when the other lights are on so that he can jump on for a few quick swings! Of course, Stop rarely takes advantage of his swing because, as mentioned before, he takes stopping the traffic very seriously. They refer to their home as Traffic Light Central, TLC!

Work at TLC can be rigorous and is certainly routine, but the triplets take pride in there never being a traffic jam! No sir! Their work is top-notch, and they keep everything ship-shape. The residents of Friend Town depend on the triplets to keep the cars running smoothly beneath the one traffic light that dons the single intersection of their fair town with the population of 425 friendly people!

And with that, I have conjured back up my story that I imagined from when I was nine years old! I now have the makings of either a children's book or a young reader's book. What have you imagined lately? What did you imagine long ago? THINK about it!

TERESA CUNDIFF

About Teresa Cundiff: Teresa hosts an interview digital TV show called Teresa Talks on Legrity TV. On the show, she interviews authors who are published and unpublished—and that just means those authors haven't put their books on paper yet. The show provides a platform for authors to have a global reach with their message. Teresa Talks is produced by Wordy Nerds Media Inc., of which Cundiff is the CEO.

Cundiff is also a freelance proofreader with the tagline, "I know where the commas go!," Teresa makes her clients' work shine with her knowledge of grammar, punctuation, and sentence structure.

Teresa is a two-time International Best-Selling Contributing Author of *1 Habit for Entrepreneurial Success and 1 Habit to Thrive in a Post-COVID World.* She is also a best-selling contributing author of *The Art of Connection; 365 Days of Networking Quotes,* which has been placed in the Library of Congress.

Author's Website: *www.TeresaTalksTV.com*
Book Series Website & Author's Bio: *www.The13StepsToRiches.com*

Vera Thomas

JUST IMAGINE!!!!

IMAGINATION is the fuel that drives

Creativity in our lives

Do not let your IMAGINATION die

Where there is no vision, we perish (Prov 29:18)

Our IMAGINATION must be cultivated and cherished

Child-like IMAGINATION that has no limits and is not bound

Is the key to success that will astound

Having the IMAGINATION of a child

Is the key to how we thrive

In addressing the issue of IMAGINATION and looking at the two types of IMAGINATION that Napoleon Hill talks about, "synthetic" and "creative" IMAGINATION, my focus is on "creative" IMAGINATION. Of course, incorporating synthetic IMAGINATION is necessary. We learn from and enhance our IMAGINATION when we are willing to explore what others have imagined that is proven and effective. While creativity and IMAGINATION may go hand-in-hand, they are not the same. "IMAGINATION is the act or power of forming a mental image of something not present to the senses or never before wholly perceived in reality" (Webster). It is what we see or perceive in our mind's eye. "Creativity is having or showing an ability to make new things or think of new ideas" (Webster). There can be no creativity without IMAGINATION! Hill talks about creativity as the source's expression and IMAGINATION or vision that comes from the source. He defines source as your faith or belief. That source for me has been the Holy Spirit. When I have learned to trust what is given to me in words and deeds, I find I am more at peace, and creative juices can flow. The child-like IMAGINATION can be hindered when life takes over our mind and replaces faith or belief with doubt, fear, and worry.

IMAGINATION is not bound by circumstances or situations. The thing is, we get so caught up in events and situations that can thwart our IMAGINATION and limit our ability to "hear," "see," or "imagine" what the source has given us. I must admit, there have been times when I have allowed situations and circumstances to clog my IMAGINATION. My IMAGINATION has been directed toward creating poetry, training, coaching, speaking, community-oriented programs, and, more recently, being an author.

The initial realization of my creative IMAGINATION was spawned through emotional pain from rejection, societal woes, and the human condition. On a personal level, the ability to imagine and create poetry was not only my way of expressing it, but it was also my way of encouraging myself! It is as though my source gave me the IMAGINATION to endure through struggles and life challenges. Interestingly, what comes to me is creativity to emote primarily about our society and the human condition. I imagine a world of love, peace, and joy on a professional and business level. Therefore my IMAGINATION has provided opportunities to develop and design tools to change the work environment, family lives, and society.

I imagine workplaces where everyone has the opportunity to live up to his/her full potential with management that is supportive, caring, and just as concerned about their most valuable resource, their employees, as they are about their bottom line. The result from synthetic, along with my creative IMAGINATION, companies are transformed through customized programs to meet their specific needs.

I imagine happy, capable and self-assured children with parents who are the same. My creativity includes an all-school motivational presentation where children leave feeling uplifted and encouraged. The anti-bullying programs have children who are bullied and empowered; children who bully are transformed and bystanders gain the confidence needed to speak up on behalf and alongside those victimized. In other programs, children gain confidence through their creative expressions and learn how to embrace their greatness. Parents assess the attitudes, behaviors, and unresolved issues that eliminate on their children and develop a plan of action for change. Teachers and administrators become more sensitive to the needs of students. Fathers become more engaged in their children's lives. My IMAGINATION!

I imagine our society transformed by the renewal of our mind where there is a spirit of cooperation, acceptance of each other, and hate replaced with love. I used my creativity and worked with others to develop town halls to address the issues of race, education, health, and the criminal justice system. I challenge each of us to let our light shine on one another, one person at a time! Where there is light, there can be no darkness. Can you imagine?

How do we get beyond what we see and focus on innate and inherent IMAGINATION? Child-like IMAGINATION is innate in that children don't have to think about or contemplate imagining. They just do. I am amazed by the IMAGINATIONs of children. One of my granddaughters, in particular, can spend hours using whatever she gets her hands on, and she creates scenarios and makes up her own songs in the process. She has a beautiful voice. Another grand uses her IMAGINATION to create video skits! It is great to watch the four younger ones create imaginary characters and do what looks like a whole theater production. Their ages range from 5 to 10 years old.

I believe IMAGINATION is inherent as it is a permanent and essential attribute necessary to succeed in whatever we choose to do. We can get so stuck in our ways, so overcome with situations and circumstances that we block our IMAGINATION. We forget how to let our IMAGINATIONS run wild! Prayer, meditation, and being still is what works for me. Being intentional and consistent can be a challenge. As a result of the source of my IMAGINATION, when I let go and let my source prevail, I know there is no limit to where or what our IMAGINATION can reveal to us. Just imagine!

Think about ways to revive your IMAGINATION. One of my suggestions is to be still and focus on your breathing to open the channel to your IMAGINATION.

In addition, I read an article in Psychology Today by Fran Sorin. This is her list. I can attest to these seven ways from a personal perspective. Start imagining your responses as you complete this exercise. It is my desire you add to the descriptions with your own account. Begin to imagine!

7 Simple Yet Effective Ways to Jump-Start Your IMAGINATION

1. **Change Your Self-Perception How do you see yourself?** Are you an optimist or pessimist? Do you say a glass is half full or half-empty?

_____

_____

I am optimistic about? _____

_____

Negativity is a weight and can block creativity and IMAGINATION. I demonstrate negativity when I _____

_____

You can change your perception through affirmations and self-talk out loud 3x each time you say it. An affirmation is a positive word or phrase that we say out loud three times as if it already exists. It must be spoken in the first person, and it must be positive. Example: *Every day, my IMAGINATION is leading me to my success!* You can choose to use this affirmation or create your own. Say your affirmation three times NOW.

_____

_____

2. **Observe.** Be observant of people, places, and things. Watch mannerisms and non-verbals and put your spin on things.

What did I observe today? How did it peak my imagination?

_____

_____

3. **Access Childhood Memories**

As I reflect – One of my childhood memories

_____

_____

_____

As a result of this memory, I imagine

_____

_____

4. **Open to Possibility Be "green and growing."** Remove "I have been like this all my life, I cannot change" from your thoughts and vocabulary. We change by moving forward or back. We do not stand still! Be open and imagine the possibilities!

The opportunity or possibility I can say yes to now or my immediate future is

_____

_____

5. **Be Curious**

Be curious about things that happen throughout your day.

_____

_____

Be curious about the weather.

_____

_____

Be curious about people.

_____

_____

Be curious about nature.

_____

_____

6. **Be Playful N**ot everything should be so serious. Play with your grandchildren or other children. Board games with other adults can be fun. Intentionally set aside time to play!

My play

_____

_____

7. **Spend Time in Nature** I remember sitting in a park one day observing three pigeons. One female and two males. I was fascinated by their interactions that went on for quite a while. Both males seemed to be vying for her attention. I begin to imagine the conversation they might be having. The female seemed to get annoyed by both of them and eventually flew away.

My nature experiences

_____

_____

Again, as you reflect on this list, begin to use your IMAGINATION! Get excited as you imagine your life, your success! Just imagine!!!!!

(This worksheet was created as a result of my IMAGINATION!)

Reference

Psychology Today Posted February 1, 2017, Retrieved 1/15/22 from https://www.psychologytoday.com/us/blog/tools-innovative-living/201702/7-simple-yet- effective-ways-jump-start-your-IMAGINATION

VERA THOMAS

About Vera Thomas: Vera Thomas lives in the state of Georgia. She is to date a 4x best-selling author, podcast host, certified transformation coach and family mediator, Classroom Management Advocate/Trainer/Speaker/poet. She works with parents, children, schools, organizations and churches.

Vera's life story directed her towards work with organizations that provided hope and empowerment to people like her to better themselves. It is her goal to help others overcome a circumstance that diminishes and help them to surge ahead with their dreams. Vera graduated "Cum Laude" with a Bachelor in psychology from Walsh University in Canton, OH.

Vera's work as a facilitator, for more than three decades and includes developing training programs for youth and adults. Hear her story and think about your own. Vera is available for companies who want to transform their teams or individuals who want to transform their lives.

Author's Website: *www.VeraThomasCoaching.com*
Book Series Website & Author's Bio: *www.The13StepstoRiches.com*

Yuri Choi

MEDITATION IS THE PORTAL TO THE REALM OF INFINITE POSSIBILITIES

Have you ever followed your "gut feeling," even though logically it might not have made the most sense to follow them?

This is something that I talk to my high-achieving clients about.

As a performance coach, I work a lot with entrepreneurs and high achievers who are often experiencing burnout and need to reset. Often, it is because they have gotten stuck in working in the traditional paradigm of "do more, do more," thinking it will produce more. But what they find out is that eventually, that engine gets tired, and "do more" doesn't always work linearly. Typically, it creates a very turbulent flow as one goes hard, crashes, and repeats this cycle, leading to burning out. How do I know this? As a recovered Type A myself, I also lived on this paradigm. However, everything changed when I learned to create a healthy relationship with meditation and mindfulness practices many years ago.

Mid 2020, as most people know, globally, there was a big pause in the world due to the pandemic. In the early part of 2020, I was living in Southern California, where we were all in lockdown mode at the time. The world was in a chaotic, stressed-out place. Meanwhile, as a lightworker, I felt the intuitive added responsibility to stay clear and be a guiding light for many. And due to this responsibility, I felt, during that time in California, I chose to meditate a lot, up to two hours a day, to ensure that I stay clear and grounded. And it worked. While the world was going into a state of chaos, I felt like I was clearer and more intuitive than ever before.

While meditating every day, something interesting happened. I was being creative in all different directions, effortlessly. I started writing spoken poetry and even performed them to a virtual audience for the first time. I even wrote a fun song about being in quarantine which went viral on my social media. I wrote more chapters of my book I was working on at the time, Creating Your Own Happiness. I was singing more. I was dancing. I started a fundraiser, and we raised over $175,000 for families of frontline workers affected by Covid-19 with other leaders. I recorded many videos for my YouTube channel. I was wildly creative and in flow when most people were frustrated, scared, and anxious.

I even started to have vivid dreams and visions in a way that I've never had before. One day specifically, I was meditating for another 2 hours, after an hour of yoga, and I received this intuitive hit that I should be going to JeJu Island in Korea. I had gone there once with my dad and my mom years ago, and that was the last family trip we took together to Korea. Then a few days after, I had a dream that my dad (who has transitioned) showed up in my dream and handed me a planner. When I opened the planner, there was just one big sentence there, and it read, "Plan a trip!" So the message to get out and go to Korea seemed to be loud and clear.

At the time, international travel was considered almost "impossible." Yet, with this dream and this message I received during my meditation, it became a question of "how will I make the trip to Korea happen at this time," rather than, "can I make this trip to Korea happen?" Once I had planted a seed in my mind that this was a possibility, every atom in my body was telling me that this was precisely where I should be.

Long story short, I was able to find my way there. I learned that I could go to Korea as long as I was quarantined for 14 days (which was not that bad considering I had been quarantined for over a month at the time in California) and that I had to prepare some official documents.

So, in July of 2020, while everyone was still in lockdown in California, I was able to go back to my home country for the first time in a long time. I initially planned to be there for a month, which turned into 13 months. But, the longer I stayed, the more I realized that was exactly where I was supposed to be.

During my time in Korea, I lived and traveled my home country as an adult for the first time, which was a monumental rite of passage for me as I reclaimed my identity as the "Korean" part of Korean American. Having moved to the U.S. when I was 11 years old, I felt that I had abandoned that part of me, and it felt so aligned to learn more about my country. In addition, I met some incredible humans, some of whom became my lifelong friends, some of them clients, and some of them great networking connections. I even got invited to host a workshop in Seoul, Korea, which was a dream come true.

I, of course, also traveled back to Jeju Island, where I got to do one of the most beautiful hikes, hang around some of the most exotic beaches, and eat amazing seafood. I truly felt like I was creating my own reality, where I got to travel and see some of the most beautiful places in Korea, reclaim my roots, spend time with my family and felt so free and abundant every day. My business grew more than it ever had, and I got to spend quality time with my family in a way that I hadn't got to since I was 11 years old. I even got to spend my grandpa's 94th birthday together, and he passed away shortly after I returned to the U.S.

Looking back, listening to this "gut feeling" was exactly what I was supposed to do for me to continue the momentum of expansion I was on at the time. It just worked out in every single way.

In *Think and Grow Rich*, this type of divine expansion is coined as "creative IMAGINATION." It is different from "synthetic IMAGINATION," where it is solely based on what we know in our own brains based on what we learned. Instead, creative IMAGINATION happens through accessing the collective consciousness or collective wisdom through activities such as meditation.

My genuine belief is that because I was meditating so much during the pandemic, especially while many others were in an anxious, panic state, I became the vessel for divine messages and creativity to come through.

I teach this to my own clients, and I refer to this type of expansion through intuitive messages from something bigger as a "quantum leap." It means that we no longer play and live in 2D or even 3D reality. Instead, we are entering a realm of infinite possibilities through meditation.

These types of "gut feelings" have been reported in many others as well. One example that comes to mind is the story that Jack Canfield, one of the co-authors of the *Chicken Soup* book series, shares in the documentary, the Secret. He talks about how he was meditating for an hour every day, with the intention of receiving messages around this book. Not only did he get to name this book through this type of creative IMAGINATION through meditation, but also, he credits his meditation for being able to get divine ideas on how to get the book out there to the public. And as he followed these intuitive feelings, he created a reality where the Chicken Soup series became an international bestseller.

If this sounds too "woo-woo," another way to think about this is that when we meditate, we actually calm our nervous system down, and we can turn off the fight, flight, or freeze mechanism of our brain. What this allows us to do physiologically is that we are no longer reacting due to heightened cortisol levels; instead, we can enter into a state of creativity. However, when we don't have this sense of calmness in our brain and our bodies, our mind is so focused on "surviving" the moment that it has a hard time accessing any new ideas or seeing things from a different perspective to allow creativity to come through.

One of the things I work on with my high achieving clients is to help them access this level of calmness and, therefore, an innovative state by assisting them in learning how to come back to their bodies as well as meditate at times. This has caused such powerful differences in my clients on their quality of life and business.

And when you're able to allow this creative IMAGINATION to be activated within your mind, you will have more ease and flow as you create the outcomes you want.

Being able to access this "creative IMAGINATION" is how some people are able to create massive leaps in their realities. And in this process, people learn to collapse time and enjoy the journey more.

So, my question for you today is, have you meditated today? What could happen if you allowed yourself to step into the realm of infinite possibilities today through your meditation?

Journaling Question:

Journal about a time when you followed a "gut feeling," which turned out to be a good thing?

YURI CHOI

About Yuri Choi: Yuri is the Founder of Yuri Choi Coaching. Yuri is a performance coach for entrepreneurs and high achievers. She helps them create and stay in a powerful, abundant, unstoppable mindset to achieve their goals by helping them gain clarity and understanding, leverage their emotional states, and create empowering habits and language patterns.

She is a speaker, writer, creator, connector, YouTuber, and the author of *Creating Your Own Happiness.* Yuri is passionate about spreading the messages about meditation, power of intention, and creating a powerful mindset to live a fulfilling life. She is also a Habitude Warrior Conference Speaker and Emcee, and she is also a designated guest coach for Psych2Go, the largest online mental health magazine and YouTube channel. Her mission in the world is to inspire people to live leading with L.O.V.E. (which stands for: laughter, oneness, vulnerability, and ease) and to ignite people's souls to live in a world of infinite creative possibilities and abundance.

Author's Website: *www.YuriChoiCoaching.com*
Book Series Website & Author's Bio: *www.The13StepsToRiches.com*

GRAB YOUR COPY OF AN OFFICIAL PUBLICATION
WITH THE ORIGINAL UNEDITED TEXT FROM 1937
BY THE NAPOLEON HILL FOUNDATION!

THE NAPOLEON HILL FOUNDATION
WWW.NAPHILL.ORG

Paperback ISBN: 978-1-63792-277-4
Hardcover ISBN: 978-1-63792-281-1